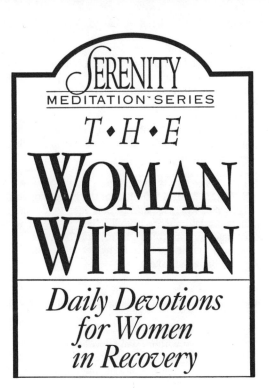

SERENITY
MEDITATION·SERIES

T·H·E

WOMAN
WITHIN

*Daily Devotions
for Women
in Recovery*

Janet M. Congo, Julie L. Mask, Jan E. Meier

D0595783

THOMAS NELSON PUBLISHERS
Nashville

Published in Nashville, Tennessee, by Thomas Nelson,
Inc., and distributed in Canada by Lawson Falle, Ltd.,
Cambridge, Ontario.

Unless otherwise indicated, Scripture quotations are from
the NEW KING JAMES VERSION of the Bible. Copyright
© 1979, 1980, 1982, Thomas Nelson, Inc., Publishers.
Scriptures marked NIV are from The Holy Bible, New
International Version, copyright 1973, 1978, 1984
International Bible Society. Used by permission of
Zondervan Bible Publishers.

Library of Congress Cataloging-in-Publication Data

Congo, Janet, 1949–
    The woman within : daily devotions for women in
recovery / Jan Congo, Julie Mask, Jan Meier.
        p.   cm. — (Serenity meditations series)
    "A Janet Thoma book."
    ISBN 0-8407-3239-2
    1. Women—Prayer-books and devotions—English.
2. Twelve-step programs—Religious aspects—
Meditations.   3. Devotional calendars.   I. Mask,
Julie.   II. Meier, Jan.   III. Title.   IV. Series.
BL624.5.C66   1991
242'.4—dc20   91–30876
                                                         CIP

Printed in the United States of America
1 2 3 4 5 6 7 — 96 95 94 93 92 91

The Twelve Steps of Alcoholics Anonymous*

1. We admitted we were powerless over alcohol—that our lives had become unmanageable. 2. Came to believe that a Power greater than ourselves could restore us to sanity. 3. Made a decision to turn our will and our lives over to the care of God as we understood Him. 4. Made a searching and fearless moral inventory of ourselves. 5. Admitted to God, to ourselves and to another human being the exact nature of our wrongs. 6. Were entirely ready to have God remove all these defects of character. 7. Humbly asked Him to remove our shortcomings. 8. Made a list of all persons we had harmed and became willing to make amends to them all. 9. Made direct amends to such people wherever possible, except when to do so would injure them or others. 10. Continued to take personal inventory and when we were wrong, promptly admitted it. 11. Sought through prayer and meditation to improve our conscious contact with God, as we understood Him, praying only for knowledge of His will for us and the power to carry that out. 12. Having had a spiritual awakening as the result of these steps, we tried to carry this message to alcoholics, and to practice these principles in all our affairs.

*The Twelve Steps are reprinted and adapted with permission of Alcoholics Anonymous World Services, Inc. Permission to reprint and adapt the Twelve Steps does not mean that AA has reviewed or approved the content of this publication, nor that AA agrees with the views expressed herein. AA is a program of recovery from alcoholism. Use of the Twelve Steps in connection with programs and activities which are patterned after AA but which address other problems does not imply otherwise.

Introduction

I've been sick, but I'm getting better."

If that phrase describes you in any sense, this book of daily meditations is for you.

You may not have been physically sick or mentally ill. But you probably have struggled with self-destructive behaviors and unhealthy relationships. You may have developed an addiction or an eating disorder. Guilt and shame from your past may have crippled your relationships. Or life may have dealt you a cruel blow that challenged all your coping ability.

Whatever your specific problems, you have made the choice to face them, seek help, and move on. We commend you. And we have tailored the meditations in this book to uplift and encourage you on your journey of recovery. In each daily selection we share insights we have gained both as professional therapists and as women trying to live positively in today's complex world.

The meditations in this book assume you are familiar with certain aspects of the so-called "recovery movement." Several refer to the Twelve Steps followed by Alcoholics Anonymous and its sister groups. Others speak of codependency (relationship addiction) and shame (the emotional foundation for most addictions). We refer you to one of many excellent books on the market for a more detailed explanation of these fundamental principles.

You will find that some of the meditations in this book are directed to specific experiences—such as eating disorders, depression, or abortion. Some refer to the single life; others are about marriage and motherhood. For this reason, certain meditations may not seem to apply to your particular journey. But we encourage you to search each devotion for a common thread that applies to your own life.

Recovery is both a specific and a universal journey. Each person faces a unique set of challenges and opportunities—yet the general principles of growth apply to us all. The attitudes and principles that help one woman overcome the pain of living with an alcoholic parent can help another survive the loss of a spouse. We hope they can help you as well.

The principles of recovery described in this book are firmly rooted in the Christian tradition. God wants to be your companion on the journey toward recovery, and we are convinced that true health is impossible without His transforming power. We encourage you to turn to Him as your Higher Power—to talk to Him, meditate on His Word, ask His guidance. If you do, we are confident that you will feel His presence as you continue down that long, sometimes exciting, sometimes frustrating road toward physical, emotional, and spiritual health.

JANET M. CONGO
JULIE L. MASK
JAN E. MEIER

That we may lead a quiet and peaceable life in all godliness and reverence.   —1 TIM. 2:2

Quiet, please! We live in a noisy and busy world. We rush continually from one important meeting to another. As wives, mothers, workers, homemakers, and housekeepers, we sometimes feel led by our schedules. We long for solitude, yet few of us are willing to make room for a quiet time in our lives.

Christ was only on earth for thirty-three years and spent only three years in active ministry. He had an immense mission to fulfill. Yet He considered His quiet time with His Father a necessary part of His mission.

What happens when we find the time to be quiet and listen? God's wisdom looms larger and our problems shrink. Silence changes our perspective and forces us to look within ourselves. It helps us understand our hidden motives and see our relationships more clearly. We gain more meaningful knowledge of what is really going on inside our heads, and we become more accepting of others.

Although quiet times are not a cure-all, they are a start. But I find I must redecide daily to get away to a quiet place where I can talk with God and meditate on His Word.

―――――――

My quiet time today is not wasted time.

J.E.M.

Look at the birds of the air, for they neither sow nor reap nor gather into barns; yet your heavenly Father feeds them. Are you not of more value than they?
—MATT. 6:26

As I sit and watch the wind blow through the trees, the birds soaring, and the sun glimmering on the water, I marvel at God's ultimate power and wisdom. And look at the little creatures—the ants busily working, the frogs hopping, the turtles sunbathing. God must have a marvelous imagination!

Then, a storm blows in with all its force—thunder and lightning, trees nearly blowing in half. And I wonder what will happen to all the animals. But after the storm, as I look out over the same lively scene I saw earlier, I realize that God's design is still working well.

This experience helps me see that when a storm comes into my life—when I start to panic and feel as if God has forsaken me—God will protect me, just as He protects the creatures of the earth. Things may not always work out exactly as we want, but that's true for the creatures of the earth too. Sometimes they must start picking up the pieces after the storm and rebuild their homes. But God remains in charge. And if we can just allow Him to comfort us through the storm and allow Him to rebuild our characters afterward, we will be able to experience the joy He has planned for each of us in life.

Lord, thank you for putting us in a world that helps us better understand your power and wisdom.

J.L.M.

*My food is to do the will of Him who sent Me, and
to finish His work.* —JOHN 4:34

Discovering whom we are trying to please simplifies
life and reduces stress. Jesus decided pleasing God was
His goal. Others—Satan, the Pharisees and Sadducees,
the disciples, even His family—tried unsuccessfully to
divert Him from His purpose. Even at His trial, people
couldn't manipulate Him to be or do something God
hadn't planned.

Dianne also had to decide who she was going to
please. Her mother was constantly telling her how she
should take care of her new baby. If Dianne let the
baby cry for more than one minute, her mother would
pick him up. When Dianne decided to nurse on demand, her mother wanted her to nurse on a fixed
schedule. Finally, Dianne took her mother aside. She
affirmed her for being such a concerned grandparent.
Then, she firmly and warmly told her mother that she
needed to do what she felt was right with her baby.
There was a period of awkwardness between them,
but Dianne stuck to her position—and all three of them
were happier.

In your recovery journey, you will have to make this
decision too. You must choose your path and follow it,
even if not everyone is pleased with your plans. And
you will be wise if you make God the Person you try to
please above all.

---

*Today, Lord, help me to stay on the track I have chosen. Let me look
to you for encouragement and direction.*

J.M.C.

For you shall go out with joy,
And be led out with peace;
The mountains and the hills
Shall break forth into singing
*   before you,*
And all the trees of the field shall
*   clap their hands.*

—ISA. 55:12

Nature continually reminds us of the power and creativity of God. In springtime, when the rain pours and later the sparkling sun appears, we are confronted with the magnificence of His creation. Every unique tree with its own special leaf, every animal with its own shape and color, every single star in the night sky reminds us anew that we are not ultimately responsible or in charge—that God is the Master and Creator of the universe in all its beauty and variety.

It is easy to become so absorbed in ourselves and our own life that we forget about God and all the wonder He provides. We can use His creation as a source of retreat and relaxation from our struggles. The simple love of a pet can bring us comfort and laughter. And being able to sit in a park, walk at a lake, stroll down a tree-lined road, and look at the stars can remind us that God is powerful and creative and able to assist us with any problem we might have.

Lord, help me to see your wonder wherever I live. Help me to enjoy your creation and trust that you are here for me.

J.L.M

And you will be sorrowful, but your sorrow will be turned to joy.
                                        —JOHN 16:20

One night during my husband's last year of medical school, I was watching the ten o'clock news on television. The commentator announced the need for a couple to live with eight girls in a nicely furnished home. When Paul came home from his rotation at the hospital, I excitedly told him I had found a job for us. After some calls, we got the job.

A word of caution, if you hear about a job on the ten o'clock news, you know there must be some drawbacks. There were! Our girls came from emotionally bankrupt homes. One had been sexually molested. Another had been passed from foster home to foster home. Still another had been severely beaten by both parents. Paul and I thought that if we showered these girls with affirmation and provided well for them materially they would be forever grateful. So we couldn't understand why they weren't instantly overjoyed in their new home with us. We now know that even though the girls did appreciate us, they needed time to work through the pain of their losses before they could truly start their lives over. Lost things and people can never be totally replaced. Before we can go on, therefore, we must mourn our losses.

I must grieve over my lost relationships if I want to grow into new ones.

                                        J.E.M.

> *By pride comes only contention,*
> *But with the well-advised is wisdom.*
> —PROV. 13:10

Pride ruins relationships. Susan fluctuates between striving to impress others and belittling them. It is impossible to have any degree of honesty or intimacy in a relationship with her. Carly treats men as objects to be possessed and manipulated. She says, "I use them. I enjoy them. And then, when I'm tired of them, I throw the relationship away." Both these women have become so puffed up with pride that they have trouble connecting with other people.

Pride exaggerates our strengths and denies our weaknesses. Love, however, frees us to be realistic about our strengths and honest about our weaknesses. Love is the effective—and healing—antidote to pride.

Truckers tell us that an empty truck makes the most noise. People are like that too: the emptier the person, the bigger the boast. Next time we are tempted to inflate ourselves or deflate someone else, let's check our empty spots and allow God's love to fill them.

Swallowing our pride may be distasteful, but it's not fattening.

J.M.C.

*Even a child is known by his deeds,
Whether what he does is pure and right.*
—PROV. 20:11

Whether our adolescents are failing in school, abusing drugs, or simply breaking rules, the most important thing we can do for them is allow them to accept responsibility for their actions. We as parents must not be manipulated into taking responsibility for our adolescents. Certainly we must guide them and be concerned about them, but the best way to do that is by helping them learn that there are natural consequences for making wrong choices. Making their choices for them only teaches them to be dependent on us and later resentful of us.

Allowing our kids to take responsibility and suffer the consequences can be painful. It may mean watching them fail when they don't do their homework or even allowing them to spend the night in jail when they've broken the law. It's tempting to bail them out of trouble because we cannot bear to watch them in pain or—even worse—to try to hide their actions so we won't be embarrassed. Whatever the situation, we must step back and ask ourselves if what we're doing is best for our adolescent . . . or best for us.

Father, help me be strong enough to allow my child to learn from his or her mistakes. Teach me self-control when I feel the urge to fix things and make things right for my child.

J.L.M.

> *Our offenses and sins weigh us down, and we are*
> *wasting away because of them.*
> —EZEK. 33:10 NIV

Garbage is more and more a topic of conversation these days. An archaeologist at the University of Arizona sorts through fresh trash for its sociological significance. And overflowing landfills have made us realize we are a nation of too much garbage; we must make better decisions about what to recycle and what to throw away.

I find that counseling recovering women is a little like going through a garbage dump. The client and I wade through her past life, deciding what can be used and what needs to go. Abuse victims, for example, must work through their experiences and see what they can "recycle" (understanding for other victims, empathy for people in pain, the strength that comes from surviving) as well as what they must "throw away" (shame and guilt over the attack, bitterness toward their attacker and God, fear of relationships).

There is much we can keep even from bad experiences, but too much garbage in our mind can push out all the good things God wants to give us. Let's determine that today, with God's help, we begin to make wise choices about what to do with the garbage that fills our minds.

Today, I will give God all the garbage in my mind that I can't use for my betterment. He has plenty of landfills to hold it all.

J.E.M.

*Therefore you are inexcusable, O man, whoever
you are who judge, for in whatever you judge
another you condemn yourself; for you who
judge practice the same things.* —ROM. 2:1

Most often when I judge someone I am battling in
them a quality of my own that I don't want to face.
When I say that I don't like someone's judgmental
spirit, I exhibit mine. Yet neither of us changes. When
someone's lack of patience irritates me, I am being im-
patient.

Carolyn accused her husband of being controlling.
He was. But no movement could be made in their recovery until Carolyn faced the controller in herself. He
would demand sex; she would refuse just to show him
who was stronger. He'd dole out small amounts of
spending money, so she got a credit card in her name
that he knew nothing about.

Judgments and condemnations don't change people.
People change by being accepted. Those of us in recovery have to remove the black robe of a judge. We
have to let go of our opinion of what should be and
dare to face what is. Acceptance suspends judgment.
Acceptance says, "I am responsible for me, and you
are responsible for you; now let's walk beside each
other."

Judgments always boomerang.

J.M.C.

Her children rise up and call her blessed;
Her husband also, and he praises her.
—PROV. 31:28

Carolyn's three children were almost grown. Last year, Carolyn had taken a few classes at the local junior college to brush up on her typing skills and shorthand. Now Carolyn's husband and her kids were encouraging her to get a job. She had taken care of them all these years, they said; now they wanted her to do something for herself.

For years, Carolyn had been the one saying, "You can do it" or "Just be yourself." This time her husband and kids were giving her pointers, helping her find something to wear and encouraging her about the interview. Carolyn was excited when she landed a position, and her family was proud of her. Everyone beamed as she started her new career.

The encouragement Carolyn's family gave her was just an echo of the encouragement she had always given them. She loved her children and taught them by example how to love others. While caring for your children, it is good to remember that they really will retain what you teach them. As you parent, pray for guidance to make wise decisions.

Father, help me to care for my children with the same devotion you give to me.

J.L.M.

So then, my beloved brethren, let every man be
swift to hear, slow to speak, slow to wrath.
—JAMES 1:19

We often say, "Did you hear what I said?" How often do we ask ourselves, "Did I hear what you said?" How often do we really listen when those we love have something to say to us?

Real listening involves more than just hearing. First, listening takes time. When we give our time to others, over a period of time they'll get the message that we care. Listening also takes heart. Our ears will often miss what our hearts won't. Our loved ones are sometimes afraid to express their true feelings because of fear of pain and rejection. Our hearts can often accept things our ears will reject. Finally, listening takes looking. They say the eyes are the window to the soul. Often our ears and hearts miss what our eyes may catch.

Just as we must train ourselves to listen to our loved ones on earth, we must train ourselves to listen to God. He speaks through His Word, His creation, and His people. We must take the time to listen with our ears and our hearts and to look with our eyes at what God has done for us.

I will take the time today to listen with my ears, heart, and eyes.

J.E.M.

> *Cast your burden on the Lord,*
> *And He shall sustain you;*
> *He shall never permit the righteous*
> *to be moved.*   —PS. 55:22

I travel a lot to get to speaking engagements, and I usually carry my own baggage. Recently, however, someone met me at the airport and offered to carry my luggage for me. I gladly accepted. And as I walked down the long corridors I felt ten years younger and fifty pounds lighter. I guess I didn't realize how heavy my baggage had been until I stopped carrying it.

So it is in life. We walk around burdened down by debilitating guilt, past failures, unspoken secrets, and so much else. We don't realize how heavy our burden is. After all, we have been carrying it forever. Only when we stop, admit that our baggage is too much for us, and then hand it over to the Lord will we feel lighter.

So often in my life this truth has become real to me through another person's loving touch, kind words, caring eyes, and committed action. I have had to learn to accept God's support through human support. I have had to be willing to be vulnerable to God and to a significant other. As I have risked trusting, my load has become lighter, my understanding of God's love has deepened, and my acceptance of my humanity has increased.

If I hadn't had a burden, Lord, I wouldn't know the extent to which you can be trusted. I wouldn't have learned how to receive. Thank you, Lord.

J.M.C.

*If we confess our sins, He is faithful and just to
forgive us our sins and to cleanse us from all
unrighteousness. If we say that we have not sinned,
we make Him a liar, and His word is not in us.*
—1 JOHN 1:9-10

If we repeatedly slip into old ways of thinking, old
habits will be impossible to break. That is why recovery must begin in our minds. And the only way truly to
heal our thoughts is through Christ. A constant consciousness of God enables us to break old patterns of
thought and behavior. It is when we become complacent with recovery that old habits emerge.

A part of allowing Christ to heal our thoughts involves admitting our mistakes. We can discover
strength from allowing ourselves to be wrong, and a
new willingness to change emerges when we decide
that only Christ is perfect. Many of us tend to beat ourselves up for not being perfect instead of admitting imperfection and praying for strength. But it is only when
we stop competing with others and relying on ourselves to be strong and self-sufficient, that we can see
God's healing power at work. Begin today to make a
commitment to increase your awareness of God's
power. Practice admitting mistakes and then forgiving
yourself, just as Christ forgave you.

*Lord, give me strength to be honest about my mistakes and turn to
you for guidance.*

J.L.M.

Who can understand his errors?
Cleanse me from secret faults.
—PS. 19:12

Denial is a trait we often find in codependent relationships. Matt, for instance, refused to acknowledge that his wife, Sue, was an alcoholic, even though he found her passed out on the porch from time to time. And Matt even denied his denial, insisting to himself that neither he nor his family had a serious problem.

But denial is not only found in codependents. We all block out reality at times. Some people delay going to the doctor because they already know something is wrong and don't want to face it. Others can get a direct diagnosis and still tell themselves the doctor was wrong. Counselors are frequently confronted with statements of denial:

"It's not as bad as it appears."

"If I were better, or tried harder, things would be all right."

"It's a minor problem—certainly not an addiction."

"We're making progress on our own; we don't need help."

Denial isn't easy to break.

Let's ask God to show us our own denial, wherever it may be in our lives.

Lord, help me not to deny my denial.

J.E.M.

All the paths of the Lord are mercy and truth,
To such as keep His covenant and His testimonies.
—PS. 25:10

A few years ago, our then six-year-old was diagnosed as having cancer. Never will I forget the pain that knifed through me as I heard that word. Why would such a dreadful thing happen to such an innocent child? And how could a good God let it happen?

Often we hear easy, flippant praise of God's goodness. Usually it comes from people who have gotten exactly what they wanted, when they wanted it. "I have a new home, a wonderful family, a Mercedes parked in my driveway. Isn't God good?"

But is God equally as good when a child has cancer, finances look bleak, or a precious relationship is disintegrating? The passage we are meditating on today says so. It states that God is both merciful and truthful to those of us who trust Him.

I believe the prayers and support of my friends opened my eyes to God's goodness during that painful time. Their faith and their love for me helped me face my doubts and then to open myself again to the possibility of love and truth. I had to realize that God never promised us a rose garden; He just promised us His presence. But His presence—His mercy and truth, and goodness—is what can carry us through the bad times.

Life isn't fair, but God is good!

J.M.C.

> *A [woman] who has friends must [herself] be friendly,*
> *But there is a friend who sticks closer than a [sister].*
> —PROV. 18:24

My friend who sticks closer than a sister is a blessing as she comforts me and allows me to comfort her. As our relationship has endured throughout the years, I have come to believe that she is a gift sent to me from our Lord. And just as I treasure other gifts from God, I treasure my friend and try never to take her for granted. As we relax in the security of our friendship, it is important that I let her know how much she is appreciated. She means more to me than words can express, and she may never know how much she is valued.

The companionship of my friend in times of trouble, the tenderness in times of rest, and the strength in times of growth help give me confidence that life is worthwhile. She gives me the ability to touch others in their times of need because, without knowing it, she teaches me how to give and receive love. The way she lives is an inspiration to me as I learn more about myself and as she shares about herself. Even though my friend may be miles away, I cherish our shared giggles, our tears, and our agreement in the Spirit. The precious gift God bestows has added both excitement and calm to my life.

I thank you, Lord, for my dear friend, with whom you so graciously have blessed me. I pray that our friendship will always include you and be pleasing in your sight.

J.L.M.

*Guard what was committed to your trust, avoiding
the profane and vain babblings and contradictions
of what is falsely called knowledge.*
—1 TIM. 6:20

Carol walked into my office, sat down, and started
crying. Through her tears she told me the story of her
marriage.

"It was like being packed for a warm Hawaiian vacation. Our shorts, swimming suits, and sunhats were
neatly packed. We got off the plane and were instantly
hit with a gust of cold wind. As we looked out of the
airplane, we saw snow-covered mountains and snow-
drifts at the edges of the runway. We weren't in Hawaii.
We were in Switzerland! I think marriage would have
been fine if we had been prepared for it," she went on.
"We had so many ideals that were crushed. We're both
so disillusioned, I don't know if we can ever get our
marriage back together."

Carol and Tom were an example of many couples
who had been swept away by the myths of marriage.
But they came for counseling ready to do away with
the myths and face reality. Together they erased such
myths as "Having to work on marriage means we
weren't right for each other in the first place" and "If
you can't meet all my needs, I need to find someone
else." And together they relaid the foundation of their
marriage.

---

*Lord, grant us the courage and the love to base our marriage on
reality, not myths.*

J.E.M.

> *In a multitude of counselors there is safety.*
> —PROV. 24:6

Helen lives with a shame-based husband. He can't talk to her without putting her down. He expects her to be the go-between with people he doesn't want to face or confront. And if she refuses, he accuses her of being unsupportive.

Helen, who grew up in an alcoholic home, also used to be shame-based. But two years ago, Helen joined a recovery group of loving, accepting, and honest people. With their help, she is learning how to set limits, take responsibility for what is hers, and live as an equal partner in her marriage.

Helen could try to change her husband, but that would only lead to bitterness and frustration; besides, changing him is not her responsibility. Instead, she surrounds herself with a wealth of healthy counsel—people who are a little further in the recovery process than she is and who understand grace at the point of their deepest failure. Rather than turning her against her husband, this support strengthens Helen so she can approach her most challenging relationship with both grace and truth.

Lord, thank you that I can't be a Lone Ranger and be in recovery. Thank you for the supportive counselors in my life. Give me wisdom to see ways that I can be there for them.

J.M.C.

*Do not let your adornment be merely outward—
arranging the hair, wearing gold, or putting on
fine apparel—but let it be the hidden person of the
heart, with the incorruptible beauty of a gentle and
quiet spirit, which is very precious in the sight
of God.* —1 PETER 3:3–4

We women wear many masks that hide who we really are. There are professional masks, mothering masks, secure masks, alluring masks, innocent masks, and more. Sometimes we try to hide behind pretty clothes, jewelry, and hair—or competence, intellect, and wit—because we fear that people would reject us if they really knew us. Unfortunately, we end up hiding the hidden beauty that is our true asset. When we wear masks, we can never risk getting to the honest feeling level with people or sharing our true personalities—the "real me" whom God loves.

Developing the courage to allow people to know us for who we are—without masks—takes reliance on God. God will support us as we take the risks involved, and He will provide the strength to endure any rejection we might encounter. The payoff is true intimacy with those who like the real, undisguised person behind the mask.

Lord, help me to remove my masks and allow my hidden beauty to be revealed to those with whom I desire intimacy. Remind me that my inner beauty must be my main focus instead of my outer beauty.

J.L.M.

> *A man's foes will be those of his own household.*
> —MATT. 10:36

Pam came into my office with the look of a martyr. She hadn't bothered to fix herself up, and her overall demeanor showed me she didn't want to be there; her pastor had referred her. Pam told me a story she had repeated to many others before me. She talked about her alcoholic husband, Joe, and the abuse she had received all of her married life.

As we talked, it became clear that both Pam and Joe were trying to complete unfinished business passed on by their parents. Pam's unconscious message from her mom had been, "Pam, I can't change my alcoholic husband, but you marry a similar man and heal him." Joe's message from his alcoholic dad had been subconsciously received as, "Carry on, son; try to be a success—even if you have to be an alcoholic."

Pam and Joe had done a great job of receiving these messages, but they were not doing a very good job of carrying them out. Pam certainly was not healing her husband! Through therapy, however, Pam came to realize that the only person she could change was herself. As she gradually stopped responding to her mother's message, Joe was forced to look at his own unfinished business. He is now in recovery through an Alcoholics Anonymous program.

Lord, help me live my own life under your guidance instead of spending all my energy trying to complete my parents' unfinished business.

J.E.M.

*And may the Lord make you increase and abound
in love to one another and to all, just as we do to
you.*   —1 THESS. 3:12

Have you ever failed at something that meant a lot to
you? Perhaps you didn't get the promotion you were
hoping for. Perhaps you dared to go back to school
after twenty years out of school and then failed your
first test. When something like that happens, many of
us feel inadequate. We doubt we will ever succeed
again. And if we were raised in a family that used
shame and embarrassment as a predominant weapon,
the darkness of our adult failure seems even blacker.

To overcome these feelings of shame, we may lash
out at those who are closest to us and most dependent
on us—a child, our spouse, our ex, or a co-worker. It's
as if we believe we'll somehow feel more adequate if
we can reduce someone else's self-esteem. But it
doesn't work that way.

Shame is never healed by shaming someone else. Instead, shame retreats in the face of love, grace, and
acceptance. Loving relationships with imperfect human beings who are themselves on the road to recovery give us the encouragement we need. And a
relationship with Jesus Christ, who doesn't condemn
us, doesn't embarrass us, and will never knock us
down to make Himself look good, gives us the strength
to recover.

---

*When I feel shamed and inadequate, help me to admit it and to reach
out to you and to others so that love can warm the frozen places in
my soul.*

                                                          J.M.C.

> *Search me, O God, and know my heart;*
> *Try me, and know my anxieties.*
> —PS. 139:23

Do you ever find yourself anxiously wishing you had been born with a different set of circumstances or blaming your parents for not being what you would have desired? Perhaps you have said, "If only I had a better childhood . . ." or "If only my parents had been there for me. . . ." Dwelling on such "if onlys" is hurtful because it keeps us from accepting reality. That doesn't mean we should ignore or repress the past. Identifying all the ways we were wronged, talking about our pain, and praying about our past can actually help us come to terms with reality. Eventually, however, the time comes to move on. Focusing on the here and now and looking forward to new opportunities to come help us proceed. The present and the future will have their setbacks, but also their joys and pleasures. As we get our focus off the anxieties of life, we can start noticing the pleasant things around us. Acceptance of life, for better or worse, enables us to mature into healthy women with a full range of emotions—women who can both grieve the negative and rejoice in the positive.

Lord, I no longer want to spend my time fretting about what I wish my life had been. Help me to accept my life for what it is and to believe you can make it better.

J.L.M.

*The steps of a good man are ordered
  by the Lord,
And He delights in his way.*
                    —PS. 37:23

Do you know where you're going and can you get there from here? Many of us go through life with a distant, fuzzy picture in our mind of what we want out of life and how we're going to get it. But we don't make the effort to define our goals clearly, and so we don't make much real progress. I often say that if you aim for a star, you'll at least end up in outer space—if you don't end up a little spacey!

When I set my own goals, I think of a few long-term objectives I want to reach. Then I ask myself, "Are these goals really achievable for me, and if I do achieve them will I feel satisfaction?" I also ask myself if these goals are consistent with my relationship with God and what I feel He wants me to do with my life. If these criteria are met, then I am ready to map out my strategies for goal achievement.

I think of small steps that will help me reach the goals I have chosen. Each day I try to take a few small steps toward my long-term goals. Even on those days when my goals seem far away, I can pat myself on the back for taking a few small steps.

Small steps are better than no steps. And if you take a few small steps every day, you'll be at your destination sooner than you think.

Today I will take small steps to eventually reach big goals.

                                        J.E.M.

> *Your word is a lamp to my feet*
> *And a light to my path.*
> —PS. 119:105

Imagine you are hiking a trail you have never tried before. As you study the map, you realize it will take you longer than you had planned to get back. Darkness settles in. The night feels oppressive. Everything sounds different and looks different—are you heading the right way? Nervous, you stop to check your supplies. And then your hand touches a flashlight. With relief you turn it on and the path ahead becomes clear.

Have you ever felt as if you had lost your way in life? Your spirit, energy, and hopes are low. Painful memories flood your mind. Someone you loved has died. Someone you needed has abandoned you. Someone whose opinion you valued has rejected you. All seems hopeless. Then, in the darkness of your soul, a Bible verse you memorized long ago clicks in your consciousness. With it comes a ray of light and hope and clarity.

God's Word is a light to our path. Rather than being negative and restrictive, it is a positive guide to all that is good, healthy, and wholesome. The more we immerse ourselves in God's Word, the more hope we will feel, even in seemingly hopeless situations.

Lord, I want the light of your Word to enlighten me today and in my tomorrows.

J.M.C.

God has spoken once, . . .
That power belongs to God.
—PS. 62:11

It is difficult for most of us to admit how controlling we are, especially when we talk about having controlling husbands or fathers. The truth is, many of us hide our controlling behind a passive manner. We may even see ourselves as the giving, considerate ones. But if we honestly start evaluating how many ways we attempt to control our family, we may be prompted to change some behaviors.

How many of us control others by worrying to the point of hovering over our loved ones? Or what about when we feel uptight and get that look on our face that tells everyone, "Stay clear"? Making our mate or children feel guilty and thus manipulating them into doing what we want is also a classic control tactic.

Turning over our controlling tendencies to God can be a daily relief. Admitting we are powerless and that we need help from Jesus Christ places our life in perspective. Honestly admitting our weaknesses and calling out to God for assistance not only is healthy for us, but makes living with another controller bearable—since we no longer are trying to "outcontrol" another person.

Jesus, I want to let go of my control today and turn it over to you. Please remind me throughout the day to rely on you to be in charge.
                                                                                J.L.M.

*For we dare not class ourselves or compare
ourselves with those who commend themselves.
But they . . . comparing themselves among
themselves, are not wise.* —2 COR. 10:12

When we get to Heaven, God is not going to say,
"Why weren't you more like Moses or another one of
the saints?" God is going to say, "Why weren't you
more like you?" God did not put us on earth to be
someone else, but to be our unique selves. I try not to
spend my time comparing myself to others. Instead I
strive to identify how I, in my own unique way, can
serve God and live a growing and fulfilling life.

Jealousy is always caused by a low self-concept. We
feel threatened by how little we have and how much
we feel others have. What we're really saying when we
feel jealous is that God made a mistake in how He
made us or what He gave us. *If I only had a little more*,
we seem to think, *everything would be OK.*

Jealousy prevents us from feeling happiness. We are
so busy feeling sorry for ourselves because someone
else got a promotion at work, a new car, a new dress,
or a new baby that we can't experience happiness at
our friends' successes. Even sadder, we can't feel joy
over the good things in our own lives.

---

*Lord, help me keep jealousy out of my life today so I can have room
for loving and being loved.*

J.E.M.

Direct my steps by Your word,
And let no iniquity have dominion
over me.   —PS. 119:133

Anger is a protective emotion. It can protect good things like love, freedom, talent, or attachments. (Just let someone try to harm your child!) It can protect personal boundaries—we become angry when someone pushes or shoves us. And it can protect our right to be human. When other people don't allow us to be real—when they idealize us or expect us to be something we're not—anger is a natural response.

Anger is healthy when it protects good things. But anger can also protect things that are not good—like isolation and illusions. Such unhealthy protective anger can keep us from facing reality, cut us off from other people, and hinder our growth. And that is why we need to test our anger.

The next time you feel angry, stop and consider: What is my anger protecting? If it is defending something healthy, then you need to process the emotion, own it, and approach the offender with honesty and grace. If it is protecting something that is not healthy, you need to seek out a counselor who can help you in the process of discovering why you are defending against love rather than moving toward it.

Lord, help me analyze whether my anger is protecting healthy or unhealthy things.

J.M.C.

> *But it is good for me to draw near to God;*
> *I have put my trust in the Lord GOD,*
> *That I may declare all Your works.*
> —PS. 73:28

Acceptance of our femininity goes with acceptance of ourselves. But too many of us were taught as children that femininity means not being responsible for ourselves. This misconception may have led us to rely on others to make decisions, take care of us, or be responsible for our happiness. Wholeness comes when we realize that we do have to make decisions and, even if we are married, there are things we must do for ourselves.

Taking responsibility for our walk with God is a good place to begin. So often we depend on our family or husbands to provide us a relationship with God by expecting them to initiate prayer or Bible study. But God expects each of us, man or woman, to be responsible for establishing and maintaining a relationship with Him. No one can choose Christ for us; this is something we do on our own. As we do draw near to Him, we discover more about ourselves. He reveals to us areas that need improvement, and we become responsible for taking action in these areas. He is pleased when we elect to become accountable for our own sins and to worship Him, and this in turn brings joy and satisfaction to our lives.

Lord, I want to be accountable for my actions and to depend on you for guidance. Please convict me of my sins and help me take responsibility in my life.

J.L.M.

*And He said to me, "My grace is sufficient for you,
for My strength is made perfect in weakness."*
—2 COR. 12:9

I call it my weak link—and it hits at the most inopportune times. For me it is lower back pain. For you it may be headaches or allergies. Whatever the symptoms, they show up when we encounter stressful circumstances over which we have no control. This morning, for example, my teenager decided he didn't feel like going to school. Reasoning with him didn't work. Threatening him didn't work. Although I didn't raise my voice, I was screaming on the inside. And the anger seemed to travel right to my lower back and stayed there, causing me pain all day.

What can we do when we recognize the out-of-control feeling that stresses our weak link? If the symptom is already there, medication can help—we can take aspirin or antihistamine. But we also need to work on turning our frustration over to God. The famous "Serenity Prayer" comes to my mind:

Lord grant me the serenity to accept the things I cannot change, the courage to change the things I can, and the wisdom to know the difference.

Lord, if I become angry about things beyond my control today, grant me the serenity to turn my anger over to you instead of transferring it to my weak link.

J.E.M.

That Christ may dwell in your hearts through faith;
that you [may be] rooted and grounded in love.
—EPH. 3:17

An angelic-looking two-year-old sat in the cart in front of me in the grocery-store checkout line. Sitting in the cart was obviously not her idea of a great time, but her mother told her to stay put. And then this curly-haired, chubby-cheeked little beauty started to scream at the top of her lungs, "No, no, no, no." The checker and I watched, wondering who was going to win. The little one yelled. The mother held firm. The child was still confined to the cart when the twosome made it to the register.

Sheepishly the mother told the clerk, "I love her yes, and I love her no. It's just not easy to face the no in public." The clerk looked at the mother with amazement as he filled the grocery bags. Soon mother and daughter were on their way out the door.

"What a lucky little girl," the checker said. I agreed. And as I left the grocery store I realized that mother had given me a beautiful picture of Jesus' love for me. He loves my yes. He loves my no. He loves me. He wants a relationship with me, but He respects my separateness. And interestingly, as my no is accepted, I find myself desiring to say yes.

Thank you for your acceptance of both my yes and my no. Help me to live that kind of acceptance with those dear to me.

J.M.C.

A man has joy by the answer of his mouth,
And a word spoken in due season, how
    good it is!   —PROV. 15:23

In our desire to establish a peaceful life, many of us have mistakenly learned to withhold our true thoughts. We may try to gain approval or prevent criticism by refusing to take a stand, agreeing with whomever we are with, keeping quiet about our religious beliefs, or adjusting our opinions to suit our audience. Unfortunately, these conflict-avoiding measures block our growth, and the stress of constantly "holding ourselves in" may lead to physical problems such as ulcers, headaches, or overeating.

As we take the risk of relying on truth instead of pleasing others, we can rely on Christ to give us courage. Praying that the Lord will bring to mind what we would say if we weren't so afraid of criticism helps us to believe it is all right to speak truthful words. As we take one risk after another, we begin to relax and feel good about what we have to say. We will keep a loving attitude, but we will reveal our true thoughts. Eventually, as we develop a security in who we are, we begin to believe that honesty is something we can respect about ourselves.

Father, give me the courage to risk being myself. I want to be pleasing to you while I focus on honest and sincere communication.

                                      J.L.M.

> *Love suffers long and is kind; loves does not envy;*
> *love does not parade itself, is not puffed up.*
> —1 COR. 13:4

Envy can be defined as not only wanting what someone else has, but also wishing the other person didn't have it. And envy is a choice. We choose to compare ourselves to others, forgetting that God made each of us unique.

Envy is like a deadly cancer that consumes our souls and ruins our relationships. It causes conflicts and quarrels in our homes and on the job, and it fills our lives with resentment, which in turn brings bitterness and self-centeredness. Envy also makes us miserable. Comparing ourselves with others prevents us from appreciating God's goodness in our lives and the lives of others and blinds us to the truth that God has enough goodness for everyone.

What can we do if we recognize envy in our lives? First we can concentrate on appreciating our God-given uniqueness. Then we can use envy as a stepping stone in our lives. We can take a hard look at values which foster envy in our lives. Then we can refocus our attention on the things that will last through eternity: God, God's Word, and people.

Love does not envy, and envy blocks love. Today I choose to fill my life with love instead of envy.

J.E.M.

Go home to your friends, and tell them what great things the Lord has done for you, and how He has had compassion on you.   —MARK 5:19

Susan, a counselor for women who struggle with eating disorders, sat in front of me. She was exhausted—overworked, underexercised, not eating well, not sleeping. She couldn't get up the energy to go to work. When she was alone, she struggled with feelings of uselessness. A few of Susan's mother's friends had wanted some counseling. She hadn't really wanted to take them on, but she didn't want to let her mother down. This addition to an already busy schedule left her absolutely wrung out.

Our helping needs to be done with joy—because we have chosen to help, not because we feel cornered or because we'd feel guilty if we didn't. Rather than something we do out of compulsion, helping needs to be done with the realization of God's compassionate touch on the empty spots in our lives.

Step Twelve in any Twelve-Step program states: "Having had a spiritual awakening as a result of these steps, we tried to carry this message to others and to practice these principles in all our affairs."* This step is the last step in recovery for a very specific reason. If we have not worked through all the preceding steps, our people-helping efforts can hurt us.

Lord, I cannot pass on what I haven't received. Help me come to you first so I really have something to share.

J.M.C.

*See page v.

> *When you pass through the waters,*
> *I will be with you;*
> *And through the rivers, they shall*
> *not overflow you.*
>
> —ISA. 43:2

O, Lord, everything within me wants to stop coming before you. I'm feeling more and more desperate, and I'm afraid to ask for help because comfort doesn't come. I then get confused because I feel like my expectations and demands on you are too much. In many ways I feel like you have already withdrawn from me—but maybe it's I who have abandoned you."

Jana felt so rejected by God because she had been following Him totally in her life and now she felt alone. Where had her faith gone?

What seemed to keep her going were gentle reminders of what the Lord had done for her in the past and what He had promised to complete in her. She knew that faith was doing what she knew she needed to do. So in spite of her doubts, she also started sharing both her concerns and her beliefs in God with others. Slowly, over the months, she saw many people come to understand, and she felt as if she had gained a bigger family. They cried and shared their pain together. They had fellowship with God, and she truly felt blessed by this God-given opportunity to minister to others and be ministered to by them.

Lord, thank you for not abandoning me. Help me to remain faithful so I may receive the many blessings you have for me.

J.L.M.

Trust in the Lord with all your heart,
And lean not on your own understanding.
—PROV. 3:5

I was wondering to myself the other day why I like people who admit that they don't understand everything. I'm talking about people who are leaders in their fields, whether it be theology, medicine, or psychology. I guess I define a brilliant person as one who knows his limits.

Before my husband and I had children, we just knew we were going to be brilliant parents. After all, our parents had done a great job raising us. With all our education, surely we could do even better! We had four children in six years. And things went relatively smoothly until the first one started to school. But in the years that followed, as each child faced distinctively different cultural values and went through unique stages, my husband and I started wondering how much we knew about parenting after all.

At some point along the child-rearing way, we realized what God meant when He said not to lean on our own understanding. We were humbled by parenthood. But God showed us His mercy by intervening each step of the way.

In the challenging task of child rearing, I need God's strength to compensate for my lack of understanding.

J.E.M.

> *But the wisdom that is from above is first pure,*
> *then peaceable, gentle, willing to yield, full of*
> *mercy and good fruits, without partiality and*
> *without hypocrisy.* —JAMES 3:17

Clarice is a brilliant, accomplished woman with multiple degrees after her name. But her quest for knowledge has left her distant, arrogant, and distrustful of all around her. Being in her presence is a lot like being with a porcupine. If you disagree with her, you are certain to feel the prick of her quills. This woman is attempting to prove her worth academically, yet underneath she feels a gaping insecurity.

Elizabeth, on the other hand, has founded her self-esteem on the fact that the Almighty God of this universe valued her enough to put His life on the line for her. This woman is free from the misbelief that anything else—education, friends, or paycheck—determines her value. Her value has been predetermined, and even her failures don't detract from it.

Once that truth makes its way deep into our beings, nothing is ever the same. We are set free to be all we possibly can be—and also to affirm the value of others. We are willing to accept the possibility that we might not always be right and that another's perspective might broaden ours. Because we are at peace personally, we bring peace into all our relationships. What a difference "wisdom from above" makes.

People don't care how much you know until they know how much you care!

J.M.C.

He gives power to the weak,
And to those who have no might
He increases strength.
—ISA. 40:29

Recovery can feel like a dream in which we are trying to escape a danger, but our body is stuck in slow motion. We often throw our hands up in exasperation and exclaim, "Why won't the pain go away? When am I going to get better?" It is at that time that God must take over. In order for healing to take place, we must realize we are powerless and let God provide the daily power to walk through another battle.

I once counseled a young woman who had been physically, verbally, and sexually abused. She had a learning disability, was overweight, had no working skills, and could not drive. Yet, this incredible young woman had a childlike faith and powerful determination. During her hospital stay, she worked hard to complete the reading or writing activities, even though they took her hours to finish. When she was released from the hospital, she worked through job-assistance programs and trained to become a cashier. She went from a halfway house to a group home to her very own apartment. It was a long haul, but she never gave up. When I would ask her how she found her strength, she would smile humbly and say with utmost certainty, "Jesus gives me strength."

Father, please be my strength and help me through today.

J.L.M.

> *But as for me, I trust in You, O Lord;*
> *I say, "You are my God."*
> *My times are in Your hand.*
> —PS. 31:14–15

Imagine that you have received a letter coming in the mail. The letter contains great news; you've just inherited $1,440 per day for the rest of your life. The only stipulation is that you must spend *all* of that money every day. I'm sure you would sit down and plan carefully how you were going to spend all of the money. You wouldn't want to waste any of it.

Every morning of our lives we are given something more valuable than money—1,440 precious minutes. And as someone has said, "Life is like a coin. You can spend it anyway you want, but you can only spend it once." Time is the great equalizer. No one, rich or poor, has more or less than anyone else. The choice of how we spend our time each day is one of the most important decisions we will make in life.

As women in recovery we must choose to use our time wisely. We are tempted to fill our days, as we have in the past, with codependent or compulsive behaviors. Just as we would carefully plan how to spend our $1,440 per day, so we must carefully plan how we will enjoy our 1,440 minutes.

Today I choose to "spend" my precious minutes wisely.

J.E.M.

*You have hedged me behind and before,
And laid Your hand upon me.*
—PS. 139:5

What is the purpose of a hedge? To create a boundary, a protection, privacy. And that's the purpose of our personal boundaries, too. We all have areas of self that should not be usurped by others.

Before we start the journey of recovery, we are often unaware that we have boundaries or that they have been violated. That's why anger and resentment are often one of the first healthy signs. Anger is a signal that someone has gone too far—transgressed our boundaries—and that we know it. The next step is learning to protect our own boundaries, to say no to those who would invade our personal territory. If we've hardly ever said no, our first attempts will feel awkward and even rude. Controlling, enmeshing, irresponsible people may accuse us of being selfish. Yet others will value our honesty and clarity—and we will gain a better idea of who we are.

Boundaries are inherent in the character of God. The Trinity, with its clear distinctions between Father, Son, and Holy Spirit, demonstrates how we can live in close relationship yet maintain our separate selves. God gave us boundaries. And God hedges us behind and before with the boundary of His never-failing love.

As I learn to say no to violations by others, help me to say yes to the safety and security found in God's love and in healthy relationships.

J.M.C.

> *Fear not, for I am with
> you;
> Be not dismayed, for I am
> your God.*
> —ISA. 41:10

Solitude and loneliness are two very different things. When freely chosen, solitude can help us become acquainted with who we are and keep us in touch with God. Loneliness, however, just causes us to feel isolated and sad. We need solitude to deepen our spiritual commitment and strengthen our relationship with Christ. But even as we cultivate solitude, we must also develop a plan to avoid loneliness. In a sense, we use solitude to prevent isolation.

After a time of solitude each day, it is time to establish contact with people you can talk to and nurture. Those who are married may want to spend time with their mates, but spending time with other people as well will enrich the day. Those who live miles from children or loved ones must make a special commitment to stay in fellowship with Christ and in fellowship with others. Being able to reach out and help others enables us to avoid loneliness. Begin today to set aside time for solitude with God and then fellowship with people.

Father, teach me how to be alone with you for meditation, and then show me how to be active with others for fellowship.

J.L.M.

*But if you bite and devour one another, beware lest
you be consumed by one another!*

—GAL. 5:15

What a 'friend' she was! I was always there for her,
but where was she when I needed her?"

"This is marriage? I had stars in my eyes on our wedding day. Things were going to be so different than our
parents' marriages. But he certainly has not kept his
part of the bargain."

"Our children are such a pain to us. We looked forward to parenthood, but now we look forward to the
day they will leave."

We've all heard these or similar stories throughout
our lives. Such unmet expectations are a primary
cause of discouragement. Often we base our expectations on unrealistic and unfair standards and then expect others to read our minds and live up to those
standards. We put ourselves and our loved ones into a
pit that's difficult, if not impossible to get out of. Who
could be a good enough friend, a devoted enough husband, a lovable enough child?

We can avoid a lot of our discouragement by taking
our long list of expectations and burning it! Let's give
our loved ones the freedom to become the people God
wants them to be, not the people we expect them to
be.

Holding on to unrealistic expectations is a form of self-abuse.

J.E.M.

Who shall separate us from the love of Christ?
—ROM. 8:35

A couple who had been married thirty years took a Sunday afternoon drive to enjoy the first glimmer of springtime. As usual, the wife was hugging the car door, and they drove along in silence.

Suddenly they became aware that the car ahead of them was swerving all over the road. What was wrong? The answer soon became obvious: young lovers were in the car. He had his eyes on her rather than on the road. She was tickling the back of his neck and running her fingers through his hair. They were sitting so close that light was barely visible between them.

"We used to be like that!" the wife burst out accusingly. "But it's been so long since you looked at me that way. What's the use?"

Her husband must have had a long fuse. He put his arm out and looked straight at his angry wife. "Honey," he said, "I haven't moved."

So many of us feel as if God were distant. The truth is that He hasn't moved. He looks at us with eyes of love and compassion—with no condemnation in His gaze. He sees each of us as a highly significant woman, so significant that He sent His only Son to die for us. Why not bask in the warmth of His love and acceptance today?

If I don't feel God's love today, I need to ask myself who moved.

J.M.C.

*Brethren, I do not count myself to have
apprehended; but one thing I do, forgetting
those things which are behind and reaching
forward to those things which are ahead.*
—PHIL. 3:13

Laura's father was a good provider. He did not beat
his wife or kids, and he rarely lost his temper. But he
was an absent father in many ways. He would come
home each evening, get drunk, and fall asleep in his
chair. He didn't know how to express his feelings, address conflict, or spend time with his family.

After Laura had become a Christian, she thought her
new life in the church would help her forget that her
dad didn't talk to her or play with her as a child. Laura
soon realized that she simply could not turn off her
past like a light switch. Forgetting the past and putting
it behind her involved grieving the loss of a loving
father. Laura did this by praying, talking about it, and
receiving support from others. As she talked about her
past, she realized that she tended to be attracted to
men like her father because they were familiar to her.
For instance, she liked the idea of a man who talked
about his feelings, but she always found herself dating
"silent types." Once Laura had grieved her past, however, she was able to put it behind her. She was also
able to put her old way of relating to men behind her
and begin reaching out toward new, healthier relationships.

Father, teach me how to put my past behind me.

J.L.M.

Every way of a man is right in his own eyes,
But the Lord weighs the hearts.
—PROV. 21:2

I recently read an interesting article containing interviews with people who had robbed houses. None of the criminals were sorry about their deeds, and they all had excuses: "Their door was unlocked; they deserved to be robbed." "They had too much stuff; they didn't miss the things I took." The criminals showed no signs of guilt, only anger that they had been caught.

When I encounter patients with no guilt, I know the chances of recovery are slight. Rarely do sociopaths, people who feel that other people are put on earth for them to use and abuse, seek counseling of their own free will. A sociopath usually enters therapy to manipulate either a family member or the court system.

What can we, as women in recovery, do about the sociopaths in our lives? To the best of our ability, we must refuse to let ourselves be sexually, physically, or verbally abused. Our body is a temple of the Holy Spirit, so as God's daughters we have a duty to protect ourselves.

I will guard my heart and my body from all forms of abuse today.
J.E.M.

Being confident of this very thing, that He who has begun a good work in you will complete it until the day of Jesus Christ.
                                                —PHIL. 1:6

One of my favorite children's stories is *The Velveteen Rabbit*. In it, the Skin Horse explains to the toy Rabbit how to become "Real." He tells the floppy-eared creature that it happens "when a child loves you for a long time." And he goes on to explain how becoming real isn't an instant event. It is a process. In fact, he says, "Generally by the time you are Real, most of your hair has been loved off, and your eyes drop out and you get loose in the joints and very shabby. . . . Once you are Real, you can't become unreal again. It lasts for always."*

Tears usually fall by the time I finish reading this marvelous book. It always makes me acutely aware that what makes us all become real is God's unconditional love for us and our mutual love for each other.

At the beginning of our walk of faith, we barely dare to trust God's love. Could it possibly be as good as it sounds? Could He possibly love us as much when we fail as when we succeed? But, over the years, we realize the extent of God's love in new and deeper ways, and we come to see it in the love of friends. As we do, we open ourselves up to more and more of God's love. In the process, we, too, become real.

Lord, I want to bask in the sunshine of your love today. I trust myself to you and I commit myself to this relationship today.

                                                J.M.C.

*Margery Williams, *The Velveteen Rabbit* (New York: Holt, Rinehart & Winston, 1983), 4–5.

The Lord has appeared of old to me, saying:
"Yes I have loved you with an everlasting love;
Therefore with lovingkindness I have drawn you."
—JER. 31:3

One of the hardest challenges many of us face in life is learning to love ourselves as Christ does. So often, we try to feel loved by doing many things to build ourselves up. We perform, brag on ourselves, become "supermoms," and go to many other lengths to feel worthwhile and accepted.

I often wonder if God sometimes sits back and laughs at our futile attempts to earn love. Then He just loves and accepts us for who we are and asks that we love in the same way. We do not have to strive to hide our insecurities; we can recognize them and then lovingly push ourselves on to change.

Lord, you know I have wasted so much time and energy trying to prove myself worthy to be loved. Thank you for loving me today. Thank you for being patient with me, and help me continue to see your love for me. Help me to love myself as you do, Lord.

J.L.M.

As far as the east is from the west,
So far has He removed our transgressions
from us. —PS. 103:12

Sometimes I ask my patients if they think they're smarter than God. They always answer, "Of course not." I then proceed to explain that if they have asked God to forgive them but still feel guilty, they obviously haven't forgiven themselves. If God has forgiven but we can't, we must think we know better than God. Because we live in a sin-filled world that accepts us very conditionally, we tend to accept ourselves conditionally too. Most of us find it very difficult to understand how a just God can forgive us completely when mortals seem to keep score of our every wrong. For forgiveness to go from head knowledge to heart knowledge takes a lot of practice.

The Lord's Prayer tells us that our sins will be forgiven as we forgive others. This is another important point. I see clients who hold grudges toward themselves because they are holding so many toward God and others. They think that our unforgiveness will somehow result in vengeance on those who have hurt us. But it is more likely to make them sick, depressed, and miserable. Forgiveness is absolutely necessary for recovery.

I choose today to release my grudges toward myself, God, or others. Lord, help me to grasp the reality of your forgiveness.

J.E.M.

> *But when Jesus heard that, He said to them, "Those who are well have no need of a physician, but those who are sick."*
>
> —MATT. 9:12

On a beautiful spring morning, four women were meeting for croissants and coffee at a harbor cafe. Their chatter was lively and animated. I sensed that they knew each other well. And I couldn't help but overhear their conversation, which was about their battles with alcohol.

As I listened, it quickly became obvious to me that only one of these women was on her way to recovery. She acknowledged her problem, her inability to handle alcohol; the others didn't. She shared that her neediness had led her to a personal relationship with God, a deeper relationship with others through a Twelve-Step group, and personal therapy.

The others laughed uncomfortably and exchanged knowing glances. One of them acknowledged that she had a problem, but only because she needed a man in her life. A new relationship would give her life meaning, and she wouldn't need to drink so much. Another woman believed she could get over her craving by sheer willpower. Yes, she had a hangover, but it wouldn't happen again; she would just try harder. Neediness to her was a sign of weakness. She didn't need help from anyone, thank you.

As the women left, I was left thinking, "needs are the fuel for growth." And I thanked the Lord for my own neediness.

———

My needs are the avenue to God.

J.M.C.

*Praying always with all prayer and supplication
in the Spirit, being watchful to this end with all
perseverance and supplication for all the saints.*
EPH. 6:18

Claire looked at the tiny face and smiled at the precious innocence of the child. The baby's fingers wiggled, and Claire ached to pick up her eight-month-old dark-headed bundle. She could still hardly believe they were sitting at the hospital and little Lisa was imprisoned in that plastic tent.

Many days Claire had been tempted to ask "Why? Why did this happen to me? Why was I singled out? Why my baby?" But the "whys" only led to frustration. So Claire had focused instead on the question of "how": "How can I survive my baby's illness? How can I manage to care for my other children through this? How will my marriage hold together?" And it was that second question that led Claire to a deeper understanding of God. For God answered, "I will provide the 'How,'" and then He gave her the strength and support she needed. Lisa recovered with no further problems, and Claire still remembers the comfort the Lord provided during her baby's illness. Today Claire continues to believe that question "why" leads to more confusion, whereas the question "how" leads her to a greater reliance on Christ.

Father, thank you for the hope and strength you provide through my tribulations. I want to rely on you for support instead of questioning you.

J.L.M.

> *Better to dwell in the wilderness,*
> *Than with a contentious and angry woman.*
> —PROV. 21:19

Anger is a natural and normal reaction to physical, psychological, or sexual abuse. It is also the second stage of grief. When anger seems to lurk just below the surface in a woman's life, we usually assume it is mixed with the first stage of grief, which is denial.

Anger mixed with denial is a deadly twosome. It may result in a person who goes around like a bomb, ready to explode over trivial provocations.

If you have a tendency to "blow up" over small matters, you may need to look for the true source of your anger. Are you really furious that the paper boy didn't throw the paper on the porch, or was he just a safe outlet for underlying anger you haven't acknowledged? Your outbursts may be a signal that you have anger just "under the surface" that you need to process.

Anger is like a toothache. If I don't get to the root cause, it won't go away.

J.E.M.

> *These six things the Lord hates,*
> *Yes, seven are an abomination to Him:*
> *A proud look,*
> *A lying tongue,*
> *Hands that shed innocent blood,*
> *A heart that devises wicked plans,*
> *Feet that are swift in running to evil,*
> *A false witness who speaks lies,*
> *And one who sows discord among brethren.*
> —PROV. 6:16–19

Has anyone ever treated you with arrogant disdain? Have you been on the receiving end of falsehoods or rumors? Were you abused as an innocent child? Did someone lay wicked plans that would hurt you? Were you unfairly labeled and dismissed? Were you the child who could never do anything right? Have you ever hurt anyone else in any of these ways?

Today's passage tells that God *hates* what happened to you—and whatever you did to others. To hate something means to differentiate oneself from it. God doesn't relate to people in ways that destroy and hurt them—and He hates it when people relate to each other in those ways. However, God *loves* you, and He loves the wounded person who hurt you.

In our own lives we need to learn to differentiate ourselves from evil so that we are not infected by it. Then we need to use this hate to help us confront evil, solve problems, and forgive.

When I stand against what is evil and destructive in myself and to others, I take a stand for love, honesty, freedom, and responsibility.

J.M.C.

> *Show Your marvelous lovingkindness by*
> *Your right hand,*
> *O You who save those who trust in You,*
> *From those who rise up against them.*
> —PS. 17:7

Elizabeth flipped back through her journal and realized how much the Lord had healed her over the year. Her early entries were full of pain:

I've always believed that God would help me in times of trouble. Lately, with so many prayers unanswered, with questions only building more questions, with the Bible offering so little solace, with my Christian brothers and sisters sharing compassion but no solutions, I'm wondering where you've gone, God. Why did Brad leave the children and me for another woman after fourteen years of marriage? Nothing in my life prepared me for this. Our marriage seemed to be going along happily, then I was suddenly thrust into a pit filled with negative emotions and destructive thoughts I don't know how to handle.

After a year of therapy, Elizabeth wrote:

Thank you, Lord, for standing by me and helping me to regain my dreams. This year has taught me so much about your marvelous lovingkindness. Whenever I had doubts or just wanted to give up, you would give me a new breath through an encouraging word from the Bible, a friend to listen, or just gently holding my hand when I thought it was hopeless.

———————

Lord, thank you for your "marvelous lovingkindness" and for the dreams you have given me.

J.L.M.

God is our refuge and strength,
A very present help in trouble.
—PS. 46:1

Whenever we experience a loss, big or small, grief and healing proceed in recognizable stages. Knowing what these stages are can help us understand ourselves and be patient with ourselves as we process our pain.

When Linda first expected that her husband of twenty-two years was having an affair, she immediately went into the first stage, *shock* and *denial*. She convinced herself nothing was going on. And since the affair was short-lived, she managed to stay in denial until her husband confessed. Then came the *anger*. For almost two months, Linda spewed fury on everyone around her. As the anger began to subside, she began *bargaining* with God, asking Him to kill her husband and send her a fine, faithful Christian man.

When *depression* set in, Linda entered counseling. Her therapist helped her sort through the events of the preceding month, separating lies from truth. Then Linda, armed with a healthier self-concept, proceeded to the last stage of grief—*acceptance and adjustment*. She chose to stay with her husband, but to continue in therapy for awhile. They have now renewed this commitment to God and to each other.

When I experience loss, I will patiently work through my grief with the help of God and, if possible, another person.

J.E.M.

*And now abide faith, hope, love, these three; but
the greatest of these is love.* —1 COR. 13:13

*In the presence of fear, paralysis happens.
In the presence of guilt, negativity happens.
In the presence of compulsiveness, stress happens.
In the presence of insecurity, imitation happens.
In the presence of selfishness, conflict happens.
In the presence of worry, procrastination happens.
In the presence of anger, attacks happen.
In the presence of arrogance, intimidation happens.
In the presence of criticism, insecurity happens.*

*In the presence of God, love happens.
In the presence of love, forgiveness happens.
In the presence of forgiveness, acceptance happens.
In the presence of acceptance, faith happens.
In the presence of faith, hope is restored.
In the presence of hope, love is renewed.*

In the presence of love, miracles happen.

*Help me to see the daily miracles that your love brings into my
life, Lord.*

J.M.C.

Bear one another's burdens, and so fulfill the law of Christ. Therefore, as we have opportunity, let us do good to all, especially to those who are of the household of faith. —GAL. 6:2, 10

Michelle had never had a friend like Beth—in fact, she had never had a real friend. Her parents had raised her to believe that getting close to people would only hurt her. They had instilled in her that a person should get married, have children, and keep to herself.

Then Michelle started a new job and met Beth. Beth was persistent about trying to get to know Michelle. She did not expect anything; she only desired her friendship. Michelle was not sure what to do with this turn of events. She had been taught that you cannot trust people. But Michelle started to trust Beth. After time, Michelle could not resist Beth's kindness. She finally let down her guard and began to realize her parents were wrong.

Now Michelle believes God brought Beth to her. Their friendship has positively affected her husband and children. Michelle has started to make other friends. Michelle's husband was also a loner, but he has started doing a few things with Beth's husband. And Michelle encourages her children to invite children over to their house. The entire family is growing through these new experiences.

Father, show me how to help myself by allowing others into my life.

J.L.M.

> *There is a way which seems right to a man,*
> *But its end is the way of death.*
> —PROV. 14:12

Someone once put a frog in a pan of cold water and turned on a fire under it. The water slowly heated and the frog, who could easily have jumped out, sat still. The increase in temperature was so gradual that he didn't notice it. By the time the water boiled, it was too late; the frog was dead. Had he been thrown into a pot of boiling water, he would have jumped out right away.

The principle that killed the frog is called erosion, and it has ruined the lives of many people. It's the process of gradually adjusting to evil. We may gradually start to accept dangerous practices we rejected before. We may begin to accept abusive actions from others that we didn't tolerate before or give in to addictive tendencies. We may also slowly change our standards to be more self-centered than other-centered, or else we may become more masochistic. If we become successful, we may gradually begin thinking we are an exception to rules we used to follow.

Solomon, the wisest man who ever lived, went from a humble man, full of wisdom, to a compromising fool in his later years. If the wisest man who ever lived died a fool, we certainly should take note and learn.

I will stay out of hot water today, even if it only feels lukewarm.

J.E.M.

Every branch in Me that does not bear fruit He takes away; and every branch that bears fruit He prunes, that it may bear more fruit.
—JOHN 15:2

Don't miss the forest for the trees." We as therapists can learn a lesson from that well-known statement. We are often guilty of dwelling on one "tree" and missing the beauty and majesty of the entire forest of our clients' lives.

I often tell my clients that I can't assess how sick they are until I know how well they are. I encourage them to tell me all the things that are going right in their lives as well as the things that are going wrong. Many times we find that one or two trees of bitterness and sin are spoiling their perspective. Once those trees are removed, they begin to see the forest for what it is.

Sometimes there is a fire in the forest. Burning trees must be tended quickly and carefully. We must prune away the branches that are burned and not functional to save the strength and fruitfulness of the surviving tree and surrounding trees. After putting out a fire in a specific area, we may even clear away the damage and plant new trees. Then, if all goes well, the client can take on the primary job of tending the forest.

My life is a beautiful forest, so I will enjoy it even while pruning an occasional tree.

J.E.M.

> *Love never fails. But whether there are prophecies,*
> *they will fail; whether there are tongues, they will*
> *cease; whether there is knowledge, it will vanish*
> *away.*
> —1 COR. 13:8

Theresa worked hard to make sure she acted the right way at her party and that every detail was in order. She would feel her stomach twist into knots whenever she saw anything out of place. A classic perfectionist, she needed to always feel in control. Her emotions frustrated her most of all, because she couldn't control and dictate how she felt.

Theresa was a compassionate person to others, but not to herself. Then came the Sunday that her pastor preached on 1 Corinthians 13:8. As she listened, Theresa became aware of the fact that she hadn't been loving herself and that perfection was an impossible goal. That Sunday she embarked on the journey of recovery. Gradually she came to see that she rarely acknowledged the depth of her feelings and that denying her feelings had caused her to become more and more rigid and demanding. She began to understand how critical it is that she talk about these feelings and situations so they wouldn't continue to cloud her perspective. She developed more of a sense of humor and became much more relaxed. Best of all, Theresa learned that loving is so much easier than performing.

Lord, teach me to be patient and to show kindness to myself.

J.L.M.

Wait on the Lord;
Be of good courage,
And He shall strengthen
 your heart;
Wait, I say, on the Lord!
 —PS. 27:14

Fear is a basic fact of life, not a barrier to success.

Many people in the Bible were acquainted with the emotion of fear. When God asked Moses to represent His people to Pharaoh, Moses began to shake, saying, "I'm not a good speaker." God's reply was "I will help you to speak well, and I will tell you what to say" (see Ex. 4:10–12).

God also talked to Jeremiah, and Jeremiah's response was "I'm too young." God promised Jeremiah that He would be with him and would see him through (see Jer. 1:7–8).

Nothing breathes fresh air into our lives like doing something we didn't think we could do. If God's love is strengthening our heart, then we know that God loves and accepts us whether we succeed or fail. Our value doesn't change. Our worth doesn't change. Our security doesn't change. Forgiveness is always available to us. When God's love is the source of our security, fear is not a signal to stop or retreat, but a sign that there is adventure ahead.

Lord, I will feel the fear. But I will forge ahead anyway.

J.M.C.

And He said to them, "Go into all the world and preach the gospel to every creature."

—MARK 16:15

One evening Frances, a single mom, came home from work more exhausted than usual. She struggled to get dinner and do the dishes, all the time dreaming of her easy chair and a magazine. But then her little son, Danny, wanted some attention. He interrupted his mother every two seconds.

Finally, Frances looked down at the magazine page in front of her, which pictured a map of the world. She found a pair of scissors and cut the map into tiny pieces. "Danny," she said, "I will cuddle you and read you a story when you have put this puzzle together." With that she sunk into the comfortable chair and let out a deep sigh.

Five minutes later Danny was back. The puzzle was completed. Amazed, Frances asked Danny how he could possibly be finished so soon. Danny grinned. He said, "Mommy, there was a man on the other side of the page. I put the man together, and the world came together, too."

Frances hugged Danny and asked him to go choose his favorite story. While Danny was choosing one, Frances pondered the truth Danny had spoken. As God's love transforms us and puts us together, we affect our world. That is what ministry is all about. Even though our words are important, what we are speaks louder than what we say.

Lord, transform me today so that everything I do is done out of love.

J.M.C.

I sought the Lord, and He heard me,
And delivered me from all my fears.
—PS. 34:4

Post traumatic stress disorder" is the clinical term for a reaction many people experience weeks, months, or years after going through a painful event. It is like taking that painful event, deep-freezing it, and then thawing it out a long time afterward. Once the event starts to "thaw," the person experiences it as if it had just happened.

For example, one woman was sexually abused in elementary school and had no memory of it for years. When she started to remember, she reacted as if the abuse had just occurred. She had recurrent thoughts and dreams about the abuse. Her distress was so great that she could not function at work or at home. The more she remembered, the more anxious she became. She tried to push the memories to the back of her mind, but she was unable to "refreeze" the thoughts. This woman was able to recover by talking with others about the past, by writing about it, and by praying about the past. The process took her several months, but she diligently kept working through the memories until gradually they became less debilitating. Now she may think back on the abuse, but her memories have lost their paralyzing power.

Father, give me the courage to talk about my greatest fears and memories from the past as I remember them.

J.L.M.

Let no one despise you.
—TITUS 2:15

Everybody hates me, nobody likes me, I'm going out to eat worms." This was a little chant we children used to say when we felt sorry for ourselves. As adults we're a little less dramatic; we just say, "I'm worthless." But both the childhood and the adult sayings are lies we must confront.

I often ask my clients to provide support for their self-accusations themselves. For instance, I asked Kay to prove her contention that she was worthless. It was as if she had rehearsed her speech for years. She proceeded to tell me about being molested from childhood through adolescence, about being addicted to sex, drugs, and alcohol. I then said to Kay, "I'm not convinced. Does doing worthless things make a person worthless?" She answered, "No." Then she began to understand what I was getting at. She said, "Maybe I'm not worthless, maybe I just feel worthless."

Correcting the lie of worthlessness was important because as long as Kay believed she was worthless, she would continue to do things that made her feel worthless. When she learned to forgive herself and others and to replace her lies about herself with truth, her actions began to change.

Lord, help me to see the lies I'm telling about myself for what they are. Thank you for being a dependable Source of truth.

J.E.M.

For as he thinks in his heart, so is he.
—PROV. 23:7

Gem Gilbert was a British tennis star who died a most unusual death. But that's getting ahead of the story.

As a young girl, Gem watched her mother die of shock in a dentist's chair after having a tooth pulled—a tragic but unlikely accident. And Gem became convinced that she would die the same way. For thirty years Gem carried this image in her mind. Understandably, she avoided dentists! But finally Gem developed a toothache so painful that she had to visit a dentist. Terrified, she took along her pastor, her medical doctor, and her best friend. But their support was not enough. Gem died before she could even get into the chair.

The British press worded the obituary this way. "Gem Gilbert had been killed by thirty years of thought."

Certainly this is an extreme example. But many women do the same thing that Gem did. Perhaps their mother was an alcoholic, and they are terrified of being like her. Or, like a friend of mine, they had an abusive mother and fear that is their destiny too. It doesn't have to be. Self-defeating cycles can be broken, but only if the heart is touched at an emotional and thinking level. And that happens if, every day, we dedicate our minds and our thoughts to Jesus.

Lord Jesus, I dedicate my mind and my thoughts to you today.
J.M.C.

*And above all things have fervent love for one
another, for "love will cover a multitude of sins."*
—1 PETER 4:8

Many of us are in marriages that take a great amount
of work due to the union of two stubborn personalities.
But we frequently get so caught up in working on the
weaknesses in the relationship that we forget the joy
and contentment we share. Our husbands may be our
friends with whom we can act silly and play around
with, our partners with whom we work side by side to
accomplish our goals, and our lovers, with whom we
share our intimate secrets. They may gently encourage and spur us on to accomplish far more than we
would have on our own, but do it in such a way that it
seemed like our own idea, laugh at our jokes even
when we mess up the punch line, or act interested as
we recount entire conversations we had with our
mothers.

Husbands are to be valued and cared for tenderly.
They may try to act strong and secure, but they need
kind words and encouragement. Our husbands may
have areas they are working to improve, and they
need to know how many things we appreciate about
them. Each of them has strengths that can multiply
when we acknowledge those strengths.

*Lord, thank you for my husband. Help me to remember how many
things I really appreciate about him, and help me to tell him those
things instead of concentrating on his weaknesses.*

                                                J.L.M.

If we say that we have no sin, we deceive ourselves.
—1 JOHN 1:8

We call them zebras at our clinic. They're black and white thinkers—people who believe that everyone in their lives—themselves included—is either a complete saint or a complete sinner. The trouble with this mentality is that it keeps people from looking at their lives realistically. If they see themselves as saints, they just can't accept the fact that they really did something wrong. Or they may flip to the stance of "Well if I did that, then I must be a sinner, so I might as well give in to it." These people often hide their pain with addictions, which drive them further down the "all good" or "all bad" road. When they're yielding to the addiction they're "bad," but when they're not, they're "good."

Our job with the "saint-sinner" client is to gently help them see themselves as whole people, capable of doing almost anything. We point out that it takes arrogance for a person to believe she is either the worst sinner or the best saint in the world. Humility is the key for the black-white thinker. We must help them realize that we are all sinners saved by grace.

I am neither all good nor all bad, but a sinner saved by grace and a saint through the righteousness of Jesus Christ.

J.E.M.

> *For the good that I will to do, I do not do; but the*
> *evil I will not to do, that I practice.*
> —ROM. 7:19

After Whitney became a Christian, she was shocked to find that she was still struggling in some areas of life. If she still had faults, then she wondered, had God really done His job? Whitney couldn't pick up a Christian book or hear a sermon without feeling guilty. But instead of sharing her struggles with another person, Whitney made a decision which has made her life a living hell. She decided simply to *pretend* she had it all together.

Can't you just feel the pressure, condemnation, and phoniness that decision brought? Need became something to deny; confession, something to fear. And because Whitney was trying so hard to look perfect, she grew critical and judgmental—excellent at spotting everyone else's guilt.

But even focusing on everyone else's dark side couldn't keep Whitney from feeling inwardly miserable. Why? Because she overlooked the truth that God doesn't expect us to be perfect. If we were innocent, we would not need God. We are all dysfunctional—every one of us. We live in a fallen world. We are fallen people—raised by fallen parents, married to fallen spouses, raising fallen children. Whitney needs to stop pretending. She needs to see herself as in process, not as a finished product. At that point, perhaps she will be able to believe that God really does love her.

I'm not OK, and you're not OK—and that's OK. Thank you, Jesus!
J.M.C.

I press toward the goal for the prize of the upward call of God in Christ Jesus. —PHIL. 3:14

Just as the apostle Paul reached for the goal of serving Christ, we need to reach toward recovery goals. Such goals will increase our motivation, reduce frustration, and give us a clearly defined purpose for living.

Establishing recovery goals involves three steps. First, *identify your strengths and use them to your advantage.* One young lady named Susan was very persuasive. When Susan was using drugs, she could always get people to give her drugs. In recovery, she learned to use her asset differently. Instead of asking for drugs, she learned to ask for support and companionship. Second, *review your experiences and learn from your past.* One of Susan's mistakes was avoiding conflict with her parents. She would run away after a blow-up and find her drug-using friends. In recovery, she focused on learning how to deal with adversity without leaving. Finally, *find out what is really important to you and make necessary sacrifices.* Susan's sacrifice was giving up her "using" friends, many of whom were more accepting of her than her new friends.

Susan recovered from her drug addiction by identifying her strengths, learning from her past, and making some sacrifices. She now tries to help others do the same as she continues to enjoy her new life.

Father, guide me to set goals for myself today.

J.L.M.

He who is devoid of wisdom despises his neighbor,
But a man of understanding holds his peace.
—PROV. 11:12

My mother said I was perfect. My mother is always right. All I ask is that you think the way I think and do whatever I say." That's the essence of the "You should be like me" lie, which some people learn in childhood. When I face a couple who both live by that lie, I know we are in for a difficult counseling session.

Some couples seem to thrive on putting each other down. If she wants to stay home and rest, he tells her she's lazy. If he wants to clean the garage, she tells him that it's stupid to do that when the kitchen floor needs to be waxed. These couples appear to get their good feelings from making their mate feel bad.

God is creative. He made each of us different. And it would be completely boring to be married to a clone, although many couples seem to be pursuing that goal. Differences can be used to broaden our perspective. One reason God gave us a mate was so that we could have two opinions on everything. He wants us to continually meld our two opinions together, even though that may sometimes mean we agree to disagree. Most of the time the blending results in a stronger appreciation for each other and a different perception of the problems—and this makes life more enjoyable and productive.

Today I will create at least one specific way to weave two "me's" into one "we."

J.E.M.

I will praise You, for I am fearfully and
wonderfully made;
Marvelous are Your works,
And that my soul knows very well.
—PS. 139:13

It took me many years to make this verse mine. When I first read it, all I could think of were the critical comments of my peers, teachers, and parents. Healthy, loving relationships—with God and other people—helped me abandon those old, negative self-perceptions. But even then, comparing myself with other people got in my way. I could admire a beautiful, original fashion creation, but I would downgrade myself because I wasn't just like someone else. And I usually compared my worst, of which I was most aware, with everyone else's best.

When I finally realized that my negative self-image had led me away from gratitude, I sat down to list the things I valued about myself. That list took a long time to create. Then I listed the things I didn't like about myself—an easier task. Imagine my shock when I realized I could change all but one thing on my "negative" list if I really tried. That was the day I acknowledged that I was a unique creation of the unique God of the universe—a divine original. True, God isn't finished with me yet. But that's OK—I'm not finished with myself, either.

If I follow the herd, I risk ending up as a pork chop. Thank you, Lord, that you created me to be unique.

J.M.C.

> *Therefore I say to you, do not worry about your*
> *life, what you will eat or what you will drink; nor*
> *about your body, what you will put on. Is not life*
> *more than food and the body more than clothing?*
> —MATT. 6:25

For many, life is merely a period of time in which to accumulate more—more possessions, more food, more money. We want more clothes, cars, and furnishings than we need, and much of our time is taken with obtaining, preparing, and consuming food. We have such a sense of ownership over our personal items. We may even try to own things that are not possessions—for instance, our husband, our children, our relationships.

The only real things of value in life are the relationships we have with Jesus Christ and with those around us. If we spent as much time on these two areas as we do on satisfying our food and material appetites, we would live in abundance, but our get-rich attitudes rob us of spiritual wealth and leave us emotionally destitute.

An attitude that reflects enjoyment of rather than entitlement to our possessions can be sensed by others, and sharing who we are and what we have with others can give our life purpose and meaning. Our food and possessions will become stepping stones to relationship when others see generosity instead of greed.

Lord, I want to value my relationships far more than my things. Help me to see my possessions as sand in my palm and my relationships as clay to be molded.

J.L.M.

Uphold my steps in Your paths,
That my footsteps may not slip.
—PS. 17:5

My husband and I were nearing the end of a long trip. It was two o'clock in the morning, and the rain was pouring steadily. We came to what we thought was an intersection where we could either continue straight or turn right or left. My husband, in his tired condition, decided to go straight. We quickly found out that we had chosen an alternative that wasn't there. We were on a high bank with our car dangerously close to tipping over. We carefully got out of the car, walked through the rain to a nearby motel, and called a wrecker. We spent the night in the motel, then continued our trip the next day.

Many of us take the wrong roads in life and we end up on a cliff, in great danger of tipping over. The rain, the dark, and our fatigue kept my husband and me from seeing reality that scary rainy night. Often, I feel my clients are blinded by the misperceptions they have carried with them through life. And it's difficult to choose the right road in life when you can't see it.

Let's make it our goal in life to find truth. Our faith in God and in His Word will guide us there. When truth is hidden we will continually make errors in judgment. But when we see the truth, we will begin to make wise decisions.

_____

Truth leads to the right road, so I will look for it by meditating today on God's Word and on my personal relationship with Him.

J.E.M.

> *I have learned in whatever state I am, to*
> *be content.*
> —PHIL. 4:11

What does it take to make you content? Contentment rarely finds us by accident. We must choose it on a moment-by-moment basis.

Julie believed that she couldn't be content unless her life was problem free and everything was going her way. She blamed her discontent on job stress, family conflicts, personal conflicts—and she was always dissatisfied.

Then Julie met Tanya. Tanya's life seemed to be in constant turmoil. Her sick and elderly mother lived with her. One of her children had a learning disability which required constant testing and extra tutoring. Her husband worked for a firm that would soon be shut down. Circumstances seemed overwhelming. And yet Tanya was at peace.

"How can you be so calm when so much is going wrong?" Julie asked Tanya. And Tanya answered, "In the middle of a tornado is a quiet place. That quiet place in me is maintained by Jesus. I invite Him in. I listen to His voice. I talk to Him and read His Word. I base my life on His principles. He is my center. He is my peace. The winds of my life continue to whirl about me, but in my core self I am at rest in Jesus' loving arms."

Contentment is the natural result of being rooted and grounded in Christ's love.

J.M.C.

Let not mercy and truth forsake you . . .
Write them on the tablet of your heart.
—PROV. 3:3

Vivian had felt so much rejection from the men in her life. Her father had always blamed her for all the family problems. Her only brother had ridiculed her unmercifully. Then she married a wonderful man, but after sixteen years of marriage he had died of cancer. Vivian just couldn't trust men anymore—and in her mind, God was a man. Surely He would reject her too.

Vivian began to look and realize how many woman friends she had, although men seemed to reject and control her. Gradually she began to confront her problems with her father and brother. She realized how she had taken in the lies they had fed her all her life—for instance that women couldn't manage money, couldn't think methodically, couldn't get along without a man. Then she started replacing these lies with the truth—for instance, that for the last three years she had been a single parent to teenage boys and that she had successfully taken care of her bills and even saved some money on her own. Finally, she began to realize the difference in how she had looked to men and how she looked to God. She again replaced lies with truth and saw God's unwavering love for her instead of rejection.

Lord, help me to see the persistent lies which cause me to reject myself and you.

J.L.M.

The Lord is my light and my salvation;
Whom shall I fear?
The Lord is the strength of my life;
Of whom shall I be afraid?

—PS. 27:1

Our whole family had traveled up the mountain on an aerial gondola in Vail, Colorado. The trip up went smoothly, but some strong winds rose as we started down. The gondola started rocking, then stopped its forward movement. There we were, just hanging there a hundred feet above the ground, with the wind whipping us back and forth. We prayed and held hands and hugged each other. Finally, after what seemed like a long time to us, the gondola started again and we made our descent with sighs of relief.

Fear comes in many forms. Fear of failure. Fear of heights. Fear of death. Fear of moving away. Fear of staying where we are. Fear of being abandoned. Fear can threaten our sense of well-being.

When moments of fear come, how do we respond? One helpful response is to join the psalmist in affirming, "I will fear no evil; For You are with me." I know that God was in command of the winds that blew our gondola that day, and He is in control of every area of fear in our lives today.

Today, I will give my current fears to God, knowing He is in ultimate control.

J.E.M.

I have come as a light into the world, that whoever believes in Me should not abide in darkness.
—JOHN 12:46

Darlene didn't really live in a basement, but she felt that way. Life to her seemed cold, damp, dark, and dingy. Her footsteps reverberated through the silence, and she was often overcome with feelings of loneliness and isolation. But as awful as her feelings were, they also seemed almost normal to her. She was used to basement living.

When the loneliness became unbearable, however, Darlene allowed another person, a therapist, to come into her dungeon and to see the hurt and anger hidden there. They explored what life felt like to Darlene, and she felt accepted. But then Darlene's therapist invited her to take a scary but hopeful journey—up the basement stairs. Would Darlene leave the darkness and denial and risk bringing the hurt, anger, and isolation to the light? Darlene said yes. Supported by her therapist, she began the lengthy journey toward the light. Step by step she inched her way upward toward warmth, acceptance, love, and grace. Finally, Darlene realized she had left the basement behind. And Darlene wouldn't think of going back. She really has seen the light.

Thank you, Lord, that your light dispels my darkness. Help me dare to expose my darkness to your light.

J.M.C.

> *Because your lovingkindness*
> *is better than life,*
> *My lips shall praise You.*
> —PS. 63:3

One simple question from God echoed in Maria's heart and mind: "What do you need from me?" Deep inside she knew the answer: "Love me." But she was afraid to speak that answer—not because she thought God would not honor it, but because she feared He would. Maria felt she did not deserve the matchless love of God. She had felt that way all her life.

Then Maria began to think back to all the things God had done for her. She thought back to bad times, such as when she was left to more or less raise herself at age fourteen because her divorced parents had wanted to spend time with their new mates. Even as she reviewed this terrible ordeal, she saw that God had always put someone in her life to let her know He loved her. An aunt had taken her in and helped her get through college. One dear friend had led her to the Lord, and another had gently discipled her into a closer walk with God. Looking back, Maria realized that these loving acts were really manifestations of God's extraordinary lovingkindness and His wonderful plan for her life. God had known her answer and met her need all along.

Lord, remind me to praise you daily so that I don't hold on to the lies of my past and overlook your acts of love for me.

J.L.M.

But may the God of all grace, who called us to
His eternal glory by Christ Jesus, after you have
suffered a while, perfect, establish, strengthen,
and settle you. —1 PETER 5:10

That isn't fair" is an often-heard phrase among children and adults. The truth is that often life is not fair. From a personal level to an international level, in fact, we are constantly bombarded with the unfairness of life.

Doris was only fifteen when she was brutally raped by an eighteen-year-old neighbor. She was so ashamed she didn't tell anyone. Then she got morning sickness and eventually discovered she was pregnant. Doris had loving parents who stood by her, but no one could give her childhood back. When she graduated from high school she had to go to a junior college so she could take care of her two-year-old little boy. Matthew, her baby, was precious, but he was also a constant reminder that life isn't fair. Doris learned through counseling that she could either dwell on the past and be filled with resentment or she could be thankful for her healthy baby and face the future with faith and hope. She chose the latter.

The test of my character is how I react when life isn't fair.

J.E.B.

> *In all your ways acknowledge Him,*
> *And He shall direct your paths.*
> —PROV. 3:6

Someone asked, at my twenty-fifth college reunion, how many of us were now doing what we had originally trained to do. In our group, the answer was "No one."

I started out to be a kindergarten teacher. Then, after teaching awhile, I entered graduate school. That led to teaching education and psychology on the college level, which I enjoyed immensely. Then my husband went back to school for his doctorate, and his studies took us to Southern California, where I resumed my teaching. Enter the United States Immigration Service, which told me I couldn't teach because I was a Canadian taking a job away from a U.S. citizen.

At that point, I went through a dark period which required me to face the reality that I didn't feel valuable without my career. Then I started teaching women's Bible studies, leading retreats, and writing. These pursuits made me aware of the need for further education and for counseling skills. That resulted in my entering the field of counseling.

Never would I have envisioned the interesting path my life would take. If you had told me in college what was to take place, I wouldn't have believed you. I don't have any idea what the future will hold, but I do know who holds the future—it is God who directs my path.

Lord, thank you that through the ups and downs of life, you are directing my path. I want to keep my eyes on you.

J.M.C.

Delight yourself also in the Lord,
And He shall give you the desires of your heart.
—PS. 37:4

Joy was four foot eleven and had short, curly, auburn hair that fit her bouncy personality. Usually Joy stayed home only long enough to change clothes, get some friends together and be gone again. Joy dated many different guys and had girlfriends she did things with, but she was afraid to let anyone really get to know her because she feared rejection. She thought that being happy-go-lucky and active would fulfill her needs, but it wasn't really enough. Joy yearned for a meaningful friendship where she could express her opinions and feelings and be fully accepted. But ironically, she couldn't develop such a friendship because she held back from sharing her true thoughts and feelings. She had been that way ever since age seven, when her mother died. Her mother's death left her feeling empty. She had lost that special intimacy with her mother and was never able to replace it.

Last year, Joy met a friend who told her about Jesus Christ. He told her how God had changed his life. Joy called upon Him to be her Savior. Through the gradual process of beginning to know Christ, she started learning about intimacy. Now Joy is beginning to take a few risks with friends. She has a long way to go, but the intimacy she is beginning to experience with Christ makes trying worth the effort.

Lord, help me become intimate with you so I may become intimate with others.

J.L.M.

Therefore do not worry about tomorrow, for
tomorrow will worry about its own things.
Sufficient for the day is its own trouble.
—MATT. 6:34

What other people say about you usually reflects much more about them than it does about you. Your reaction to them, however, usually says much more about you than it does about them. Think about the last confrontation you had. Instead of taking it personally, step back and analyze what really happened.

Say, for example, that it is late on Monday afternoon. You're traveling the speed limit in the right-hand lane on the freeway, and a car behind you starts honking. You continue to drive within the limit, and he continues to honk and ride your bumper. The driver of the car behind you is telling you by riding your bumper that you are going too slow. But what is he saying about himself? He's saying he wants to disobey the law and he feels you're keeping him from it. By not being swayed by the honking and the tailgating, you are saying, "I'm going to do what's right for me no matter how much pressure I get from you."

The man on the freeway who was riding your bumper was probably not mad at you. He was probably mad at the authority figures he grew up with or the people he thinks limit him in his life now. But he is taking it out on you. Don't take it personally. You're a great driver of your car and your life.

I will not be offended today by other people's problems. I have enough trouble of my own to deal with.

J.E.M.

*I would have lost heart, unless I had believed
That I would see the goodness of the Lord
   in the land of the living.* —PS. 27:13

*A*s a therapist I would have lost heart
   in the face of man's cruelty to man . . .
I would have lost hope
   in the face of marriages that seemed to be
      crumbling . . .
I would have lost love
   in the face of incest and abuse . . .
I would have lost courage
   in the face of fury and rage . . .
I would have lost joy
   in the face of depression and despair . . .
I would have lost perspective
   in the face of anxiety attacks and
      panic . . .
I would have lost honesty
   in the face of denial and secrecy . . .
I would have lost patience
   in the face of defense and deception . . .
I would have lost self-control
   in the face of drug and alcohol abuse . . .
I would have lost peace
   in the face of personal disintegration . . .

*But I believed that I would see the
goodness of the Lord in the land of the living.*

I didn't lose anything.

Help me see your goodness today, Lord.

J.M.C.

Peace I leave with you, My peace I give to you; not as the world gives do I give to you. Let not your heart be troubled, neither let it be afraid.
—JOHN 14:27

The following passage is Sheila's account of her recovery from divorce:

It's only Wednesday, but it has been such a long week. I am exhausted, but for once the exhaustion is not defeating, for I am able to rest in God's peace. It is so much easier to cope with my divorce with God's help.

I'm afraid of being alone and uncared for, but I must let go of this fear. I know that there will be times when the excitement and the desire to work on my fears won't be there, but remembering the peace God has given me provides the power I need to go on. I know that now, while God has wrapped me in peace, I must take advantage of everything that will help me progress and build a sure foundation to sustain me so that I can stand firm when times are difficult.

I can hardly believe these thoughts are coming from my mind. I feel like shouting to everyone "Hey! It's me! I've found God's peace!" I feel such relief even though it's been a hard week, and I am so thankful I want to cry.

Lord, help me to remember that you give me your peace not because I deserve it, but because of your grace.

J.L.M.

Let nothing be done through selfish ambition or conceit, but . . . let each esteem others better than himself.
—PHIL. 2:3

Sally and Fred had never learned that any relationship that works takes work. Like many in our "instant" society, Sally and Fred were unwilling to put hard work into making their marriage strong and stable. Sally was starting to feel attached to a man she was working with. Fred was an engineer who seldom listened to Sally's feelings. As soon as they noticed that things weren't going smoothly, they began to wonder if they were "meant" for each other. As their therapist, I asked them to be careful of the lie of "There is someone with whom I could easily live happily ever after."

Elisabeth Elliott, a wise woman, once said, "The first thing to remember when you get married is that you're marrying a sinner. The second thing to remember is that he is marrying one too." But many married people prefer to leave the marriage instead of looking at their own sin, laziness, and impatience. Often, however, when couples who are fighting can calm down and humbly listen to each other, they often find that they can complement each other wonderfully. Sally and Fred eventually made that discovery. They even enjoy each other and look forward to their times together.

Lord, help me be willing to be willing to work at my relationships. Open my eyes to ways my mate and I can complement each other.

J.E.M.

> *He delivered me from my strong enemy,*
> *From those who hated me,*
> *For they were too strong for me. . . .*
> *But the Lord was my support.*
> *He also brought me out into a broad place;*
> *He delivered me because He delighted in me.*
> —PS. 18:17–19

When Alicia stopped smoking, she gained sixty pounds in three months. Shaken, she made her way to a therapist, who gently probed into her family background. Alicia volunteered that her father had disciplined her harshly. Gradually, over the course of therapy, she began to face the fact that he had also abused her sexually. Alicia had survived emotionally by "forgetting" that the abuse ever happened. She had become a self-assured, self-confident, high-achieving woman. She just never talked about her feelings: she smoked and overate to keep them under control.

Among other things, the therapist introduced her to a God who had been betrayed by those He loved—a God who loved and accepted Alicia, who declared that she had done nothing to deserve the abuse, who covered Alicia with His shed blood and declared her clean. This God allowed her to be angry; He did not condemn her for her feelings, and He offered her a comprehensive forgiveness. Because of her heavenly Father's love, she was eventually able to forgive herself and understand her earthly father.

Thank you, Lord, that you delight in me.

J.M.C.

*Therefore if there is any consolation in Christ, if
any comfort of love, if any fellowship of the Spirit,
if any affection and mercy, fulfill my joy by being
like-minded, having the same love, being of one
accord, of one mind.*
—PHIL. 2:1–2

Barbara was an efficient legal secretary. At forty-six, she had never married, and she had no desire to. Although she behaved professionally at work and was cordial socially, Barbara basically hated men. Most men picked up on her dislike for them and kept their distance, but one attorney kept seeking her out. Finally Barbara told him that she couldn't stand men, she couldn't stand him, and she would appreciate his leaving her alone. Barbara saw the hurt on his face and realized her own hurt. She had never verbalized her attitude toward men. After that experience, Barbara started to reflect on her childhood and to talk to her mother about it. An illegitimate child, Barbara had never known her father, and she had absorbed her mother's deep anger at being left alone with a child to raise. When Barbara looked into her past, she saw her present attitude for what it was: hurt manifesting itself as anger.

As Barbara continues to address her hurt, she feels different toward men. She has apologized to the attorney and even gone to lunch with him a few times. She even jokes that one day she may marry. Who knows?

Lord, help me see how events from my past affect my current attitudes.

J.L.M.

All of you be submissive to one another, and be
clothed with humility.   —1 PETER 5:5

Being married is a little like being on a teeter-totter.
It's no fun for one mate to be always up and the other
down. No one can move if both partners insist on absolute equality. And if one partner jumps off, the other
partner has no choice but to leave as well. In order to
enjoy being on the teeter-totter, both partners must
learn to give and take.

"You owe me and you'd better pay up." John and
Jennifer both used this phrase when they first came to
therapy. Each seemed to carry a little scorebook in his
or her head and to give themselves points for every
"good deed." They were constantly arguing about who
had done more for the other. Their goal seemed to be
to have complete equality and end up with the perfectly balanced teeter-totter. Instead, their teeter-totter
was jolting up and down, with each of them being
bumped as it hit the ground.

Can you imagine a couple so loving that they argue
about how much they want to *give* to each other instead of how much they want to *get* from each other?
As John and Jennifer's marriage therapist, I was never
able to persuade them to get *that* humble. But after
nine months of therapy, they had begun to develop a
give and take marriage instead of the "take and take"
marriage they had.

The more I give true love, the more likely I am to get true love.
                                                    J.E.M.

*Because, although they knew God, they did not
glorify Him as God, nor were thankful, but became
futile in their thoughts, and their foolish hearts
were darkened.*
—ROM. 1:21

How would you complete this sentence: "I would be a much happier person if . . ."?

Sylvia spent her entire life waiting for happiness and fulfillment. When she was in high school, she was anticipating college. Then she received her college acceptance and she became career oriented. Once her career was established, she lived for the weekend. Marriage became her next goal, and once she married she had a desire for children. Sylvia never really tasted life because she was always waiting.

Many of us, like Sylvia, persist in believing that happiness will be just over the next hill. This might not be so bad if we could enjoy ourselves after that hill. Instead, yet another hill always looms on the horizon. Lasting satisfaction remains elusive. And eventually "I'll be happy if . . ." becomes a nostalgic "I was happy when . . ." Many women live the first half of their adult lives postponing satisfaction and the last half with regrets.

Happiness is not a destination; it is a journey. Don't brood over what would make you happy tomorrow or what made you happy yesterday. Instead, let's be grateful for today.

Lord, help me develop the attitude of gratitude today.

J.M.C.

> *Let the words of my mouth and the meditation*
> *of my heart*
> *Be acceptable in Your sight,*
> *O Lord, my strength and my redeemer.*
> —PS. 19:14

Sometimes the more we determine to think of things we can appreciate about ourselves because of God's gifts to us, the more we are flooded by thoughts about what we hate about ourselves. Because of the lies we have held onto, we are afraid to allow ourself the luxury of accepting God's truth that He loves us and wants the best for us.

We must continue to meditate upon the truth that we are beloved children of God, and we need to be around other Christians who will reinforce that truth. God has placed others in our life, some of whom also struggle with the lie that they are worthless. When we are together, we can remind each other of God's love and acceptance.

The more we accept ourselves, the more at peace we feel. But the greatest thing about believing God thinks we are valuable is being able to help others see that about themselves. Helping others confront the way they think about themselves and sharing with them that God sees them as clay to be molded, not dirt, gives us joy and reminds us we need also to meditate on that message.

Lord, give me the insight to see the truth by meditating on your love and acceptance so I can share these truths with others.

J.L.M.

For my mouth will speak truth.
—PROV. 8:7

Mind reading is a magic trick that few of us have mastered. Yet that is exactly what Raquel and Peter expected each other to do. "If you loved me you would be able to read my mind. You should be able to anticipate my needs without me having to express them." These two assumptions were a real hindrance to growth in their marriage.

"Love is magic. If it isn't magic, it isn't love." That expressed their opinion of marriage. Every couple must eventually realize that a good marriage is not to be had by magical thinking, but by honestly discussing needs, expectations, and priorities. Some items will be a source of negotiation. Raquel and Peter had some disagreements about how to handle some items on their lists of expectations, but eventually they developed verbal contracts with each other that they both chose to live with. More important, they learned good communication skills that enabled them to be lovingly assertive and to speak the truth in love. It sure beats "magical" mind reading!

Today, I will be honest about my needs and expectations and not expect my mate to read my mind.

J.E.M.

*Now this is the confidence that we have in Him,
that if we ask anything according to His will, He
hears us.*   —1 JOHN 5:14

Betty entered therapy because although she had been a Christian for years, she could not feel God's love. She had been on a treadmill of performance, afraid to say no for fear that God would view her as selfish and disobedient. As we examined Betty's earliest relationships, we discovered a workaholic dad who had been physically and emotionally absent during much of Betty's life. She had tried to please him, but he had been unpleasable.

In therapy, Betty came to see that she had transferred all her feelings about her father onto God. She mourned the dad she never had and traced the losses she had sustained as a child. And she began a new relationship with God—not the God of her father's image, but the God of the Scriptures. Betty pulled out of all commitments she had undertaken for the wrong motive. Now she had time to get quiet, to risk an openness to God and to ask Him to do for her what she could not do for herself—to make her aware that she was loved. And it happened! Friends, nature, books, insights during therapy, circumstances all started to speak to her with words of grace and love. If you were to ask Betty today if God loves her, she would give you a resounding yes.

Thank you, Lord, that you are even more willing to answer my prayer than I am to ask.

J.M.C.

*Now may the God of patience and comfort grant
you to be like-minded toward one another,
according to Christ Jesus.* —ROM. 15:5

God has such patience with us, and we have so little
patience with ourselves. Yet patience is a part of accepting who we are and being satisfied with how we
have been created—as growing individuals with whom
God is not yet finished. We run from ourselves to avoid
facing this fact. We are masters at diverting attention
from our incompleteness through constant activity and
preoccupation with our outward appearance. But real
growth comes when we patiently and lovingly examine our inner selves, which God sees and loves regardless of how we look or what we accomplish.

Our inner self is who we are—personality, mind,
emotions, and faith. And patience with ourselves
means trusting that growth in all those areas will continue. It also means that they will never reach a point
in this life where they cease to need refinement. We
can learn to endure our own limitations by recognizing
this truth. And as we begin to get accustomed to these
limitations they become manageable. We can then
take what we know about who we are and patiently
work towards growth.

*Father, I want to continue developing my faith, mind, and emotions.
Help me to view myself as being under construction instead of unrealistically expecting a finished product.*

J.L.M.

> *Confidence in an unfaithful man in time of trouble*
> *Is like a bad tooth and a foot out of joint.*
> —PROV. 25:19

The unspoken motto of codependent women seems to be, "Pour on the shame and guilt; I deserve it." One of our biggest problems we face as women in recovery is getting rid of shame and false guilt. The sad truth is we often allow our loved ones to make us feel guilty and ashamed. And letting people take advantage of us is wrong.

On many Monday mornings, Marilyn would call her husband's boss and tell him her husband, Dennis, was sick when he was really suffering from a hangover. On the few occasions when Marilyn would refuse to cover for him, Dennis would try to fill her with shame and guilt. Like Marilyn, some women allow their families and friends to bully them into taking on responsibilities that are not theirs or to accept the false shame and guilt when they don't comply.

For our loved ones' sakes as well as our own, we must daily draw our boundaries to protect ourselves— and we should probably apologize to those we love for having taken away from them their opportunities to grow away from them. Let's commit our lives to asking God to help us resist manipulation, false guilt, and shame.

I will ask God today for His insight into opportunities to express my love by saying no in codependent situations.

J.E.M.

By faith Abraham obeyed when he was called to go out to the place which he would afterward receive as an inheritance. And he went out, not knowing where he was going. —HEB. 11:8

Have you experienced a major change in your life, one that put you on an unknown path? That happened to Anne. She and Chuck had been happily married for seven years and had two beautiful little girls. They were both committed Christians. Everything seemed fine. But one evening Anne came home to find a piece of paper. Chuck had written, "Anne, I don't think I love you anymore, and I don't want to be married. I'm going away to find myself."

That message turned Anne's life upside down. Chuck had never talked with her about his private struggle. He left his job, he left the state, and to this day Anne and her daughters have no idea where Chuck is.

Overnight, Anne became a single mom forced to walk an unknown and unchosen path. Sometimes she stumbled. But Anne made one decision during this time that helped more than anything else she did. Like Abraham, she anchored herself to the character of God. She affirmed on a daily basis that God was good and that He wanted to work out good in Anne and her family's life. Anne's faith in God's goodness gave her hope even when she didn't know where her life was going.

Lord, keep me anchored to your character when major changes and senseless tragedies come into my life.

J.M.C.

> *For our light affliction, which is but for a moment,*
> *is working for us a far more exceeding and eternal*
> *weight of glory.* —2 COR. 4:17

I have just realized," wrote Eileen, "just how afraid I am of venturing out of the house. This will be the first year since John and I got married that I won't have any children at home. I have always been a mother; can I do anything else? I think of my options: I can get a job, do volunteer work, or continue to stay at home. But while I think of all these things, I get a very hollow, empty feeling in the pit of my stomach. I feel like someone who had crawled out on a high ledge in the dark—like I am just sitting in one spot, unable to move . . ."

Two weeks later, Eileen wrote, "As I look back at that moment of fear, I wonder if I am the same person who had those thoughts. Today I volunteered down at the community center, working with young mothers and their children. I can clearly see that God has given me the skills and experience to teach mothers about parenting and how to be a good wife. Surely I knew I had these strengths, but I let fear paralyze me for awhile. Now, although the fear has not disappeared, I see that God has taken me through my own set of tribulations so I can bring understanding and insight to help others."

God, don't let my "light affliction" and my fear of change paralyze me. Help me to see it as preparing me for greater things.

J.L.M.

*Let all bitterness, wrath, anger, clamor, and evil
speaking be put away from you, with all malice.*
　　　　　　　　　　　—EPH. 4:31

Do you ever struggle against bitterness? My own struggle could have been called the bitter battle of the suffering saint—although now I prefer to call it the better battle of the recovering masochist.

Actually, I think I hid my bitterness pretty well most of the time. Even my closest friends and my family would have told you that I was a happy person who nearly always had a kind word and a contagious laugh—and that really is part of who I am. But there was also another person inside me—a bitter woman who felt life should treat her better since she tried so hard to do what was right. My bitterness was private, but I know it influenced my loved ones. Hidden feelings often have a profound effect on our own lives and the lives of others.

Looking back now, I realize I was trying to play God and decide what results I should get for the efforts I had exerted. Through prayer, Bible study, and quite a bit of self-confrontation, I finally began to let God be God. I realized I'm not smart enough, nor is it my place, to figure out what is fair and what isn't.

Do you have a bit of bitterness? Don't let it get the best of you. Give it to God. He knows what to do with it.

I will let go of my secret bitterness today. I will trust God to even things out in His own way and His own timing.

　　　　　　　　　　　　　　　　　　　　J.E.M.

> By faith Sarah herself also received strength to
> conceive seed, and she bore a child when she was
> past the age, because she judged Him faithful who
> had promised. —HEB. 11:11

Sarah was almost ten years younger than her husband, Abraham—but he was ninety-nine years old. So she must have been amazed when Abraham told her God had appeared to him and promised that Sarah would bear a son. In response, Abraham had fallen face down in front of the Lord and laughed.

Sarah laughed too, when she overheard three visitors talking to her husband outside their tent. He had invited them to enjoy his hospitality, unaware that one of them was the Lord. While the guests were eating, the Lord told Abraham that ninety-year-old Sarah would have a son by the same time next year.

If Sarah had really believed him, she might have cried instead of laughing. Would you like to be one hundred and five when your son goes on his first date? (Imagine trying to stay awake waiting for him.) What about the first day of school, when you try to explain that you were the mother, not the great grandmother?

The Lord asked Sarah as she giggled, "Is anything too hard for the Lord?" And Sarah learned firsthand that the answer is no. One year later, she had her miracle baby. And he was named Isaac, which means "laughter."

Lord, help me to walk out my belief that nothing I am facing today is too hard for you.

J.M.C.

For You, O God, have proved us;
You have refined us as silver is refined.
—PS. 66:10

Refining silver is a process that takes out the impurities, and refinement of character is a process that reveals our flaws and gives us the opportunity to work on them. This often happens during difficult times in our lives. An illness or an accident, for example, may challenge us to examine our strengths and weaknesses, then concentrate on developing our strengths and overcoming our weaknesses. But although such external trials strengthen our faith, we do not need them to develop character and godliness, strength and perseverance.

We can refine ourselves on a daily basis by opening ourselves to self-examination, asking God to reveal areas that need improvement. We can also refine ourselves by opening ourselves up to new challenges. Taking risks with goals and relationships gives us the opportunity to see qualities in ourselves we didn't know existed. Any activity that exposes our weaknesses, improves our relationship with Christ, and renews us can be a source of refinement. May our growth come not only from calamities, but also through a daily, Christ-guided process of refinement.

Lord, bring about in me a spirit of new life that seeks continually to improve my faith, character, and relationship with you.

J.L.M.

*And let us not grow weary while doing good, for in
due season we shall reap if we do not lose heart.*
—GAL. 6:9

Chameleons are animals that can change colors depending on the setting they are in. God created them to do that as a protection against their enemies. They blend into rocks or grass and can be almost invisible to the untrained eye.

Mary Jane would have liked to be a chameleon—to blend into every situation. Mary Jane thought that if she could become whatever those around her expected her to be, then she would be loved by everyone. She avoided any situation where she might lose the "loved and respected" title. She defined happiness as having the whole world's admiration.

Let's look at the truth. Jesus Christ was perfect. But was He a chameleon? No! Was He loved and respected by everyone? No! In fact, He was hated, resented, and ultimately crucified.

God didn't create human beings to blend in with their surroundings. He made each of us unique, and His goal for us is to become the best we can be—not like everyone else. He wants us to stand up in a crowd when we feel we're right. He wants us to be like Christ, secure in our mission and secure in the One who sent us on that mission.

I will determine today to not lose heart. I will keep doing what is right, not necessarily what people expect.

J.E.M.

I acknowledged my sin to You,
And my iniquity I have not hidden.
I said, "I will confess my transgressions to the Lord,"
And You forgave the iniquity of my sin. —PS. 32:5

A few years ago, I experienced a major financial setback. It was only partly my fault, but I felt responsible—furious with myself. And I soon found myself slipping back into old, self-defeating behaviors such as rehearsing my failure over and over again to God. A loving friend who heard me praying asked, "Don't you believe that once you have confessed this area to the Lord, He wipes your slate clean? Are you trying to pay penance?" That was exactly what I was doing. I also was downgrading myself for not being perfect, trying to make up for my failure by working harder, and becoming irritable toward those I loved—another old pattern.

One day I stopped my frantic activity and did a self-evaluation. I had to admit that in response to this crisis I had regressed—fallen back into old, dysfunctional habits. What I needed to do instead was to fall back on the stability of God's grace. I needed to confess my failure but affirm my value. I needed to move toward relationship rather than away from it or against it. And I needed to say, "Of course I made a mistake. I'm human. Only God is perfect." Once I did that, I could begin to deal with the consequences of my poor choices and put them behind me.

Lord, when I face my weaknesses and mistakes, help me to confess rather than to regress.

J.M.C.

> *Do you see that faith was working together with his*
> *works, and by works faith was made perfect?*
> —JAMES 2:22

Whenever Celia looked at her one-year-old son, Ryan, she felt a rush of mixed emotions. She could not stop thinking about the abortion she had in college. At the time, it seemed like an easy solution. Now shame and guilt over that long-ago event were robbing her of the joy she should be feeling with her son. She had asked God for forgiveness, but she couldn't accept it. How could anyone, especially God, love someone who terminated a human life?

Celia had kept the abortion a secret for a long time. But finally, when the pain became too much, she shared her situation with a woman she respected in her church. This woman put her in touch with a small group of women who met together regularly to work through their problems of guilt and shame. After a few months, with the group's support, she began to put her past behind her and move forward to a new freedom. One day, as she sat in her backyard watching Ryan play, she felt overwhelmed by the wonderful blessing that God had given her. She realized at that moment that she needed to put away her fears, embrace God's comfort, and use her mistakes to help others.

Thank you, Lord, for forgiving me and staying by me while I stumbled along to find your grace.

J.L.M.

*And we know that all things work together for
good to those who love God.* —ROM. 8:28

Do bad things happen to good people? Yes. Do good
things happen to bad people? Yes. One of the most difficult concepts to grasp is that life is not always fair. As
children, we were obsessed with everything being fair,
but it wasn't. Life wasn't fair when we were children
and it's still not fair now that we're adults.

Why does God allow bad things to happen to good
people? Theologians give us three reasons. It might be
because God wants to show us His *power*. Sometimes
God wants to use the incident to help us *mature*. And
sometimes bad things happen because of our own *sin*.

Whatever the reason bad things happen, here is a
truth we can always rely on: God can bring good out of
bad. We can't be sure, in our limited human perspective, why things happen. But we can be sure that God
is with us. We can also be sure that no matter what
happens, God loves us. He will help us overcome—not
become overcome by—our problems in life.

*God will bring good out of bad when we are committed to His pur-
pose in our lives.*

J.E.M.

For by me your days will be multiplied,
And years of life will be added to you.
—PROV. 9:11

Kay had been happily married for forty-five years when her husband was stricken with a fatal heart attack. He had always been an encourager in Kay's life. Why, he had even prompted her to go back to college during a time when that was an unusual choice for a mother. Kay misses him terribly. But she has not let his death keep her from living.

Kay's bathroom mirror is fascinating. On it she keeps a list of the people she is praying for, the names and interests of the people she has just met, and a new word for each day of the week. Is it any wonder that people delight in her company? Last year Kay was hospitalized for an extended period of time. The nurses accused her of having the phone permanently attached to her ear. Even from her hospital bed, her vibrancy and love reached the people she was committed to. Now Kay has enrolled in a computer course because "after all, the world is changing. I don't want to be left behind."

Is it any wonder that Kay is an inspiration to me? No matter what age Kay gets to be, she will not grow old. One of her favorite sayings is "You do not grow old. You become old by not growing."

Lord, I want to keep growing. I will age in years, but I don't want to stagnate.

J.M.C.

Now godliness with contentment is great gain.
—1 TIM. 6:6

Contentment and satisfaction are more often seen in animals, nature, and children than in ourselves or others. Contentment is the family cat sleeping at the head of our bed on our pillow. It is our dog sprawled lazily at our feet after inhaling his dinner. Contentment is a brook gently flowing over softly rounded stones, an infant securely nestled in our lap.

Material possessions, relationships, jobs, children, and even addictions may bring us pleasure. But unless we are content, nothing fulfills us. Contentment must come from within, and it occurs when we are at peace with God and ourselves.

Contentment is different from happiness. Happiness is a brief emotion that comes and goes, but contentment endures. We find it when we have learned to respect struggles and unhappiness as a part of life, when our joy is a result of how we lead our lives instead of what life gives us. Leading our life in a manner that contributes to the welfare of ourselves and others is what contentment is about. And it is our faith rather than life experiences that produces true contentment.

Lord, help me to pursue contentment through you, and as a result of how I live my life, instead of expecting life to make me happy.

J.L.M.

> *The Lord will strengthen [her]*
> *on [her] bed of illness;*
> *You will sustain [her].*
> —PS. 41:3

Marilyn came for counseling with physical, emotional and relational problems. Her doctors had diagnosed her as having multiple sclerosis, a progressive neurological disorder that leads to blindness or paralysis. The disease can progress for a time and then go into remission for two or three years before recurring. There is no known cure.

Counseling helped Marilyn see that she did have choices. She could try to ignore her pain by continuing life as usual or run from it by becoming busier than ever. (The stress of this choice would probably make the disease progress more quickly.) She could make excuses about her illness or just worry about what would happen next. Resentment toward God was a possibility. So was just giving up and going to bed.

Marilyn looked at all these possible responses, and she tried many of them before and during counseling. Finally, however, she made the difficult decision to face her problems every day. This meant acknowledging her illness and its consequences and determining, with God's help, to live with the truth. Marilyn decided to live one day at a time, make the best choices she could, and share her honest feelings with her loved ones.

When pain comes my way, I will acknowledge it, verbalize my honest feelings about it, and discover how facing my pain helps decrease its intensity and duration.

J.E.M.

Yes, I have loved you with an everlasting love;
Therefore with lovingkindness I have drawn you.
—JER. 31:3

A young girl was wandering through a beautiful garden when she came upon a clump of daisies. She picked one and started pulling off the petals, saying, "He loves me, he loves me not, he loves me, he loves me not . . ." As I watched her from my quiet corner in the garden, I became overwhelmed with thoughts of gratitude to God for His gift of unconditional love.

The people in our lives say "I love you" so easily, but so often there are major strings attached. These messages come through: "I'll love you if . . . ," "I'll love you when . . . ," "I'll love you but . . . ." There are so many conditions, and as a result we go around insecure, trying to please other people, looking for approval. Our emotions stay on a constant roller coaster; we fluctuate from happiness to despair and back again.

God sent His Son, Jesus Christ, as a living demonstration that His love is radically different from conditional human love. If God had that daisy in His hand, as He pulled off the petals His message would be, "I love you, I love you, I love you!" That's inner security!

Thank you, God, for your love. Truly it is good news.

J.M.C.

A false balance is an abomination
to the Lord,
But a just weight is His delight.
—PROV. 11:1

Once again Caroline had to work late, and her irritation level was high. On the drive home from work she just wanted to scream at the other drivers. Upon arriving home she was glad to see that her husband was not yet home, and she was both panicked and relieved when her husband called to say he would be late. She went into the kitchen to start dinner. But when the catch on the cabinet stuck—again—she lost control. Next thing she knew, she was staring down at a pile of shattered china on the floor.

Where had this intense anger and frustration come from? Outwardly, Caroline's life seemed to be going well, but lately she had found it hard to read her Bible or talk to God because she didn't feel she measured up to His standards. She called an old friend, who suggested that she start reading one Bible verse in the morning and one at night. The friend also suggested that she share her feelings with others so she could receive support and stay accountable. As she read Proverbs 11:1, Caroline realized she really did need to balance her stressful life with more godly input. As she shared with others and meditated on God's Word, she began to feel her anger subside.

As I call upon your name and spend time in your Word, teach me the secret of a balanced life.

J.L.M.

Stop contention before a quarrel starts.
—PROV. 17:14

And the winner is. . . ." That's what Mike and Meg wanted me to announce during their early therapy sessions. They entered counseling on different sides and proceeded with one central question, "Who's right?" My job was to convince Mike and Meg to join forces and fight together against their problems in life.

My first task was to help Mike and Meg recognize there was indeed a war going on. And the next step was negotiation. When both partners began to recognize their own individual selfishness, the differences in the marriage could begin to be addressed from a stance of "What's in both of our best interest?"

When Mike and Meg began to realize that they both win when one wins and both lose when one loses, I knew they were on the right track. One step farther was to begin to teach each of them the concept of putting the interests and needs of the mate above their own interests and needs. My therapeutic goal was to combine their forces and send Mike and Meg out as equipped allies headed toward victory in the war of life together.

———————

Lord, help me see my loved ones as allies, not adversaries.

J.E.M.

Speaking the truth in love.
—EPH. 4:15

But it's so much more natural to speak the truth in anger," Sue said. "I don't know the first thing about speaking it in love."

Can you relate to Sue? So often we associate speaking the truth with criticism, verbal abuse, or sarcasm. After all, that's how many of us heard it in our family of origin. The problem is that what we heard was not necessarily the truth. Verbal abuse and sarcasm tell us more about the criticizer than the person being criticized. Constructive honesty builds people up. Destructive honesty tears them down. Words leave a permanent imprint on people's lives. And relationships do not give a license for rudeness.

When you talk, is the other person touched by your acceptance, understanding, and empathy? If so, your communication demonstrates love. But is your communication also characterized by truth? That's equally important. Love and mental telepathy are not the same thing. If you're upset, afraid, feeling neglected or angry, you need to say so.

The only person who lived this principle of "truth in love" perfectly was Jesus Christ. Let's ask Him to help us be more aware of our communication.

Today, Lord, help me to be lovingly honest.

J.M.C.

The Lord your God in your midst,
The Mighty One, will save;
He will rejoice over you with gladness,
He will quiet you in His love,
He will rejoice over you with singing.
—ZEPH. 3:17

This passage reveals God's pleasure in us. We often think of God as angry and condemning, ready to devour us if we slip up. But this verse shows clearly that the Lord loves us and desires good things for us. He yearns for us to turn to Him and rely on Him for His guidance. The Lord also gives us a model for us to follow in our relationships. Just as He rejoices over us, we should express our delight in those who are special in our lives.

We can rejoice over our loved ones in many creative ways. We can come up with little poems or notes to give them or surprise them with small gifts or cards. Our expressions of love may be as simple as putting a chocolate kiss on their pillow or a card in their lunch or briefcase, or it could involve selecting a meaningful song for them to hear or playing soft music during dinner. And most certainly it involves *telling* them how much they mean to us. Showing our loved ones how much we care not only helps them feel special, but helps us feel good about ourselves, while adding spontaneity to the relationships.

Father, help me to show others how much I love them, just as you continually show love to me.

J.L.M.

> *Finally, brethren, whatever things are true,*
> *whatever things are noble, whatever things are*
> *just, whatever things are pure, whatever things*
> *are lovely, whatever things are of good report,*
> *if there is any virtue and if there is anything*
> *praiseworthy—meditate on these things.*
>
> —PHIL. 4:8

The Christian life involves proper thinking. Compare your mind to a video recorder. If your "recorder" is continually tuned to a channel that broadcasts sleazy "soaps," brutal "action," exploitive "comedy," and sensationalist "news," these broadcasts will, in time, affect the way you live.

Our verse encourages us to think on things that are true, noble, just, pure, lovely, and of good report—that have virtue and are praiseworthy. *True* is the opposite of dishonest and unreliable. *Noble* means dignified and worthy of respect. *Just* involves conforming to God's standards, not the standards of the world. *Pure* is wholesome, unmixed with moral corruption. *Good report* talks about that which promotes peace rather than conflict. *Virtue* and *praiseworthy* refer to those things which are positive and constructive, as opposed to negative and destructive.

Think about it! How different our lives could be today if we switched our channel of thinking from worldly thinking to godly thinking.

Staying tuned to God's channel keeps my life on the right frequency.

J.E.M.

And you shall know the truth, and the truth shall make you free.
— JOHN 8:32

The Chinese tell the story of an old man whose horse ran away. The man's friends, trying to console him, said, "We're so sorry about your horse." But the old man's reply was, "Bad news, good news—who knows?" A few days later the horse returned home, leading a herd of wild horses. This time the friends congratulated him, but he answered, "Good news, bad news—who knows?" When the old man's son, trying to break in one of the wild horses, broke both legs, the father's reaction was similar: "Bad news, good news—who knows?" And when all young men in the village were drafted but the farmer's son was excused, he said, "Good news, bad news—who knows?"

Our journey towards wholeness begins when we face the truth and stop avoiding pain. Identifying our childhood wounds and tracing their influence into our adult life is not easy. But by facing the often-painful truth about ourselves, we are choosing to get well. We are trusting that what we learn will not be all bad news. Good news will also result from facing our pain and problems. Miracle of miracles, we find that not only can we stand the pain that we were terrified of facing, but we can also move beyond it to freedom and fulfillment.

Thank you, Lord, that in the pursuit of truth, I am set free.

J.M.C.

> *Now may the Lord direct your hearts into the love*
> *of God and into the patience of Christ.*
> —2 THESS. 3:5

Trudy hid behind her weight because she felt so guilty about her past. She also feared that if she lost weight she would have another affair. Trudy had been married to an abusive man. Instead of seeking help, she had become involved with another man. She then divorced her husband and married her lover. One month later, Trudy and her new husband had both accepted the Lord. She had been forgiven. So where was all this guilt and shame coming from?

Trudy talked to a girlfriend about her problem, and they began working together on choosing to accept God's forgiveness and unconditional love. Trudy began to confront her fear that she would have another affair. She wrote her ex-husband to apologize and ask his forgiveness. She then made the decision to forgive herself as God had forgiven her. She started meditating upon God's love and patience in the Scripture and began to reach out to other women in her church. To her great delight, after several months of working at these tasks, Trudy found she was no longer consumed with eating. The pounds began to come off. More important, as she focused on Christ's love, the weight of her guilt began to lift.

———————

Lord, help me to be consumed with your love, to know I deserve it, and to know that your grace is sufficient.

J.L.M.

God is able to make all grace abound toward you,
that you . . . may have an abundance for every
good work.   —2 COR. 9:8

Corrie ten Boom, a Dutch woman who was imprisoned by the Nazis for hiding Jews in her home during World War II, once told of a valuable lesson her father taught her as a girl. Corrie was worried about being able to face all the trials and suffering that might come her way as a Christian. Her wise father reminded her of her frequent train trips to a nearby town. He said, "Corrie, when do I give you the money for your train ride?" She answered, "Just before I go." He said, "That's right, and that's when God will give you the grace for any problem—just when you need it."

God hasn't promised a life without trials, but He has promised us grace for the journey. God gave Corrie ten Boom the grace to endure a flea-infected Nazi concentration camp. He even used the fleas as a defense to keep the guards out so the women could have their Bible studies.

Think about the areas in your life where you are suffering and in need of help. Mentally dump them all into a cardboard packing box. Then picture Jesus as standing by your side, ready to lift one end of the box and carry it with you. Then relax in the assurance that His grace will always be there—ready when you need it.

God's grace can be mine—if I will accept it.

J.E.M.

> *It is vain for you to*
> *rise up early,*
> *To sit up late.*
> —PS. 127:2

Every Mother's Day some well-meaning pastor reads the section on the virtuous woman from Proverbs 31. No doubt you have sat in the congregation and gritted your teeth as this woman's many accomplishments were extolled. Verses like "She also rises while it is yet night" (v. 15) seem guaranteed to lay a guilt trip on any woman.

But nowhere does this passage say that the woman in question accomplished all her feats in a day or even a year! In light of the entirety of Scripture, I am certain she did it in the appropriate seasons, in accordance with her family's needs and her gifts and energies. To accomplish what she did, she must have known the value of rest.

Rest is so important for human beings that God made it the basis of the Fourth Commandment. When we don't take time to be refreshed, little issues become big issues, and problems mount. The warning signs that we have been overdoing it are chronic fatigue, apathy, and the inability to make it through the day without caffeine. In our fast-paced, overstimulated world, it's easy to experience one or more of these symptoms. That's why our Lord tells us to get some rest. It's part of His plan for even the most accomplished woman.

Lord, give me the good sense to know when I am tired. At those times, help me to leave my cares in your loving arms.

J.M.C.

Talk no more so very proudly;
Let no arrogance come from your mouth,
For the Lord is the God of knowledge;
And by Him actions are weighed.
—1 SAM. 2:3

Many of us were taught from an early age that education is the key to success. Our experiences with education were valuable since it was in our school years that we learned how to socialize and make friends, deal with difficult people, set goals, and recover from failure. It was also there that we experienced how much value the world places on intelligence. It isn't surprising that people are often judged by how "smart" they are, where they went to school, or what degrees they hold; that attitude has been drilled into us since elementary school. We forget that God is the one who blesses us with the gift of intelligence and the ability to retain knowledge.

Boasting about intelligence is like an apple tree's bragging to an elm tree about how much more valuable it is. God made both, and He made them for different purposes. If we respect intelligence as a gift from our Lord, we will not be prideful about it. And knowledge is pleasing to the Lord when we use it to glorify Him, serve others, and help ourselves, not when we pride ourselves in it.

Lord, help me to value intelligence and knowledge as gifts from you to help others and to live a responsible life, not as reasons to glorify myself.

J.L.M.

> *Do not say, "I will recompense evil";*
> *Wait for the Lord, and He will save you.*
> —PROV. 20:22

Greta was an angry woman who was addicted to food, money, and control—and her addictions were working together to make Greta miserable. How could she get rid of these insidious emotional leeches that seem to hang on so tightly? In her own power, she couldn't! Step Two of the Twelve Steps is: *We came to believe that a Power greater than ourselves could restore us to sanity.** This is a big step. Greta had to turn upward as she looked inward.

The oral tradition of Alcoholics Anonymous breaks this step into three parts that Greta learned to use every day. First, she *came,* which means she reached a place in her life where she realized she was needy and the answer was not within herself. Next, she came *to;* she faced the fact she could live a healthier life without the emotional crutches of her addictions. Finally, she came to *believe*—she accepted that she couldn't do it by herself, but she *could* do it through God.

I remember when Greta prayed, "Lord, I can't get over all my anger toward others and my shame about myself without your power. Give me the power today to have love and not hate for myself and others. Lord, help me to come to believe that you are the strength I need to meet my trials for today. Amen."

I will "come to believe" today, trusting that the Lord—not I myself—will save me.

J.E.M.

*See page v.

*For now we see in a mirror, dimly, but then face to
face. Now I know in part, but then I shall know just
as I also am known.* —1 COR. 13:12

When we are little children, the adults in our life are
our mirror. But the reflection they provide is inevitably
distorted—influenced by the imperfect reflections they
received of themselves when they were tiny.

There is only one mirror that will give us a true reflection of ourselves: God's mirror. In His Word, He reflects back to us the truth that we are acceptable,
valuable, lovable, forgivable, and capable. That knowledge provides a solid foundation for our self-esteem.

God declared us acceptable and valuable when He
sent His only Son to die in our place. He knew we
needed to be forgiven, that we could never be good
enough on our own to make ourselves acceptable to a
holy God. And He offered that forgiveness freely—
telling us that all we have to do is ask. Then He went on
and declared us capable, urging us to act in behalf of
others.

When God mirrors back to us this positive picture of
ourselves, He reverses the curse put on us by distorted
human reflections. Your self-esteem is shaped by how
the most important person in your life feels about you.
Make Jesus Christ that person.

Thank you, Jesus, for the reflection you mirror back to me.

J.M.C.

> *Do not cast me off in the time of old age;*
> *Do not forsake me when my strength fails.*
> —PS. 71:9

Sally was getting older. Although her mind was still keen, arthritis made it difficult for her to get around. One day Sally told her daughter, "Everything within me cries out at the futility of my efforts and wants to give in, to give up hope and quit. Sometimes I just want to lie down and not get back up." Somewhere deep inside, however, she knew her spirit had not given up.

After Sally's great-granddaughter came and visited her for a few days, Sally began to realize what she had known all along—that God's infinite wisdom surpasses all understanding. During those two days she felt adored and comforted by her granddaughter. And the greatest of the many blessings she received during that time was that of leading her granddaughter to the Lord. She praised God for giving her the opportunity to affect someone else's life for eternity, especially someone she loved so much.

Sally is still persevering—giving up control of her life to God while trusting His infinite wisdom. She knows the Lord is her pillar of strength, and even though her body aches she refuses to allow Satan to defeat her. She no longer thinks she is too old to be of any use, and she now serves as a "telephone granny" for latchkey children.

Lord, let me lean on your infinite wisdom, and give me the opportunity to spread the greatest message of all time.

J.L.M.

*"But let him who glories glory in this,
That he understands and knows Me.
—JER. 9:24*

Marci was sexually abused by her stepfather, a deacon in a local church, from the time she was two until he was killed in an automobile accident when she was eight. Marci told her mother about the abuse, and her mother replied, "That's no big deal! It happens to lots of girls." A couple of years later, Marci's mother married another "religious" man, but this one was physically rather than sexually abusive.

Marci came to me when she was thirty. She was married to an abusive atheist. I worked with her for over three years, trying to be a loving listener. Marci knew I was a Christian, but because of her circumstances I tried to *exhibit* Christian character in my therapy work without saying a lot about my faith. As we neared the end of therapy, Marci asked, "Well, is that all there is?" I felt we had gotten to a place she was ready for the "good news." So I shared the gospel with her and worked to help her begin a relationship with God to fill the vacuum her "fathers" had left. Like many people, Marci had to learn to see her heavenly Father without the "dark glasses" of her experience with earthly father figures. Eventually, however, she came to see Him as He is—loving, kind, forgiving, and compassionate.

Today I will try to see my heavenly Father as He really is, not through the glasses of my earthly experience.

J.E.M.

> *And a great windstorm arose, and the waves beat
> into the boat, so that it was already filling. But
> [Jesus] was in the stern, asleep on a pillow. And
> they awoke Him and said to Him, "Teacher, do
> You not care that we are perishing?"*
> —MARK 4:37–38

What is rocking your boat today? Our boat rocked when our precious six-year-old son was diagnosed as having cancer. It rocked when our financial plans went awry and I couldn't keep teaching in the States because I had been born in Canada. And it has rocked many times since—and it will rock again. Because we live on a dysfunctional planet, such crises are unavoidable.

One of the worst things about a crisis is that awful feeling of being out of control. But the truth is that most of life is beyond our control; the crisis simply rubs our faces in that reality. But while we cannot really control what happens, we can control our *response* to what happens.

In this story the disciples gave in to panic; Jesus was at peace. Calmness in crisis is a direct result of concentrating on God's closeness and care. We fear too much because we trust God too little. But the disciples did do something healthy in the midst of their crisis; they went to Jesus. Why don't you try that in the midst of your next crisis?

Nothing is out of control when it's in God's control.

J.M.C.

In a dream, in a vision of the night,
When deep sleep falls upon men,
While slumbering on their beds,
Then He opens the ears of men,
And seals their instruction.
—JOB 33:15–16

Shirley felt sad as she thought about finishing the project without her Mike. Since her husband's death, she had thought about giving up on their dream of building an orphanage. Her heart ached; they had grown so close through the years as they had grown closer to God. Now she wondered if she would be able to keep their dream alive. The foundation wasn't finished, and she couldn't even read a blueprint!

Then one night Shirley had a dream. She saw the site completed, landscaped, surrounded by trees and playgrounds. And she woke with new confidence that, with God's help, she could make the orphanage a reality. She had some money from Mike's life insurance, so she began to look at her options. She started a board of directors for advice. And slowly but surely, over the next five years, she saw her dream come true. Later, she looked back at how God had started her on a small and seemingly impossible project. With a few assets, a bit of determination, and the Lord's help, her dream became a real home for children who needed one.

In my times of despair, God, help me to hang onto the dreams you have given to me and my family.

J.L.M.

*Not that I have already attained, or am already
perfected; but I press on, that I may lay hold of that
for which Christ Jesus has also laid hold of me.*
—PHIL. 3:12

We all know her (or think we do). She looks like
Cheryl Tiegs and cooks like Betty Crocker. Her children rise up and call her blessed. Each morning, her
knight in shining armor rides off to work on his white
horse.

We also know her next door neighbor. She looks like
Betty Crocker and cooks like Cheryl Tiegs. Her children rise up and call her. Some mornings her husband
gets up, and some mornings he doesn't. He doesn't
own a horse.

Romantic that I am, I always dreamed of being the
perfect mother and wife. I'm not sure what my definition of perfection was. But when I was around thirty-
five, I had to face the sad facts. Nothing in my life was
perfect. My children were great kids, but they certainly weren't perfect. My husband was nice, but not
perfect. No one in my family had "arrived."

I realize now how far off my perspective was. Of
course, none of us is perfect. Perfection will come only
in Heaven. And here on planet earth, true significance
comes not from looking like Cheryl Tiegs or cooking
like Betty Crocker, but from "laying hold" of specific
ways we can use our God-given talents to benefit
others.

*Instead of trying to be perfect, I will keep pressing on to discover how
God wants to use me in His service.*

J.E.M.

*And I was afraid, and went and hid your talent in
the ground.* —MATT. 25:25

How often we crucify ourselves between two thieves:
regret for yesterday and fear of tomorrow. What a
waste of a life!

I remember a time when I wanted to write a book,
but I was afraid I couldn't do it. All I could see were
those *B*s and *C*s that had come back from professors in
college when I thought I should have gotten *A*s. What if
I didn't have the stuff to be a writer? What if no one
would read my book?

One day I woke up and realized I was facing the
wrong enemy. Instead of being afraid of failing I should
have been afraid of not trying. The one who never
risks anything is the ultimate failure.

Failure is not final, and it even provides some major
benefits. Failure is a great educator. It certainly teaches
us what doesn't work. It develops and refines our skills,
it helps us discover our true talents, and it makes us
more sympathetic and less judgmental.

Each of us needs to make one good mistake a
week—just as long as it isn't the *same* mistake. Either
we will be failure avoiders or success seekers. The
choice is yours.

---

*Lord, help me to remember the turtle. He makes progress only when
he sticks his neck out.*

J.M.C.

> *For where envy and self-seeking exist, confusion*
> *and every evil thing will be there.*
>
> —JAMES 3:16

In Jody's mind the same tape kept running over and over: "I'm fine!!! I'm fine!!! I'm fine!!!" But the scream got louder and louder, and Jody knew she wasn't fine. She was capable and efficient at her job; she could do more at work than her colleagues and in less time. Her boss had recently put an arm around her and told her how proud he was of her. But he had also told her in a concerned voice to take care of herself and not to worry so much. Jody was so confused. Was she really fine and just telling herself she wasn't, or was she really sick?

Jody began attending a Bible study at her church. Gradually, as she studied about God's love with other women, she became less confused. She realized that much of her efforts at work were really self-seeking attempts to earn praise and feel loved. She came to understand that God, not other people, was the only dependable source of love—and God's love can't be earned. Then she was able to take her newfound knowledge and comfort to work with her. She was able to see her strengths and weaknesses more clearly and to turn her energies from self-seeking to serving.

Thank you for giving me the knowledge of your true love and for helping me accept it. My confusion vanishes in the light of your truth.

J.L.M.

For the lips of an immoral woman drip honey,
And her mouth is smoother than oil;
But in the end she is bitter as wormwood. . . .
Her ways are unstable. —PROV. 5:3, 4, 6

These verses refer to an adulterous woman, but they can also be applied to an addictive personality. (Sin, after all, is addictive.)

Addictions, in the beginning, are usually pleasant—like honey or olive oil; it is only later that they turn bitter. And because addictive behaviors bring pleasure, they blind us to the downward spiral. Only after all the chains have bound us do we begin to see how destructive our behavior is to ourselves and others.

As we look at who we have been and who we have become, we begin to realize that much of our destructive behavior comes from our being "unstable." Only as we understand our spiritual and emotional "wobbliness" will we begin to feel God's wisdom and His deep love and supporting strength.

God wants us to anticipate trouble, to recognize the addictive pattern ahead of time, to depend on His stable strength. If we do, we can learn to be free from sinful behaviors that we have been caught by in the past. God wants to deliver us from bondage, but He will not do it without our cooperation.

I will acknowledge my own unstable tendencies today to avoid slipping into addictive behaviors, even if they appear to be as sweet as honey.

J.E.M.

> *Finally, all of you be of one mind, having
> compassion for one another; love as brothers,
> be tenderhearted, be courteous.*
>
> —1 PETER 3:8

Where does a mother go when she needs some nurturing? Until recently, men have not been taught nor expected to nurture their wives—and many still find it difficult. Children are children; they can't be expected to meet their mother's needs. So where does a mother go for nurturing? On the human level, mothers need to go to other mothers. Who else understands so completely what it's like to be exhausted because your entire family has had the flu for a week? Who better can relate to the mortification you suffer when your children throw temper tantrums in the store? Who else understands the feeling of helplessness when you can no longer kiss your child's hurt away—or the pride you feel when your child stands on her own two feet?

Mothers share the experience of being women at a turning point in history. We also share the awesome opportunity of loving our children, of being responsible to them but not for them. What a shame if women who have this much in common didn't get to know one another.

Thank you, Lord, for the gift of friendship. Without friends, life would be like a garden with no flowers.

J.M.C.

Like a madman who throws firebrands,
arrows, and death,
Is the man who deceives his neighbor,
And says, "I was only joking!"
—PROV. 26:18–19

Humor is a quality to be desired. It helps us to create a diversion in our lives and serves as a respite from the ordinary. But sometimes humor is merely an outpouring of anger. Have you ever had someone cut you down and then laugh and say, "Just kidding"? If you didn't laugh, you might have been accused of pouting or being "no fun." But you knew the "joke" wasn't really funny.

If this scenario seems familiar, it is healthy for you to confront the jokers by telling them you feel hurt by their words and asking them not to "joke" with you like that. You may even choose to shy away from individuals who consistently use humor as a weapon. But don't shy away from humor entirely! Make an effort to bring laughter and fun into your everyday life—not only for your sake, but for those around you. You can model appropriate humor by "lightening up" about your mistakes and the mistakes of others. For example, if you break a glass, you have an opportunity to joke about it instead of griping. Finding the comical side of everyday life—not laughing at others—is what a healthy sense of humor is.

Lord, help me see the funny things in life and share them with others. I want to make a commitment to developing a sense of humor and bringing laughter into my life.

J.L.M.

Give us day by day our daily bread.
—LUKE 11:3

We have three clear choices as we live our lives. We can look back, look forward, or live in the present.

Continually looking back can cause us to stumble. Whether our past is filled with failure or success, continually dwelling on it will not help us today. We can learn from it, but we shouldn't live in it.

Living for the future can bring problems too. It's good to look ahead, to plan better ways of facing future challenges of life. But focusing only on tomorrow can either paralyze us with fear or distract us with pipe dreams.

The best way to stay on the recovery road is to choose each day to live a balanced, healthy life. We pray for God to "give us day by day our daily bread." We also need to pray for God to give us daily help for our emotional and spiritual needs. We can avoid falling into depression or despair by focusing on present possibilities instead of future problems or past failures.

I choose today to learn from my past and hope in my future, but focus on living a balanced, meaningful life with loving relationships.

J.E.M.

A new commandment I give to you, that you love one another; as I have loved you, that you also love one another. —JOHN 13:34

Nearly everyone can stand adversity. But if you really want to test someone's character, give her power.

Susan was into power. A competent businesswoman climbing the ladder of success, she wanted to get to the top, and she really wasn't terribly concerned who she used to make it happen. She made a practice of dominating and demanding. She often negated others and their contributions in order to make herself look good. Her basic question was "What's in it for me?" She valued power far more than she valued people.

Stacey also was a competent businesswoman. But her basic question was "How can we turn this situation into a double win, where both of us succeed?" She wasn't afraid to give encouragement or ideas to those around her. She made a practice of serving, discussing, and listening. She attempted to do her best, and she encouraged others to do theirs. Her love freed others to be themselves.

The difference between Susan and Stacey was love. Stacey had been touched personally by Jesus' love, which freed her from the need to always be on top. Susan had yet to discover it.

Lord, thank you for loving me. Help me to model your love to those around me.

J.M.C.

*For indeed, when we came to Macedonia, our flesh
had no rest, but we were troubled on every side.
Outside were conflicts, inside were fears.
Nevertheless God, who comforts the downcast,
comforted us by the coming of Titus.*

—2 COR. 7:5–6

The only thing I can count on in myself right now is inconsistency. Yesterday morning, I fought back tears all the way to work for no apparent reason. The day before, I wanted desperately to stay curled around my bear in bed, drawing comfort from that sense of isolated protectedness. The pain will leave when I get busy, but then it will suddenly pop up again."

All of us feel sad at times, but some have deep depressions which can be quite unsettling. Jill couldn't seem to shake her depression. She felt apprehensive sharing her feelings with family and co-workers because she thought they were probably tired of hearing her. Instead, she decided to go on a retreat and try to have fellowship with other Christian women. While there, she began to feel comforted and rested by the natural beauty of the retreat center and the uplifting of the other women. After she returned, her depression would come and go over the next few months and she saw a therapist for awhile. But she saw that God had placed others in her life to comfort her. As she got better, she was able to comfort them as well.

---

*Don't let me be deceived by my fears, Lord; let me find comfort in you
and the brothers and sisters you place in my life.*

J.L.M.

Grace and peace be multiplied to you in the knowledge of God and of Jesus our Lord, as His divine power has given to us all things that pertain to life.
—2 PETER 1:2, 3

If mechanical ability is a gift, I guess I didn't get it. I do know that if a machine has a plug, it must be inserted in a socket before the machine will work. I have also grasped that usually there is also an "on and off" switch. Beyond that I usually need to read the directions. But some Christians don't even get to the point of plugging in the plug and turning on the switch. They often try to sort their lives out without Christ's power—and end up missing out on His grace and peace. If we interpret our past without calling on His power to heal our past wounds, we will be continually turned off.

You may have had parents or other significant people who constantly gave you the message, "You are not quite good enough!" You may have had parents who pretended like you didn't exist or acted as if you didn't matter. You may have holes in your soul from your past. But Christ offers you the power to break free of your past if you will just "plug in" to Him. There will still be plenty of work for you to do, and Christ will use other people to help you. But He will be the underlying Power Source, causing "grace and peace" to be "multiplied to you."

I will plug into my Higher Power—Jesus Christ—today, so I can resolve the pain of my past.

J.E.M.

For the Lord takes pleasure in His people;
He will beautify the humble with salvation.
—PS. 149:4

A beggar agreed to let an artist paint his picture. A few hours later, he was staring in astonishment at the finished canvas. "Who's that?" he asked, for before him was a portrait of a tall, dignified gentleman. "That's the you I see," the artist replied quietly. "Then," responded the beggar, "that's the me I'll be."

Jesus sees each of us not as the sinner we indeed are, but as the saint we will one day be. We need to learn to see ourselves that way, too. This doesn't mean we are never to experience negative thoughts and feelings about ourselves. Negative thoughts may indicate that we are aware of our limitations and may motivate us to change. But by constantly putting ourselves down, we choose the pathway to withdrawal. We hide behind the smokescreen of inferior feelings rather than facing the truth about ourselves.

A positive view of myself, based on an awareness of both my strengths and my limitations, is the result of seeing myself as God sees me. He knows I am deeply fallen, but He felt I was significant enough to send His only Son to die for me. God loves me greatly. God loves you!

Thank you, Lord, for looking at both my weaknesses and my strengths with loving, accepting eyes.

J.M.C.

And they were both naked, the man and his wife,
and were not ashamed.   —GEN. 2:25

Sheri felt so happy to be married, and she couldn't believe how patient and kind Drew was, but she became uneasy when sexual matters came up. In fact, she felt so ashamed that she couldn't enjoy that part of her relationship that she started to resent Drew. Naturally, that hurt him, and he began to pull away.

With the help of a good counselor, Sheri began to realize that she was harboring deep guilt about sexual encounters she had had as a teenager and a college student. She had always been taught to wait, but after the first time it hadn't seemed to matter. Then, after leaving college, Sheri had experienced a Christian renewal and started setting limits. She and Drew had never done more than hold hands and kiss. She had told him that she wasn't a virgin, but neither was he, and he didn't condemn her. The trouble was, she was condemning herself.

As Sheri increasingly became aware of how God had ordained marriage, she realized she was in danger of letting false guilt destroy her relationship with Drew. But as she was able to talk these matters over with him, she began to feel a freedom which allowed a whole new level of intimacy. She also continued to work on accepting God's forgiveness so she would not feel shame about the sexual part of their marriage.

Lord, please remind me to let Satan know that you handle my account, so I can escape the web of shame and self-deceit.

                                                        J.L.M.

> *Having then gifts differing according to the grace that is given to us, let us use them.*
>
> —ROM. 12:6

When I sit down for dinner, I often think of all the hands it took to bring the meal to the table. Farmers had to carefully plant, cultivate, and harvest the crops. They sold the food to manufacturers, who processed and packaged it. Store personnel placed it on shelves and ran it through checkout lines. I bought many foods and mixed them together to get to the final step of a dinner for my family.

Many different people also helped me be what I am today spiritually. I became a Christian through a televised Billy Graham crusade when I was ten years old. I think of the Sunday school teachers who helped lay the foundations of my faith and the youth leaders who tirelessly worked with me when I was going through those "teen years." I think of my Bible-study leaders and pastors who have ministered to me so faithfully during my adult life.

What am I doing to give back a portion of what has been given to me? Hundreds of people with many different gifts have helped me grow spiritually. I want to use my own gifts to help others grow.

I am only one, but I am one who can choose to give back a little of myself.

J.E.M.

In labors more abundant, in stripes above measure,
in prisons more frequently, in deaths often.
—2 COR. 11:23

Do your problems cause you to lose your religion or use your religion?

Joseph, in the book of Genesis (see Gen. 37, 39—45), had plenty of reason to despair and lose his faith. His eleven brothers were jealous of him, and so they sold him into slavery. And that's good news; they originally had planned to kill him! While a slave, Joseph experienced seduction and slander. Because he wouldn't succumb to the romantic overtures of his master's wife, he was framed and thrown in prison. While in prison he helped free two men who were about to lose their heads. One of them promised to help Joseph in return, but he gave no further thought to Joseph once he himself was released.

Through it all, Joseph never lost sight of God's sovereignty. His basic belief was that God can turn other people's cruelty into good. This belief kept Joseph going. He coveted God's blessing on his life more than he desired immediate gratification. Because of this belief, Joseph did his best wherever he was. As a slave and as a prisoner, the quality of his relationship with God positively affected the quality of his work. And when troubles struck, Joseph used his religion. His faith in God anchored him for all the storms life would throw at him.

Lord, please let me view my problems as an opportunity for strengthening my faith in you.

J.M.C.

> *Bring my soul out of prison,*
> *That I may praise Your name;*
> *The righteous shall surround me,*
> *For You shall deal bountifully with me.*
> —PS. 142:7

Rebecca looked out her "prison cell," as she called it—her own home. It had become her place of confinement due to her obsession with cleanliness. She couldn't stop washing her hands over and over, even though they were rough and cracking. She felt compelled to keep everything spotless and in order.

Slowly but surely Rebecca began to realize that her behavior was a way of getting control and feeling comforted. She began to seek help by praying and getting friends to just listen and be there. She also sought help from her pastor and a therapist. She would cry out to God, "Will I feel so weak and vulnerable forever?" She knew that she was getting better, but the world still seemed such a lonely place to be. She felt as if no one could come inside and know the hurt and soothe the ache that echoed around inside her. Surprisingly, though, as she began to allow others to comfort her, the ache began to be soothed—little by little. As the ache subsided she would give thanks that all the conflict and torment was subsiding. Finally she stopped compulsively washing her hands, and she felt free to do something other than clean her house.

Thank you, Lord, for allowing me to act upon freedom instead of allowing my fears to keep me a prisoner.

J.L.M.

Jesus said to her, "I am the resurrection and the life. He who believes in Me, though he may die, he shall live." —JOHN 11:25

My grandmother was ninety-three when she died. Her husband and three sons had gone before her, but she had never lost her radiant faith in God. She died on her couch with her well-worn Bible open on her lap.

The only real certainty in life is death. There is no question that we will die; the only question is how long we'll live. And God has not promised us long life, but He has provided a way for us to meet death and face eternal life.

It always amazes me that a certainty like death is so overlooked by so many. People fall into denial even in the face of certain death. Some who have been diagnosed with fatal diseases will vehemently maintain there is nothing wrong with them.

Physical death seems so final, so frightening. For a non-Christian, death spells the end of any joyful experiences, of hope, the entrance into everlasting darkness. For the Christian, however, death is only the beginning—the beginning of an eternity we can't begin to comprehend, the entrance into everlasting life.

I will bravely reflect today on my own inevitable death, looking to Christ's death and resurrection and His promise of eternal life.

J.E.M.

> *Fearfulness and trembling have come upon me,*
> *And horror has overwhelmed me.*
> *And so I said, "Oh that I had wings like a dove!*
> *For then I would fly away and be at rest."*
> —PS. 55:5–6

Marlene had been dating Chip for a month when she invited him to a business dinner. When Chip told her he had other plans, Marlene hung up the phone and berated herself for ever having invited him. That night, she bombarded herself with negative thoughts: *He thought I was chasing him; he's met someone else; he saw a flaw in me that other men see too. I'll always be alone.*

Marlene was overdramatizing a stressful situation, and her self-talk was putting her in an emotional tailspin. How much more helpful it would be to direct her energy toward what was really upsetting her—the possibility that someone she cared about didn't care for her in the same way. She needed to remember also that, rejections are unpleasant, but not terminal.

Marlene needs to find her security in God's unconditional acceptance of her through Jesus Christ. That cannot be lost even when she experiences rejection from others. If Chip cannot meet her legitimate need for relationship, she needs to develop some other relationships, male and female, where this need can be met in a healthy way.

Lord, please remind me in the midst of rejection that it isn't terminal. Help me gain an inner security because of your unconditional acceptance of me.

J.M.C.

Train up a child in the way he should go,
And when he is old he will not depart from it.
—PROV. 22:6

As Liza dreamed of the ways things could be with her and her strong-willed daughter, she couldn't see herself acting upon what she knew would help. She knew Amber needed lots of hugs and love, but something in Liza prevented her from giving them. When she thought about how Amber might turn out because of the way she had raised her, she would begin to panic and be filled with guilt.

Liza began praying about her problems with her daughter. After several weeks of prayer, she began to understand Amber better. She realized that Amber often mirrored Liza's own imperfections, acting out many things Liza felt like doing. No wonder Amber "got her goat"! Then Liza began to act upon what she knew Amber needed—love and nurturing. She began to give Amber hugs during peaceful times and made an effort to think rationally during emotional fights when Amber was pushing to get her way. As Liza started giving her more attention, Amber actually started to act out more at first, because she wasn't used to it. Liza felt like throwing the towel in several times, but with the Lord's strength she persisted. Now Amber's outbursts have subsided, and mother and daughter enjoy a new loving relationship with its "normal" ups and downs.

Oh, Lord, when there are trying times, help me to act out of love and to look at my daughter's gifts just as you do.

J.L.M.

> *I call to remembrance the genuine faith that is in you, which dwelt first in your grandmother Lois and your mother Eunice, and I am persuaded in you also.*
>
> —2 TIM. 1:5

Two little boys once pressed their bare feet into the soft cement of a freshly paved street and ran away, leaving deep footprints. A few days later, after the cement had hardened, a circus parade complete with elephants marched down the same street. Not one of the elephants left even a dent in the pavement. Two little fifty pound boys left impressions in soft cement. Tons of elephants couldn't make an impression once the cement had hardened. And what is true of cement is true of hearts and minds. They are soft and impressionable when they are young—much harder to mark at a later age.

My grandmother was truly a woman who loved God. She passed the love and faith to my mother. My mother has lived her life as a testimony to all of her children. Now we, her two daughters and two sons, are committed to passing the faith on to another generation. My mother is praying for each of her children daily as we strive to create an atmosphere of love, faith, and prayer in our homes.

I will reach out today to make godly imprints on those whose hearts and minds are still soft enough to be impressionable.

J.E.M.

Wives, submit to your own husbands, as to the Lord.
—EPH. 5:22

What does submission mean? It is not involuntary subjection nor a trade-off in domination or self-negation. Neither is it a mathematically precise, fifty-fifty relationship. Submission in marriage is mutual. In fact, the verse before this one speaks, "Submitting to *one another* in the fear of God" (emphasis added). Submission is a deliberate, voluntary, love-initiated response to another's needs. Because it is a personal choice, it is only possible for women and men who have a strong understanding of who they are and who are confident of their full equality before God and each other.

Mutual submission results from our awareness that in serving others we are really serving God. Therefore both people in the relationship will do their best to affirm the other's gifts, talents, and completeness as well as their own. The greatest benefit of such a relationship is that of mutual growth. When one partner is not free to grow, neither partner will achieve his or her full potential. But as both submit to each other in love, both move toward becoming their best.

Lord, help me bring all of who I am to the one I am closest to. Help me value this person. Help us both in healthy ways as a result of our relationship.

J.M.C.

> *Children's children are the crown of old men,*
> *And the glory of children is their father.*
> —PROV. 17:6

While walking down a narrow cobblestone street in Mexico, I was struck by the presence and importance of family in this poverty-stricken community. All around you could see whole families pitching in to do the daily chores. Children helped with the family business or with meals. Grandparents helped keep order. Families ate together and then sat around telling stories.

Seeing this made me stop and think about how important it is in our fast-paced society to get involved as a family—to work together on projects, develop hobbies, and move toward a common purpose. A family can achieve a goal if its members work together, but a family pulling in separate directions can destroy individual members as well as the family unit.

I asked the Lord to help my family to establish a vision for our life together. We agreed that we want to have a fellowship with God and to take the time to listen to each other, as well as to share genuine concern for each other's personal needs. We have now made a commitment to support and encourage each other in our endeavors.

Lord, give us the wisdom to work together for your purpose, allowing your love to radiate from our families. Thank you for my family, and help me be a good steward with those I love.

J.L.M.

There is . . . a time to be born.
—ECCL. 3:1–2

How sweet it is to hear a newborn baby cry. For anyone who has gone through the agony of childbirth, that cry is a joyous sign that labor is over and a new life has begun. Every birth is filled with wonder.

The miracle of conception and birth is well documented but still awe inspiring. Two tiny cells unite to begin the process. The resulting fertilized egg is only barely visible to the naked eye, yet it contains all the directions necessary to form a human being. The first cell divides, then redivides, attaches itself to the womb, and the baby begins to grow.

It is truly beyond my comprehension how a baby could form in nine short months from these two cells. No human feat has ever come close to competing with the miracle of reproduction—only God could invent such a process. Yet many people today seem to have forgotten God; they do not recognize Him as the giver of life. As mothers—or as friends and children—let's give thanks to God today for the miracle of birth.

Lord, thank you for those you used to give me birth and those you privileged me to give birth to. Keep me ever aware of and grateful for the miracle of new life.

J.E.M.

*For I say, through the grace given to me, to
everyone who is among you, not to think of himself
more highly than he ought to think, but to think
soberly, as God has dealt to each one a measure
of faith.*
—ROM. 12:3

A husband and wife who had been married thirty-five years were asked the secret of their marital longevity. With a smile they answered, "We made Romans 12:3 our marital verse."

In our society, image is everything. Many don't care if there is little substance behind the image as long as the image is polished—and they are totally involved in polishing their own image. The result is troubled relationships. It's difficult to inflate ourselves without deflating the people around us.

I love the story I heard about Muhammad Ali, who was on a plane. The flight attendant asked him to fasten his seat belt. His reply was, "Superman doesn't need a seat belt." The attendant didn't miss a beat. She said, "Superman doesn't need a plane."

Paul warns us "to think soberly," which means to have sound thinking about ourselves—to be realistic about our strengths and honest about our weaknesses. Taking a daily and weekly inventory helps us do that. When we accept our humanity, humility is the natural result . . . and we're a lot easier to live with.

Lord, help me to be realistic in my estimation of myself today. Help me remember that people wrapped up in themselves make very small packages.

J.M.C.

Then you will walk safely in your way,
And your foot will not stumble.
—PROV. 3:23

Have you ever tried to walk on a balance beam? You start to fall to the left, and then you have to compensate by leaning right. Most important, you have to look straight ahead. If you look to either side, you seem to lean in that direction. If you look down, you seem to lose the perspective of where you are going. And looking back spells total disaster.

It's amazing how that simple little rule of looking straight ahead—keeping our eyes focused on the Father—is so important in our Christian walk. When I let myself become distracted, before you know it, I am off wandering in the wrong direction. My life just seems out of sync; I can't stay on the beam. If I glance down because of my fear or doubt, I always stumble or lose my footing. And if I turn and look back at something that has always enticed me, I land flat on my back. Yet one of the greatest comforts through all this is that if I just refocus on the Lord, He's always waiting to help guide my steps on the straight and narrow path toward Him.

Help me stay focused on you, Lord, and thank you for always waiting patiently for me.

J.L.M.

> *I am the Lord your God, who brought you out of*
> *the land of Egypt, out of the house of bondage.*
> —EX. 20:2

Our fourteen-year-old seems to spend a lot of time questioning rules. Her two favorite sayings seem to be "That's not fair" and "Let's change that rule." It's hard to make her understand or accept the reasons behind the rules we've made, but we try. Our goal is for her to see that we set rules for her because we love her and want only what's best for her.

God is like that. What a freeing experience it is when we truly understand that God gives us laws not to bind us, but to free us. Our verse today is an introduction to God's laws, the Ten Commandments, but the word picture it expresses is *freedom*. Imagine all the Israelites—thousands of them—trudging out of Egypt, out of the extreme bondage. God gave the Israelites the Ten Commandments not to cramp their style, but to show them how to keep from falling into bondage again.

The picture is there for all of us to see. We can choose bondage by breaking God's laws or freedom by keeping His laws. Praise God, He sent Christ and the Holy Spirit to assist us in keeping His principles. And when we fail but turn to Him, He is quick to forgive us and put us back on the path to freedom.

God's principles point the true way to freedom.

J.E.M.

When my heart is overwhelmed;
Lead me to the rock that is higher than I.
For You have been a shelter for me,
And a strong tower from the enemy.
—PS. 61:1–3

Jean was overjoyed when her only grandchild, Ruth, was born. She babysat for her often and read to her by the hour. Jean helped Ruth bake her first batch of cookies and took her to see *The Nutcracker* ballet. Every week, Jean took Ruth to Sunday school.

Then came the divorce. Ruth's mother, Suzanne, moved Ruth to another state. Not long afterward, a polite letter arrived from Suzanne, asking Jean to cut off all contact with Ruth. Suzanne's new husband wanted to adopt Ruth, and they wanted to start over. Jean's heart broke as she read that letter. "Why? Why?" she cried out to God. "I love this precious child as if she were my own!" Jean complied with Suzanne's wishes. But she put Ruth's picture on her refrigerator, and lifted her up to Jesus every day. Years went by. Then one day Jean received a phone call. It was Ruth— grown up, newly married, and pregnant. She thanked Jean for introducing her to Jesus, and wondered if Jean would like to meet her family. Two months later, Ruth took her newborn to meet Jean. "I hope you don't mind, Grandma," said Ruth, "but we want to call her Jean."

Lord, when I feel overwhelmed, help me remember that you haven't had the final word yet.

J.M.C.

He has blinded their eyes and hardened their heart,
Lest they should see with their eyes,
And understand with their heart,
  Lest they should turn,
  so that I should heal them.
  —JOHN 12:40 (from ISA. 6:10)

I did it again!" Lori chided herself. Then the memories of Friday's desperation flooded her in. Where did this desire for men come from? Every time she was around a man, her need for love would just overwhelm her—and inevitably she would end up in bed with him.

Lori kept reading her Bible and going to church, although she felt like a hypocrite. One Sunday the preacher talked about honoring one's parents, and Lori grew uneasy. Her father's strict rules and discipline had kept her from getting close to him. But now Lori decided to go and talk to her father about the past and ask him to forgive her resentment toward him. When she did so, to her surprise, he took her hand and asked her to forgive him, too. They talked for an hour about improving their relationship and decided to meet once a week just to talk. Lori also decided to begin seeing a counselor and attend a support group for people with sex and love addictions. Gradually, to Lori's surprise, her addictive desire for a man's love waned. She also began to see God in a whole new light and eventually began to develop appropriate relationships with men.

Lord, please help me to drop my pride so I can clearly see your path for me.

                                                              J.L.M.

The heart of her husband safely trusts her.
—PROV. 31:11

The thirty-first chapter of Proverbs paints an unforgettable picture of a lady to be admired. She is a wife, a mother, a homemaker, a businesswoman. She's also beautiful and dresses well! She seems to be wealthy and to have many servants, and that might make her hard for some of us to identify with. However, it is not her wealth that this chapter in Proverbs extols but her character. Verse 11, for instance, talks about her trustworthiness; she did what she said and said what she did. Her husband and children knew she was an anchor they could come home to.

When this verse talks about "heart," I think it's talking about the core of a person's being. The verse says that this woman's husband trusted her from the very depths of who he was. What a compliment to be safely trusted in the heart of your own husband!

I will strive today to be dependably trusted in the hearts of those I love.

J.E.M.

> *Finally, all of you be of one mind, having*
> *compassion for one another.*
> —1 PETER 3:8

I first met Rita after she had attempted suicide. A history of emotional abandonment and sexual abuse had left her in deep agony. Hers was a long, hard fight back to sanity, but a turning point came one night when she dreamed she was skydiving over a dark, murky ocean. Terror gripped her as she pulled the ripcord and only one side of her parachute opened. She fought with it all the way down, thinking, *Is this how I'm going to die?* She crashed into the ocean and continued to struggle with the parachute. But suddenly she was distracted by a van full of people that had just driven off a nearby pier. The people were drowning. But somehow Rita got her parachute attached to the van and pulled it into shallower water. Everyone—including Rita—was safe.

As we discussed the dream, Rita shared how her memories felt like that dark, terrifying ocean. Her recovery process had worked like the half-opened parachute. But when she had reached out and begun to relate to others who were also feeling overwhelmed and desperate, Rita had turned a corner in her recovery. The evil done to her was being transformed into something that could be used for good.

I am important in someone else's recovery. Thank you, Lord. Complete my recovery as I reach out to someone else.

J.M.C.

There is no fear in love; but perfect love casts out fear, because fear involves torment. But he who fears has not been made perfect in love.
—1 JOHN 4:18

Jenny had been depressed since her husband had died in an automobile accident almost nine months before. Now she looked around her house. Kitchen, bedrooms, and family room were all a mess. The yard needed mowing. She hadn't cooked a meal for her children in almost two weeks. The bills needed paying, and there was money to pay them, but she just couldn't find the energy to get them done. "I just can't do it, God!" she prayed.

In the silence that followed that panicked prayer, Jenny began to see how fear had taken hold and paralyzed her. Most of all, she feared being on her own. But then she realized, "I'm not really alone." With that encouraging reassurance, Jenny could risk stepping outside of her fear and begin doing things a step at a time. And Jenny found herself able to get things done. Two weeks later she thought, "I had a productive day; I got a lot accomplished." She began to feel released from her fear, especially from her fear of taking care of the family alone. Her kitchen and bedrooms were clean, and she paid her bills. When she stepped past the fear and began to understand the depth of God's love for her, she gradually became content with God Himself as her companion.

Lord, as I pull through the fear and begin to accept myself, let me be flooded with your presence.

J.L.M.

> *But God, who is rich in mercy, because of His great love with which He loved us . . .* —EPH. 2:4

The story is told of a poor woman who traveled a great distance to talk with a famous general. She begged the general to pardon her son, who was a member of his army but had been charged under military law for a serious offense. The general said sternly that justice required her son to be put to death. The mother replied, "I'm not asking for justice; I'm begging for mercy." The general replied that her son did not deserve mercy. The mother quickly replied, "You couldn't give my son mercy if he had earned it, and it is mercy I am asking for." The general granted the mother's wish, and the son's life was saved.

Think of the mercy of God. God had a plan for us from the beginning. Mercy was in His mind when He laid the foundation of the world. From the time that humanity first turned from Him, He offered us ways to return to Him. Finally, God sacrificed His own Son as a way of offering eternal salvation to everyone who depends on Christ's death and resurrection to pay for our sins.

The mercy of God is incomprehensible to the human mind. The Psalms continually speak of the everlasting mercy of God. We don't deserve it, but it wouldn't be mercy if we did.

I will thank God today for the richness of His mercy.

J.E.M.

Behold, You desire truth in the inward parts,
And in the hidden part You will make me to
*   know wisdom.*
Purge me with hyssop, and I shall be clean;
Wash me, and I shall be whiter than snow.
*   —PS. 51:6–7*

June had a dream one evening that literally changed her life. In the dream she was a little girl in a beautiful rose garden. And she was wearing the most beautiful white eyelet dress imaginable. But as she turned around, June could see that the dress was badly soiled. Suddenly June's father was in the garden, shouting to her that Jesus was coming to the garden and would be there momentarily. June looked at her dress in dismay. It was a mess. What was she going to do?

Jesus entered the garden. Paralyzed with fear, June stood like a statue. But Jesus came over to her, and He never once looked at the soil on her dress. Instead, He put His arms around her and gave her a hug. Then He picked her up and put her on the swing. They talked, played, and laughed for a long time. Then Jesus gave little June one more hug, and said good-bye. The child was left with the warm memory of His acceptance and delight in her. When she wandered back to the swing to bask in the memory of Jesus' visit she found a white package tied in a beautiful white bow. In it was a brand new white dress.

Thank you, Jesus, that I am dressed in your righteousness today.
                                          J.M.C.

> *How beautiful upon the mountains*
> *Are the feet of him who brings good news,*
> *Who proclaims peace,*
> *Who brings glad tidings of good things,*
> *Who proclaims salvation,*
> *Who says to Zion,*
> *"Your God reigns!"*
>
> —ISA. 52:7

Many of us cringe a little when we think of spending time with our mother-in-law or daughter-in-law. How does a wife compete with a mother anyway? We have all heard horror stories of being told how to cook, rear children, clean, and even to dress. Mothers-in-law, on the other hand, complain of daughters-in-law who are prickly, defensive, and jealous.

As we meditate on the verse above, we begin to see how important it is for both mother-in-law and daughter-in-law to proclaim goodness and peace. It is easier to say, "I am set in my ways" or "It's none of your business" than to appreciate the differences that make us each unique and accept the way others choose to do things. But once we understand and accept that parenting techniques and cooking methods are far less important than showing Christ's love, getting along becomes a little easier. Joy will radiate throughout our family as we are able to share how God works in our lives.

Lord, thank you for my mother-in-law/my daughter-in-law. Please help me to see we are both trying our best. Help me be a good role model to my children and grandchildren by demonstrating love and acceptance.

J.L.M.

My son, hear the instruction of your father,
And do not forsake the law of your mother.
—PROV. 1:8

Proverbs 1:8 is directed at children, but it is also aimed at parents. Children are to follow their fathers' instruction and their mothers' laws. But how can a father instruct if he doesn't understand the lessons he is to teach? Fathers have the obligation to Scripture to make sure their instruction is correct. Mothers may not make their own laws, but rather must daily seek to learn God's laws and convey them to their children.

God gave parents a sacred responsibility—to be the leaders of their families. They are their children's most significant teachers. Children inevitably learn from their parents. It is up to the parents to choose whether their lives teach good or evil.

Parents can only do so much, of course. Children also make personal choices daily, and environmental influences can be beyond a parent's control. Nevertheless, a parent's job is crucial. Let's determine today to do the best job we can, using the Word of God as a searchlight in our souls to make sure our leadership is what God wants it to be.

I cannot control my children's current or future choices, but I can determine, by word and example, what I teach them today.

J.E.M.

The Lord God said, "It is not good that man should be alone; I will make him a helper comparable to him."
—GEN. 2:18

Heidi, Amy, and Elissa work in the same office. But the similarities between the three women end there. Heidi came from an abusive home, and she hates men. Her method of revenge is to entice them, use them, and leave them.

Amy, on the other hand, adores her husband of seven years. In fact, Amy has often said that if anything happened to him she really doesn't think life would be worth living. Amy's husband chooses her friends, clothes, and activities; he makes all her decisions for her. In return, she is dedicated to stroking his ego. In a sense, her husband has become her god.

Elissa is single but contemplating marriage. And her "significant other" knows he is lucky. Because of her personal awareness of God's deep love for her, Elissa values and respects other people, male and female. She neither flaunts her sexuality nor plays fraudulent games with other people. She will not serve their egos with flattery or deceit. Elissa can enhance another's sense of personhood because she has been set free by God to be a person herself.

Thank you, Lord, that I am a woman. Help me not to be caught up in false stereotypes that inhibit healthy relationships.

J.M.C.

Be kindly affectionate to one another with brotherly love, in honor giving preference to one another.
—ROM. 12:10

When I have had a hard week, nothing is quite as meaningful as receiving an encouraging word from a friend.

One week, my husband and I seemed to be disagreeing on everything. We didn't even want to eat the same things—much less communicate. I felt as if no one else had to put up with the kind of things I was putting up with. Surely no one had such an inconsiderate husband as mine. (He had not even been carrying out the trash in the mornings!)

Then I got a phone call from my best friend. She let me express my frustration, then she began gently to remind me of all my husband's good traits. She helped me devise some loving ways to set boundaries with him. She read me Scriptures and prayed with me. She truly talked me into being "kindly affectionate" to him. Oh, what a joy it was to greet my husband that night as he walked through the door. My changed attitude helped bring pleasure back into our marriage.

Thank you, Lord, for special friends who gently remind me of your abundant joy.

J.L.M.

> *Show me Your ways, O Lord.*
> —PS. 25:4

The Associated Press recently carried a story about a "Cutest Kid in the World" pageant that turned into a free-for-all. The contest was running four hours behind schedule on the first day. Frustration built among the children and their "stage mothers." Finally, one mother climbed up on stage, grabbed the emcee's microphone, and yelled for all the parents to get their money refunded. Parents responded and rushed the stage. A computer, a cash box with all the ticket receipts, and the six-foot "Cutest Kid" trophy were all last seen being carried out by parents.

Like those parents, we sometimes get frustrated and tired of waiting. We want problems to work out on time the way we want. When they don't, we take things into our own hands, and the results can be chaotic.

Problems will come in life—that's a promise. Facing each problem *is* our problem. Let's remember that God is close, He cares, and He will be in control if we let Him, even though He won't always control our crisis the way we, with our limited insight, think He should.

Lord, I absolutely cannot ask you to eliminate all problems from my life or even to resolve them my way. But I can count on you to comfort and guide me through them your way.

J.E.M.

I will give you a new heart and put a new spirit within you.   —EZEK. 36:26

James Hilton's entertaining novel, *Goodbye, Mr. Chips,* tells the story of a shy, clumsy schoolteacher to whom something wonderful happens. He meets and marries a woman who loves him. And gradually the inept schoolteacher becomes a kind, friendly, gracious man, the most beloved teacher in the school.

Human love can do wonderful things. But God's love can change character. I believe it because I have personally experienced God's love creating in me what I was incapable of making happen on my own. Conversions are a real event. And habits really can be broken—not by willpower, but by grace.

When the little abandoned child in so many of us truly grasps the fact that God, through Jesus Christ, is committed to love us forever, it is an incredibly awesome moment. That truth illuminates the darkness in our souls. It resurrects in us the legitimate needs that we have denied or let die, and it fills our empty spaces with an unconditional validation and acceptance. As a result of being filled in our empty places, we no longer want substitutes; we want the real thing—love. And God's love transforms us at our deepest level. The story of Mr. Chips is repeated over and over again, thanks to God and His people.

Thank you, Lord, for your transforming love.

                                                                J.M.C.

> *Faithful are the wounds of a friend,*
> *But the kisses of an enemy are deceitful.*
> —PROV. 27:6

We often fall into traps with enemies who sometimes treat us kindly. A friend of mine has a mother-in-law who will smile and bring her gifts, then hatefully crush her spirit with sarcasm, criticism, and mockery. My friend has told her how she feels and tried to repair the relationship, but nothing changes. Her mother-in-law treats others that way too.

Until recently, my friend continued to set herself up for grief by seeing a little friendliness in the woman and making herself vulnerable. Now she is learning the survival skill of detachment. Completely staying away from her mother-in-law is not an option she wants, but she is learning to pull away emotionally while in her presence.

With certain individuals, our best defense is to pray for them and remove our vulnerability. We must mentally and emotionally rise above the situation instead of trying to fix the other person or getting them to understand us. Doing this brings us a calmness and an inner peace. My friend detaches by being cordial but not sharing personally, not asking for help, and not expecting her mother-in-law to change.

Lord, give me peace and help me to focus on you when confronted with those around me whom only you can change.

J.L.M.

Lord, make me to know my end,
And what is the measure of my days,
That I may know how frail I am.
—PS. 39:4

The dam broke. And in ten minutes it was all over. Their house was filled with water to within three inches of the ceiling. They weren't there, but they stared in shock at the devastation a few days later as they sought in vain to retrieve their belongings. They had lost everything—or had they?

Human lives are frail. Dams break. Children develop incurable diseases. Husbands of twenty years walk out. Houses burn. How do you go on? Only by depending on God and relying on heavenly perspectives instead of earthly positions or possessions.

I like to think of God up in the sky overlooking the whole earth. When things happen which seem so devastating, God is looking down. He sees the end from the beginning. He knows how everything is going to work out.

When dams break in your life, look up to God, realizing He sees the whole picture. Say to Him, "God, I don't understand why this happened. I know you're in Heaven and you understand the things I'll never understand while I'm here on earth. Help me to put my hand in yours and know that you are my security when there seems to be none on earth."

A heavenly perspective today will help me have peace of mind on earth today, in spite of tragedy, and through all my tomorrows.

J.E.M.

> *But the fruit of the Spirit is love, joy, peace,*
> *longsuffering, kindness, goodness, faithfulness,*
> *gentleness, self-control. Against such there is*
> *no law.*
> —GAL. 5:22–23

The fruit of the Spirit is . . . *love*." Can I see beyond myself, my needs, and my feelings in our relationship?

". . . *joy*." Are there times of laughter, lightness, and fun?

". . . *peace*." Is there a quietness and honesty in my own soul? Is there the security that even in the midst of conflict we are on each other's team?

". . . *longsuffering*." Am I open to hearing my partner's point of view? Can I accept our differences without feeling threatened?

". . . *kindness*." Do I direct kind words and actions toward my partner and hold him in high regard both publicly and privately?

". . . *goodness*." Am I attempting to be God's love connection to my partner?

". . . *faithfulness*." Am I committed to this relationship? Do I avoid all appearance of evil?

". . . *gentleness*." Do I treat him with respect? Am I a good listener and an affectionate, sensitive lover?

". . . *self-control*." Am I honest with myself and my mate? Am I taking responsibility for what is mine in this relationship?

Lord, thank you for the gift of your unconditional acceptance and love even while I am in process.

J.M.C.

To open their eyes, in order to turn them from darkness to light, and from the power of Satan to God, that they may receive forgiveness of sins and an inheritance among those who are sanctified by faith in Me.
—ACTS 26:18

Carla had been doing her own thing for quite awhile. She hadn't been to church in many years, and she was having an affair with a man at work. When she realized she was feeling depressed, she decided to begin reading her Bible again and to call an old friend from church. She was half afraid the friend would condemn her; instead, she reminded Carla of God's patient love.

After several weeks of reading her Bible and talking to her new/old friend, Carla realized what she needed to do. She wrote in her journal, "I can't run away anymore. It's time. I am at a turning point in my life, and I have to face my sin and all the pain that has come with it. God, please give me the strength and grace to do what I have to do." The next day she ended the affair. She also quit her job so she wouldn't be tempted. It didn't seem fair, but she was determined to trust God. She talked her husband into going to church again, and they began to talk about ways they could grow closer to each other and to the Lord. The next few months were painful. But for the first time in years, Carla felt really free, because she turned from her sin.

Lord, thank you for waiting for me to turn to you and for giving me an inheritance in the kingdom of God.

J.L.M.

> *When I thought how to understand this,*
> *It was too painful for me—*
> *Until I went into the sanctuary of God;*
> *Then I understood their end.*
> —PS. 73:16–17

Have you ever been overjoyed at the prospect of working through a problem and growing from it? Or do you tend to be like me, overwhelmed by the problem and oblivious to the fact that God can help solve it? Expecting a life without problems will leave us continually bitter and disappointed. Earthly existence means earthly problems—hopefully with breathing spells in between.

Our job is to eliminate, through healthy choices, as many problems as possible. How? One way is to ask, as problems come into our lives, "What was my part in letting this problem happen?" We can confess the answers to God and then learn from them the next time we encounter a similar circumstance. We can confront the problem and do everything we can to solve it.

We can also claim God's promises. God didn't say our lives would be easy, but He did say that He would be with us through all of life's storms.

Remember the story of the shipwreck in Acts 27? The ship didn't make it, but the passengers made it safely to shore. Sometimes, in our lives, our "ships" will also be wrecked, but God will guide us safely to the shores of solutions, growth, meaning, and eventually heaven itself.

God's hand is stretched out for me to hold onto. I will take it today.
                                                    J.E.M.

Ointment and perfume delight the heart,
And the sweetness of a man's friend gives
delight by hearty counsel.
—PROV. 27:9

Nope, that doesn't work, either!"

My husband crumpled up the page and threw it across the room. Then we both slumped in our chairs, exhausted and discouraged. Our manuscript was due in three days, and the ideas just wouldn't come. We were definitely experiencing writer's block.

The doorbell rang. We were expecting no one. There at the door were two of our dear friends. They were beaming and holding a bag. "Hi," they said, "we thought you might be stuck. We brought you some ice cream bars. Why don't we sit down and brainstorm?"

We could hardly believe what we were hearing. What a gift! For the next two hours the four of us sat and talked together about the thesis of the book. They prayed with us, bid us good-bye, and left. We went to bed.

The next morning we sat down to write, and the ideas just flew. By the evening of that same day, the manuscript was ready. Our hearts had delighted in the counsel of our friends.

Lord, thank you for the gift of friendship. Let me be the one who brings delight to my friend's heart today.

J.M.C.

*He heals the brokenhearted
And binds up their wounds.*
—PS. 147:3

Mary was young and vivacious. Tall and slim, she had long, thick brown hair and a smooth olive complexion. Mary worked as a first-grade teacher. She was well liked by her first graders, and the other teachers enjoyed her pleasant attitude and willingness to work hard. But even with all this going for her, Mary felt desperately alone. She saw herself as undesirable and unwanted because, although she has friends and participates in church and singles activities, she has no special male friends. Mary dreamed of being married to someone who would be her companion, friend, and lover. She blamed herself and God for her not having a husband.

Not long ago, however, Mary began to change her negative thinking. She is still single, but she has come to an acceptance of who she is. To do this Mary had to confront the "You must be married to be fulfilled" lie. She began to focus on what God and her own life had to offer instead of how she has been cheated. Mary is working hard to change her beliefs. She now is starting to believe "It's OK to be single." And although she is not totally convinced, she is working on "I can be content and fulfilled even if I never marry"!

Father, teach me how to be content with who I am.

J.L.M.

The spirit of a man is the lamp of the Lord,
Searching all the inner depths of his heart.
—PROV. 20:27

It's not my fault!" she insisted. The fifty-year-old mother tried to explain to authorities why she had embezzled one million, two hundred thousand dollars from her employer. She said that she hadn't been a good mother and she wanted to make it up to her twenty-three-year-old daughter. Her way of "making it up" landed her in jail for a five-year prison term.

"It's not my fault," she said. The twenty-three-year-old daughter had gladly taken and spent one million, two hundred thousand dollars on a condo and luxury automobiles. When the police asked her where she thought her mother got the money, she said she never asked. She is now in jail for two years.

Granted, this is an extreme example of "It's not my fault." But it's a true story, extreme only in the amount of money it involves. Each day as I sit in my office I am amazed at the stories I hear that end with, "It's not my fault."

I challenge you to look in your life today. Is there a responsibility you're trying to avoid with "It's not my fault"? Maybe today's the day to take that responsibility back.

Lord, please give me the insight today to accept responsibility for my own feelings and actions while giving away responsibility for the feelings and actions of others.

J.E.M.

> *Search me, O God, and know my heart;*
> *Try me, and know my anxieties;*
> *And see if there is any wicked way in me,*
> *And lead me in the way everlasting.*
> —PS. 139:23–24

The night before Jolene began seeing a therapist, she had a dream. In the dream, someone was scaling the cement wall outside her home. He broke into the house and went from room to room, throwing things out of the drawers and cupboards and knocking over Jolene's possessions. She woke up frightened and horrified—certain the dream related to her upcoming therapy.

After meeting the therapist, Jolene recounted her dream to him. Imagine her relief when he assured her that his role was not that of a thief, but that of an invited guest. Only with Jolene's permission would he open doors or drawers. As he talked, Jolene felt herself relaxing. Perhaps this man could be trusted.

David trusted God. He was willing to invite God in to search his heart, to test him, to know his anxieties and help him see his faults. God always comes as an invited guest; never does He act as the robber.

Is there an invited guest in your life—a person who will help you face the hidden parts of yourself, who can give you perspective and be an objective listener? If you have asked both God and a human being to assist in this process, growth is bound to happen.

Thank you, Lord, that you are willing to help me in this process called recovery. Direct me to the people who can assist me on my journey.

J.M.C.

*And you shall know the truth, and the truth shall
make you free.* —JOHN 8:32

Alice sat in her room all alone, wondering if she
would ever be happy. People at work thought she was
a strong and vibrant individual. She was active in
church and many other outside activities. She had
plenty of opportunities, but happiness seemed to elude
her.

Alice sensed that she must continue doing what she
knew was right. So she kept studying God's Word and
continued to help others in their walk with the Lord.
Then she began to see that she hadn't accepted her life
as it was nor chosen to live with the cards she had been
given. She had just kept waiting for life to get easier so
she could be happy. Now she realized she had to accept
her life just like it was now. Once she began to internal-
ize this truth, she didn't just act vibrant; she truly felt a
great joy. She saw her struggles as challenges which
would lead her closer to the Lord. She stopped wishing
for a different life and became content with who she
was by realizing that God had designed her to live her
life, not someone else's.

*Father, help me to accept where I am in life and stop looking for an
easier path to happiness. Let me feel your joy.*

J.L.M.

> *I have seen all the works that are done under the sun; and indeed, all is vanity and grasping for the wind.*
> —ECCL. 1:14

We are daily confronted with lies. Unless we can learn to identify the lies of the world, we will be continually unhappy and dissatisfied. And one of the biggest lies is, "You can have it all, and having it will make you happy."

He was president of his state professional association. He had four brilliant and athletic children, a gracious and beautiful wife, and was worth well over a million dollars. And yet he was one of the most unhappy people I have ever met. Having reached every goal he had set for himself, he was now trying to convince himself that perhaps a bigger house, a younger wife, or another million might make him happy. He was rapidly reaching a point in his life where he had to face the truth that even if you have it all, you don't. If he didn't change his focus, he would end up saying, like King Solomon long ago, "All is vanity."

If we define happiness by the world's standards, we will continually be disappointed. Happiness comes from knowing and following God, not from power, prestige, and material possessions. And that means that God's kind of happiness can come to anyone, from the lowliest worker to a king.

Lord, I want the happiness that comes from knowing you, not the emptiness of "grasping for the wind."

J.E.M.

Call upon Me in the day of trouble;
I will deliver you, and you shall
glorify Me. —PS. 50:15

Two little girls were playing on the banks of the Mississippi River and watching the stately, white paddlewheelers make their way lazily up the river. Suddenly one of the little girls turned to the other one and said, "I can make that steamer come right over here to where I am." The other little girl looked at her in disbelief. "You can't do that. You don't have that much power." "Oh yes I do," was the first girl's reply. With that she ran to the nearest dock and started waving her hands over her head. And amazingly, after a few minutes, one of the big boats turned from its course and headed toward the dock.

One little girl couldn't believe it. The other one just beamed. Finally the huge steamer was close to the dock. The weathered captain leaned over the railing and said, "Hi honey. How's my daughter? What can I do for you?"

Family connection means everything. Those of us who have accepted Jesus Christ as our personal Savior are part of God's family. God's resources become ours. When we call on Him, we can be sure that He hears and will answer us. He is a faithful, loving Father.

Thank you, Jesus, that I am a part of your family. Thank you that you are my deliverer in the day of trouble.

J.M.C.

> *As the Father loved Me, I also have loved you; abide*
> *in My love.*
> —JOHN 15:9

Watching all the young couples at the park walking hand in hand, smiling and laughing together, brings back the springs of my youth. Love just seemed to float in the air; those butterflies in my stomach never seemed to stop fluttering.

Oh, I thought that I really loved my husband back then. But after all our years together, I think I understand much more about our love. It doesn't have to be spring anymore for us to sense love in the air; I can just feel his hand gently caressing mine and know how much our love has grown. Each year my love for him has deepened. The disagreements, joys, losses, and trials have brought us closer and closer. As we sit and pray, I know that God has strengthened our love. I pray that He will help me continue being a loving wife who gently encourages the one I truly love. As I walk with the Lord, I pray that His love would shine through me to my husband every day.

God, you have blessed me with a wonderful husband. It is truly a blessing to be created in your image and to be able to share your love with him.

J.L.M.

In my distress I called upon the Lord,
And cried out to my God;
He heard my voice from His temple,
And my cry came before Him, even to His ears.
—PS. 18:6

A friend of mine had a muscle in her back that was hurting. She asked her ten-year-old daughter to pray for her, but Mary shook her head "no." My friend asked, Why not? God answers prayers. But Mary, with tears in her eyes, said, "No, He doesn't. I've been praying every night for my daddy to come home, and he hasn't come home."

Mary can't understand why her daddy left. Her mother doesn't understand, either. Her husband studied his Bible daily, taught Sunday school, and coached the girls' sports teams. Then one day, he said, "I want a divorce, I never loved you." Now she is left to raise two little girls whose faith in God has been severely shaken. And her faith is being tested too.

God gives us free choices in life, and people frequently make the wrong ones. Sadly, other people often must live with the results of those choices. But God is still there! My friend is facing her problems one at a time. She's crying, but she's also working valiantly to rebuild their lives. And she's depending on the God who has promised to hear us when we call upon Him in distress.

I can't manipulate God to force those around me to do what is right. But I can face my future with a renewed confidence in a God who cares for me and loves me.

J.E.M.

> *Let your conduct be without covetousness, and*
> *be content with such things as you have. For*
> *He Himself has said, "I will never leave you*
> *nor forsake you."*
> —HEB. 13:5

It was dark when little Shalimar awoke. As she looked around her room she saw grotesque shadows and shapes. The dresser loomed as a huge, black monster, the closet a cavernous hole. The wind was blowing outside, and the windows rattled. Shalimar closed her eyes tightly, but the horrible images wouldn't go away. She pulled the covers over her head, but the terror was too much. She jumped out of bed, tripped over some toys on the floor, and—half crying, half screaming—cried out for her mom and dad. But no one was in her parents' bedroom . . . or in the bathroom . . . or downstairs. The house was silent. Shalimar curled up in the corner of the sofa sobbing.

In the garage, Shalimar's mother and father were hard at work. The light was bright as her daddy put the finishing coats of paint on the dollhouse he had built. Her mother was busy sewing curtains to go into the windows. As they worked, they talked about how happy Shalimar would be on Christmas morning.

Two realities—one terrified; one creative, loving, and anticipating. Lord, there have been many times when this is an accurate picture of my life. I have experienced abandonment, terror, and tears—unaware that you were there, loving me.

Help me to be aware of your continual presence with me, Lord.

J.M.C.

*Oh, that men would give thanks to the
Lord for His goodness,
And for His wonderful works to the
children of men!* —PS. 107:21

Sitting here acting like a child with my husband gives me great joy. We will do silly things together, like giggling or tickling, then go out and act mature with others. What a pleasure to feel free enough to play, to share and laugh together. I praise the Lord for these times because we easily get involved in our daily routines and begin taking ourselves too seriously. Have you ever just thought about how dull life would be if we just had to be serious all the time. I never want to forget how important it is to look at life with a sense of humor.

One of the greatest discoveries of my life is learning to play with God. Play with God? Oh yes, He's the one who created this marvelous child in us. The Lord is the one who created our laughter, and I believe He enjoys our sharing the good things with Him as well as the bad. I am amazed at how much I learn about me as I am able to share my playful side with God; playing with Him lets me view life in a totally different light.

Thank you, Lord, for the laughter and joy you have brought to my soul by giving me a little child within.

J.L.M.

> An eagle stirs up its nest,
> Hovers over its young,
> Spreading out its wings, taking them up,
> Carrying them on its wings.
> —DEUT. 32:11

I was sitting in church one evening, shortly after I had my second child. We were in a prayer group, sharing our requests. And one of the older women said something I'll never forget: "Your children are only yours for a little while. God has loaned them to you, to prepare them for serving Him." That really bothered me. I thought of letting my babies go to be missionaries in a faraway land. I didn't think I could do it. Now, seventeen years later, I realize how wise that woman was.

The oft-repeated statement in sentimental cards says we must give our children "roots and wings." Real roots come from a strong faith in Christ—a faith we model and teach every day. Our children will have roots if they grow up in a home where the stability of the parents is found in God and God's Word.

Wings are more difficult to give. We can't just hand over a completed set of brand-new wings and expect our children to "fly." Instead, think of adding one feather at a time. We must daily give our children added choices and responsibilities, so they will be equipped to go out on their own when the time comes.

Teach me, Lord, when it is appropriate to carry those who are dependent on me and when it is more loving to nudge them out of the nest.

J.E.M.

*Let this mind be in you which was also in Christ
Jesus, who, being in the form of God, did not
consider it robbery to be equal with God, but made
Himself of no reputation, taking the form of a
servant, and coming in the likeness of men.*
—PHIL. 2:5–7

It had been snowing for twenty-four hours. Knowing
that it had been a hard winter, I filled the bird feeder
with an extra supply of birdseed. A short while later, a
small bird appeared in the yard. Obviously weak, hungry, and cold, he pecked at the snow, searching for
food. How helpless I felt watching this. I wanted to go
out and point to the feeder. But if I opened the door the
bird would be frightened off. Then I realized that only
if I were another bird could I indicate to the little bird
where to find food. Only if I were another bird could I
fly with him, identify with his hunger and cold, and let
him know that I understood and cared.

Our God, looking at us, knew that He must become
one of us in order that we might know His love. Jesus
disclosed God's character through a willingness to be
transparent and vulnerable. How grateful I am that
God reached out to me in a language I could understand. Because He reached out and loved me first, I am
capable of loving myself and others.

*Thank you, Lord, that you have allowed me to know you. Thank you
that you know and understand all of me, and yet you continue to
approach me. Thank you that as I have the courage to share myself
with others, I know myself, them, and you better.*

J.M.C.

Then Peter said, "Silver and gold I do not have, but what I do have I give you: In the name of Jesus Christ of Nazareth, rise up and walk."

—ACTS 3:6

Have you ever stopped and thought about what your giving does for those close to you and for the world? I guess this thought started swirling in my head because I would wonder how we were going to make it to the next paycheck if we tithed. I can remember our years as married students. We tithed consistently, but we just had to believe that God would give us enough to eat. Through this experience, I learned that God is faithful to meet my needs, although not always the way I wanted Him to. Once, for instance, we went to the store to buy a can of soup to eat. I wanted clam chowder, but we only had about fifty-three cents. We had to buy chicken-noodle soup. But we didn't go hungry.

Now as I look around I see that giving is so much more than money. Giving of my time helps meet others' needs and shows them more about Christ's love and concern. Giving of my money allows me to reach people I will never know or see. Giving of my other possessions enables me to share the blessings God has entrusted to me. If I allow God to give through me, I can change the world.

Father, thank you for the joy that giving brings. Help me remember that I can give the gift of you as well as the gift of money or possessions.

J.L.M.

Unless the Lord builds the house,
They labor in vain who build it.
—PS. 127:1

Look around you right now. What do you see? If you're like most of us, you see a home with lots of "stuff." The furniture and appliances may be sleek and modern, or they may be old and rather worn. Possessions may be scattered as comfortable clutter or be neatly stowed and carefully ordered. A home is material things, but it is more. A home is also a place where our loved ones live.

Today's verse does not give us permission to wait for God to give us a perfect home and a perfect family. Instead, we have the responsibility of working and doing our part in the daily provisions. But we also must realize daily that without God's grace and blessing, all of our labor is in vain. As we build our homes physically, emotionally, and spiritually, let us look to God and be continually dependent on Him as we strive for a home filled with God's love.

With your help, Lord, I will work to build a loving home.

J.E.M.

> *It was Mary Magdalene, Joanna, Mary the mother of James, and the other women with them, who told these things to the apostles.*
>
> —LUKE 24:10

On the morning of the Sabbath a discouraged, downcast group of women made their way to put spices on Jesus' body. Their Lord had been crucified two days before. What did their future hold now? As they approached the tomb, they started to run. Something had happened; the big stone in front had been rolled away. Cautiously the women made their way into the tomb. They didn't see Jesus' body. Instead, they saw two men dressed in garments so bright that they couldn't even look. The men told them that Christ was risen. They were to go and tell the other disciples.

A familiar story—but such a radical one to the Jewish mind. Women—that inferior breed according to the Talmud—were being permitted to bear witness to the most incredible news the world would ever hear. But then, this Jesus had always been a different sort of a rabbi. He regularly taught women the Scriptures. He wasn't afraid to hold a conversation with a woman in public. The first revelation that He was the Messiah was made to a woman. And now this—they were permitted to bear witness to His resurrection. And once again, Jesus was turning His world upside down.

Lord, Jesus, thank you that you affirm me as a person first and then as a woman, that my status is equal to men's.

J.M.C.

*When I kept silent, my bones grew old
Through my groaning all the day long.*
—PS. 32:3

For eight years, Charlotte hung onto her secret—bulimia—in silence. Because of her fear of rejection, she endured the dark pain alone. But the longer she hid the bingeing and purging, the more frequently it occurred.

She could hide the secret, but she could not seem to escape herself. Charlotte thought her life was a failure, though she acted as if it were a success. Yet to admit the emptiness she really felt was unthinkable.

Finally Charlotte summoned the courage to tell one of her friends about her disorder. As they talked, Charlotte began to realize that she used the bulimia to shut others out of her life—and that she needed help to stop. Determined to get the help she needed, she overcame her embarrassment and enrolled in a medical program for eating disorders. She also became involved in a support group at her church. Gradually she began to get better.

Until Charlotte was willing to expose herself and to turn loose of her secret, she couldn't begin to be whole. When she took the step of exposing her secrets, God began to hear her "heart hunger." Through the healing power of Christ, she was able to accept the love of her husband and friends and the love God had for her in her pain.

Lord, give me courage to expose my silent hurts in order to find healing.

J.L.M.

> *You have been weighed in the balances, and*
> *found wanting.*
> —DAN. 5:27

One of our daughters was a gymnast. Watching her routines, I learned a little about the sport. And one thing I learned was that balance is a key to success in gymnastics, especially on the balance beam. The first few years of lessons on the beam were little more than carefully walking across it without falling off. As lessons progressed, the girls learned to do jumps and flips. By high school, the challenge was to do an intricate routine without falling off.

Balance is a key ingredient in life as well as on the balance beam. Early in life we are taught the basic principles of balance. We learned that walking outside was fine, but walking in the middle of the street wasn't. That was balance. We learned that we could play after school, but we also had to do our homework. Our parents, knowingly and unknowingly, by actions and by word, taught us how to balance our lives. Some lessons we learned well; others we still struggle with.

As we walk the balance beam of life, we make adjustments in time management, in relationships, in our careers, and in the "re-creation" of our own bodies, souls, and spirits. And in life as well as in gymnastics, wisdom, flexibility, and experience all help bring success.

Dear God, please weigh my priorities in your balances today. Show me if I am "wanting" in any major areas of my life.

J.E.M.

And Jesus answered and said to her, "Martha, Martha, you are worried and troubled about many things. But one thing is needed, and Mary has chosen that good part, which will not be taken away from her." —LUKE 10:41–42

Martha and Mary were so excited. Jesus was going to visit their family. What an honor! No doubt they busied themselves making preparation for their dear friend's visit. Then came the sound of voices and footsteps. Jesus was finally coming. They flew out to meet Him. Welcoming sounds and laughs of delight filled the air. Then they brought Jesus into the house and made Him comfortable. Martha started to bustle about, making certain that everything was just so. She wanted everything to be perfect so that Jesus would feel welcome there—and, no doubt, so that she would look good. Mary, on the other hand, couldn't take her eyes off Jesus. In fact, she was so mesmerized that she sat down at His feet with all the men.

Martha was furious with her "lazy" sister, who had left her with all the work. She stormed into Jesus' presence and demanded that He tell Mary to help her. Instead, Jesus honored Mary for choosing relationship.

I have often wondered how Martha responded to Jesus' criticism. I have wanted to believe that Martha heard the love and truth in those words and joined Mary on the floor at Jesus' feet.

Lord, help me remember that relationship is more important than reputation.

J.M.C.

The Lord is near to those who have a broken heart.
—PS. 34:18

Something was wrong with Brenda. For several weeks she had felt "down" and irritable. She couldn't eat, wasn't sleeping well, and couldn't concentrate well.* Her friends at church, seeing her sadness, urged her to have more faith and increase her prayers. But Brenda knew that what she was experiencing was more than just sadness.

Brenda prayed for guidance and finally shared a problem with a woman at work. "I think you're depressed," the woman said. "It happened to my husband." She told Brenda she needed to talk over the problem with a trained counselor and that she might require medication. Brenda took her advice. She prayed that the Lord would lead her to the help she needed. Then she talked about the problem with her doctor, who prescribed a course of antidepressant medication, and with a counselor at a nearby clinic. Over time, and with help, Brenda recovered from her depression. Now she explains to others that depression is more than sadness; it is an illness that should not be ignored.

Father, thank you for being near when I am depressed. Thank you, too, that you work both directly and through others to heal me. Please give me the courage to ask for help when I need it—and to be ready to help others.

J.L.M.

*Other symptoms of depression include loss of interest in normal activities, feelings of worthlessness or guilt, hypersomnia, increased appetite, or thoughts of death or suicide.

Stand fast therefore in the liberty by which Christ has made us free, and do not be entangled again with a yoke of bondage. —GAL. 5:1

I once read about a tribe of Africans who used a unique technique to catch a monkey. They cut a small hole in a large, choice pumpkin and placed many seeds and nuts inside. The "smart" monkey comes along and sticks his hand into the hole of the pumpkin. Once inside, he gathers a big handful of seeds and then tries to pull his hand out. The hole isn't large enough for the monkey's full hand to come out. Now, the monkey could simply let go of the "good stuff," pull his hand out, and be on his way. Instead, the greedy monkey refuses to let go, so he is caught. The Africans return after a little while to carry the captured monkey home to their village.

We say, "What a silly monkey!" Yet, aren't we just like him? We greedily put ourselves into compromising positions, hoping that if we can just hold on long enough, we will go home with the "prize." Instead, we end up in bondage.

What am I holding onto that is keeping me away from God's best for my life? Is it money? Is it jealousy? Is it bitterness? Is it adulterous fantasies? Whatever it is, I will let it go today.

Lord, give me the good sense to let go of the things that entangle me and reach out to the One who sets me free.

J.E.M.

> *Therefore if the Son makes you free, you shall be
> free indeed.*
> —JOHN 8:36

Free to define who I am, but not to define who you
are.

. . . Free to reach out to others, but not to make myself responsible for their choices.

. . . Free to love, but not to lean.

. . . Free to lead, but not to lord it over others.

. . . Free to submit, but not to be a doormat.

. . . Free to talk, but not at the expense of listening.

. . . Free to believe, but not without asking questions.

. . . Free to ask questions, but not to expect all the
answers.

. . . Free to be positive, but not to be a pollyanna.

. . . Free to face issues, but not to lose sight of priorities.

. . . Free to state my beliefs, but not to harbor anger
or bitterness when your beliefs are different than mine.

. . . Free to dream, but not to forget that the dreams
come from God.

. . . Free to fail and make mistakes, but not to abandon my dreams because I've failed.

. . . Free to see living as a privilege, not as a problem.*

---

*Lord, please touch my heart with your finger of love. Leave a print
that will set me free.*

J.M.C.

*Portions of this meditation are from Janet Congo, *Free to Be God's Woman*
(Ventura, Calif.: Regal, 1985).

*Release those who through fear of death were all
their lifetime subject to bondage.* —HEB. 2:15

Two addictions that are often overlooked are perfectionism and busyness. Quite often, these two forms of bondage are combined in women who overclean, overcommit, overreact, and overdo.

Breaking free of an addiction involves figuring out what personal need the addiction is trying to hide, resolve, or fill. Keeping busy might provide an escape from emotional pain, and perfectionism often stems from insecurity. It is this underlying problem that must be addressed. The addictive behavior has been used to hide the pain and has been receiving the most attention. But as one breaks free from the addiction, the underlying need is still lurking. The key to healing, therefore, lies in addressing and filling the personal need.

Fran, for example, was a perfectionist. She began to talk about that problem with her husband, and she realized she had started her "habit" as a child, trying to please a demanding father. Her father had been dead for years, but part of her was still trying to please him. Fran talked about her past and finally was able to put it to rest by forgiving her father. Then, over a period of time, she began to allow things to be less than perfect by concentrating on the belief that God loved her for who she was and not for what she did.

Father, show me my addictions and help me to break free of them.

J.L.M.

> *Each one should test his own actions. Then he can take pride in himself, without comparing himself to somebody else.*
> —GAL. 6:4 NIV

There are lots of paradoxes in psychology. Today's verse points to one of those paradoxes—the paradox between healthy pride and grandiosity. Many times people with chronically low self-esteem try to disguise their inner emptiness by puffing themselves up. Our verse asks us to test ourselves for such false pride—in order to take true pride in ourselves as worthy children of God.

It's a delicate balance. This Scripture tells us to look in the mirror honestly; to take credit and be happy for all our real accomplishments, our areas of growth and recovery, but not to puff ourselves up into something we're not.

When we make a "searching and fearless moral inventory of ourselves" (Step Four in the Twelve Steps*), we are freed from both grandiosity and self-condemnation. In addition, as we're really honest with ourselves, we're able to pull away from destructive codependent relationships. We no longer need the constant approval of others, and we feel a new strength to "bear our own load."

I will obey scripture by examining my own behavior today. I will take healthy pride in my cooperation with God in my own recovery process.

J.E.M.

*See page v.

*Therefore comfort each other and edify one
another, just as you also are doing.*
—1 THESS. 5:11

It's a support group," Dale told Juanita, "for women
whose husbands aren't Christians. It's not a pity party;
it's a process—and it works! Amazing things are beginning to happen in our hearts." Then Dale invited
Juanita to join the group and shared the guidelines
they had drawn up:

1. We will focus on the good (Phil. 4:8).

2. We will resist the temptation to talk about our
   spouse in a derogatory way (Eph. 5:33).

3. We will focus on what we can do rather than
   what our spouse is doing or not doing (Rom.
   14:12).

4. Each day we will try to do some definite action
   for our spouse. Then we will report back to the
   support group (James 1:22).

5. We will keep as our guide 1 Corinthians 13:4–
   5: "Love suffers long and is kind . . . love does
   not parade itself, is not puffed up; does not behave rudely, does not seek its own, is not provoked . . ."

6. We will accept that no human spouse will ever
   be able to meet the deep longing of our heart.
   Only God can do that (Ps. 2:5–6).

Thank you, Lord, that change doesn't happen in a vacuum.

J.M.C.

Blessed be the God and Father of our Lord Jesus Christ, the Father of mercies and God of all comfort, who comforts us in all our tribulation, that we may be able to comfort those who are in any trouble, with the comfort with which we ourselves are comforted by God.

—2 COR. 1:3-4

It is difficult to understand why innocent people must suffer because of someone else's offenses. No one ever should be sexually abused either. But we cannot weigh out what things should happen to which people, because there is no fairness to calamity.

So often women ask "Why me?" over and over, to the point that it keeps them from recovering. I tell them that I don't know why, but I do know how to recover. Recovery comes by acknowledging our pain and by our talking, crying, and writing about it with someone we trust. We do this until everything is out in the open—then some more, until we are sick of talking about it. After this, the healing phase begins. We can begin putting our lives back together, eventually forgive those who have hurt us, and move on. Many women have recovered from pain of past abuse and are living productive lives because they had the courage to stop asking "Why me?" and start trusting the recovery process. It works.

Lord, please comfort me today. Give me the courage to tell someone about my pain and begin the process of healing.

J.L.M.

And he said, "What have they seen in your house?"
—2 KINGS 20:15

King Hezekiah had been near death but God, in His grace, chose to let him live. The king of Babylon took advantage of the situation. He sent envoys to Hezekiah's house, supposedly to find out how Hezekiah had gotten well and to congratulate him. But the Babylonian king really wanted to know the strength of Hezekiah's armies. Soon after the visit, the prophet Isaiah came to Hezekiah and asked him the question found in our verse today. Hezekiah sheepishly told Isaiah that he had shown the messengers his vast holdings, including gold, horses, and soldiers. Isaiah told Hezekiah what a dangerous and foolish thing he had done. By showing his house, Hezekiah had told his enemies too much about himself.

I often wonder about my own house. What do people see when they walk through my doors? Does my house convey the feeling of welcome to a weary traveler? Do visitors sense a feeling of calm as they walk through the house? What about my children's feelings about home? Can they comfortably bring their friends there? Does the literature and music in my home reflect the love of God? If a stranger walked into my home today and read it like he was reading a book, would I be proud of what he was reading?

My home tends to reflect who I am. Is it conveying the message I want to send today?

J.E.M.

*Be kind to one another, tenderhearted, forgiving
one another, just as God in Christ also forgave you.*
—EPH. 4:32

Jim and Gail have been married for eight years, and
they are absolutely miserable. Jim married Gail because she was beautiful and outgoing, but over the
years she has gained one hundred pounds and become
a virtual recluse. Gail married Jim because he was sensitive, wise, and godly, but after they married she
found him to be none of the above. Jim and Gail are
both furious inside. She "eats her anger"; he alternates
between verbal abuse and withdrawal.

How can these two angry people reach forgiveness?
First, they must communicate their anger to one another. Verbalizing anger is not the same as losing control or being abusive; it means acknowledging the
hurt—getting the truth on the table. Next comes
forgiveness—choosing to let the other person begin
again without handicap. Forgiveness is something that
happens inside one person, and it can take place
whether or not the other person responds. But if both
people can summon up the courage and faith to verbalize anger and then forgive, true reconciliation becomes a reality.

*Thank you, Lord, for being honest with me. I know, based on your
Word, that I have done many things that grieve you, yet you offer me
the opportunity of beginning again without handicap. How grateful I
am for such good news.*

J.M.C.

Now I pray to God that you do no evil, not that we should appear approved, but that you should do what is honorable, though we may seem disqualified.
                                        —2 COR. 13:7

Lauren had become involved with Steve primarily because she was angry with her husband, Brian, for the lack of communication in the marriage. Now she looked towards Steve for support. She wanted to restore her marriage, but she wasn't sure where to start. So she had a long talk with her friend, Lena. As they talked, Lauren realized she should have talked to Lena in the first place! Lena encouraged her to break with Steve and look to God for direction. Lauren followed that advice. And she soon came to see that one reason she and her husband had trouble communicating with each other was that they weren't communicating with God.

Lauren began to have a quiet time with the Lord each day, and she prayed that Brian would also reestablish his relationship with the Lord. Brian did start to read his Bible again after he noticed the change in Lauren. Eventually they began to pray and read Scripture together. And as their communication about God got better, so did their communication about their marriage. Brian started listening to Lauren, and Lauren stopped criticizing Brian. They now understand how much easier it is to communicate when each of them is in individual communication with God.

Father, please help me to deal honestly with my relationships. I want to continually communicate with you as well as with my mate.
                                        J.L.M.

*Whatever you do in word or deed, do all in the
name of the Lord Jesus, giving thanks to God
the Father through Him.*
                              —COL. 3:17

What do you say when you enter your kitchen each
day? We women tend to do a lot of work in that room.
But do we look at it as sacred?

Sixteen-year-old Trish, one of six children, went on a
summer missionary trip to Mexico. She worked hard
all summer, helping to build a church during the day
and teaching the little children in vacation Bible school
at night. She was introduced to a different culture and
experienced a true spiritual awakening. When Trish
arrived home, she found her mother busily working in
the kitchen. The daughter quickly began to relate to
her mother her summer experiences. Then Trish
asked, "Don't you wish you could have been working
for the Lord all summer like I did?" Her mother replied, "But Trish, I've been working for the Lord all
summer too."

Trish's mother was wise enough to know that you
don't have to be a clergyman to be in full-time Christian work. In fact I don't know of any calling that is
more full-time or more Christian than the calling of being a mother.

_____

*Lord, help me remember that every calling—even housework—is a
holy calling if I'm doing it for the Lord.*

                                              J.E.M.

> *. . . To know the love of Christ which passes*
> *knowledge; that you may be filled with all the*
> *fullness of God.* —EPH. 3:19

Cheryl has been a bulimic for years. Some days she will buy fifty dollars' worth of groceries and eat them all at one sitting. Then she will swallow two packages of laxative and make herself throw up.

Then one day Cheryl owned the fact that the binge-purge process doesn't make her remotely happy; it makes her miserable. And it keeps her in the same place that her alcoholic mother kept her for years. Through her habit, Cheryl has been recreating the familiar—the control, the abandonment, the fear, the guilt, the self-hatred, and the inconsistency.

To a child raised with these devastating messages, love, consistency, forgiveness, freedom, and self-respect are just intellectual concepts with no grounding in reality. So how can Cheryl discover a new reality? Through incarnational love. She needs to be supported by two or three friends who can know Cheryl at her worst and still be her friend. She needs to feel grace, love, acceptance, forgiveness, and consistency in relationship. When that happens, Christ's love, which is totally beyond our human comprehension, will become understandable—and it will fill Cheryl's empty spaces to overflowing.

Lord Jesus, thank you for the "grace" people you have put into my life. They have helped me feel what I have accepted as fact. Help me make your love tangible in someone else's life as well.

J.M.C.

> *Therefore, putting away lying, each one speak truth*
> *with his neighbor, for we are members of*
> *one another.*
> —EPH. 4:25

Lynn's grandfather was an alcoholic. Growing up with him, Lynn's mother had developed a variety of ways to communicate—and she modeled these bad communication techniques to Lynn. The worst of these were "walking on eggshells," avoiding conflict, and trying to please as many people as possible. Lynn learned from her mother only to express positive feelings. She learned to keep angry or hurt feelings inside until she exploded—then to act as if nothing had happened. If she ever had a conflict with someone, she tried to hide it at all costs.

After several failed relationships, Lynn started thinking that perhaps something was wrong with her set of communication beliefs. She began to pray about how God would want her to communicate. When she read in Ephesians about "speaking truth," she realized her main problem was avoiding the truth in order to keep peace. As Lynn started addressing people honestly, she felt good about her new communication styles. She learned that she couldn't please everyone all the time, but she felt all right about that. As Lynn continues to practice honesty with kindness, she believes she has broken the chain of unhealthy communication in her family.

Lord, help me to be loving toward others while speaking the truth.

J.L.M.

*Love . . . does not behave rudely, does not seek its
own, is not provoked, thinks no evil.*
—1 COR. 13:4–5

Another version of this verse is "Love keeps no record of wrongs." I once had a client who actually kept such a record. Helen seemed like a very sweet person, but I soon found out underneath the sweetness was a bitterness equal to that of any patient I had ever seen. And for years she had maintained a notebook full of all the wrongs that had been done to her. It was divided into sections: "What People Have Said about Me" and "What People Have Done to Me." She added to her lists regularly, and she read them often. And of course, she was miserable!

In therapy, Helen saw what her resentment had done to her. She realized she had been becoming like those she had hated. And so she began the process of giving up her bitterness. She prayed for her offenders and forgave them. She asked God to take over the business of revenge. Most important, she threw away her book—and asked God to help her also throw away the list of wrongdoers from her mind.

I will choose to throw away my "hit list" of grudges today.

J.E.M.

> *In the multitude of my anxieties within me,*
> *Your comforts delight my soul.*
>
> —PS. 94:19

Trudy and Fred love each other deeply, yet both are feeling an increasing anxiety about their impending marriage. Fred is divorced and has a fifteen-year-old daughter. Trudy is a widow with three young boys. Trudy and Fred wonder how they will manage the task of forging a new family.

Trudy and Fred can expect the new family to be just like their previous one, or they can expect "instant love" among all stepfamily members. But either expectation is likely to bring only despair and defeat. A better alternative would be to view the new family as a place of repair and learning and to follow God's example for living in relationship.

God never forces Himself on us. He offers His love, acceptance, and forgiveness, but He allows our relationship with Him to develop at our pace. He encourages honesty and a full expression of emotions, and He never expects us to be more than human. Rather than creating an unhealthy dependence, He gives us all kinds of freedom. And although He promises us that life will be full of challenges, He offers us His comfort and companionship in the midst of them.

When I am personally rooted and grounded in God's love, I can face .he unknown in His power and learn from His example.

J.M.C.

And you, fathers, do not provoke your children to wrath, but bring them up in the training and admonition of the Lord.　　　　—EPH. 6:4

More than anything, Danielle wanted her father's attention, but he was rarely home. As a small child, she tried to do nice things for him, but he would still go out of town for business and be gone for weeks at a time. As she grew older, Danielle began to stay out late, date wild guys, and let her grades slip. She thought this would surely get her dad's attention—and it did. It also seemed to bring her parents, who didn't get along, closer together. Her behavior gave them something to talk about when her dad was home. The worse she behaved, in fact, the better they seemed to communicate. Not surprisingly, she continued to rebel.

This is a classic example of how parents can provoke their children to wrath and rebellion without even realizing it. Danielle could not get the attention she desperately desired, so she rebelled. If your story is similar to hers, take comfort that although your earthly father may have failed, your heavenly Father won't. He notices your accomplishments, no matter how small, and you do not have to rebel to get His attention. Most important, He wants you to turn to Him.

Lord, put my rebellion to rest and show me how to start a new pattern of behavior.

J.L.M.

> *And whatever you do, do it heartily, as to the Lord*
> *and not to men.*
> —COL. 3:23

At age twenty, we worry about what others think of us. At age forty, we don't care what they think of us. At age sixty, we discover they haven't been thinking about us at all!" I love that saying; it helps me keep perspective, and it reminds me of the folly of trying too hard to please other people.

When they were in their early teens, they all vehemently proclaimed that they wanted to dress in their own particular way. Yet when I toured the school, it seemed to me that every junior higher was wearing the same jeans, the same shirt, and the same shoes. They were so afraid that someone would notice that everything wasn't "just right."

Most of us eventually grow out of the junior high obsession with being just like everyone else, but many still spend their lives trying to get approval from others and fit in. That's why the apostle Paul reminds us to be careful about whom we are trying to please. And Paul promises that if we live for the approval of God rather than that of other people, we will be rewarded for doing so.

If I live for what others think of me, I'll have an empty hand, but if I live for the Lord's approval, I'll reap a rich reward. Today I choose to live for Him.

J.E.M.

I will say of the Lord, "He is my refuge
and my fortress;
My God, in Him I will trust."
—PS. 91:2

When the alarm rings each morning the Smiths groan, turn over, and press the snooze button. A couple of minutes later, one of them sits bolt upright, looks at the clock and lets out a panicked yell. Both partners roll out of bed. Two bleary-eyed children are yanked from never-never land and commanded to be dressed. After gulping breakfast, everyone is out the door—to jobs, school, volunteer activities, lessons, and sports. Weekends, too, are an endless round of activity. Meanwhile the house is cluttered, the garden produces only exotic varieties of weeds, the Smiths' "date nights" are a thing of the past. And their stress levels, not surprisingly, are off the chart.

The Smiths have structured their lives without any conscious thought about God. As a result, they are like the pilot who radioed back to his base, "I have no idea where I'm going, but I'm making record time." Stress comes when we feel alone in the midst of pressure. God didn't make us go through the storms of life alone. He offers us a refuge. But we must take the time out of our hectic lives to turn to Him.

Lord, I accept you as my source of peace even in the midst of stress.
Be my refuge, my fortress, the source of my security so that I can
keep my activities in balance.

J.M.C.

> *Wait on the Lord;*
> *Be of good courage,*
> *And He shall strengthen your heart.*
> —PS. 27:14

Yvonne had been the assistant administrator at her firm for eight years. She knew she could run the company as well as anyone, but she had been turned down twice for the administrator's position in the past five years. The first rejection hadn't been too bad since she had been there only two years. The second time it happened, she was crushed. It seemed that no matter how hard she worked or how good a job she did, she would always remain the assistant.

Like Yvonne, you may feel cheated because you have worked hard and seem to have reached a dead end. When you begin to question what you should do now, remember that sometimes God gives us an immediate answer to our concerns, and at other times we must wait.

When Yvonne turned her dilemma over to the Lord, and waited on Him, she found a new peace about her position. She saw she really wouldn't have liked the administrator's position anyway because of the extra hours and stress it involved, and she also found herself thinking about going back to school. Yvonne decided the Lord must have been protecting her from a job He knew she would hate and preparing her to go in a completely different direction.

Father, help me to wait upon you, and discern your answers.

J.L.M.

*Looking diligently lest anyone fall short of the
grace of God; lest any root of bitterness springing
up cause trouble, and by this many become defiled.*
—HEB. 12:15

The primary reason we hold grudges is to get vengeance. Subconsciously, we somehow think that our bitterness toward someone will magically make that person miserable. Instead we are usually the ones who end up being hurt by our feelings.

Vicki had been divorced for three years when she came for counseling. Her anger toward her former husband was destroying her ability to live happily. In therapy, Vicki came to realize that bitterness was futile and that she must put it aside. But putting aside bitterness was not easy. Vicki had to recognize daily that God was in charge of judgment and that vengeance was not her job. She also had to find a way to let go of the deep-seated anger that was fueling her bitterness.

Vicki didn't feel the freedom to communicate her feelings with her ex-husband, but she did write him letters, and read them to her therapist, and then destroy them. Letter writing helped her to express her anger so she could then let go of it and choose forgiveness.

*I will prayerfully write a letter today to the person I have felt most
bitter towards. I will express my angry feelings, then ask God to help
me forgive that person. Finally, I will throw the letter away.*

J.E.M.

Be still and know that I am God.
—PS. 46:10

Genesis 32 tells the story of Jacob, who was preparing to meet his brother, Esau. Esau had been holding a grudge against Jacob because Jacob had stolen what was rightfully Esau's. Esau had even threatened to kill Jacob. Naturally, Jacob was terrified at the prospect of meeting his brother.

The night before their confrontation, Jacob had an encounter with a stranger, whom he wrestled. Only the next morning did he realize that he had been in the presence of God—without even knowing it.

How meaningful that story has been to me personally. Unless I make time daily to become still, I lose sight of the truth that God is in this place, in this person, or this situation. My perspective blurs. I forget that the God inside of me is closer than the problem facing me.

If our life is never quiet, we starve spiritually. The constant hustle and bustle of living in the fast lane leaves us empty and often angry. By contrast, a sense of peace and purpose is the result of living life from the inside out.

When my connection with my heavenly Father is unbroken, I can face all that life offers me.

J.M.C.

*See then that you walk circumspectly, not as fools
but as wise, redeeming the time, because the days
are evil.*
—EPH. 5:15–16

Paula can remember the first steps she took in her recovery from alcohol and drug abuse; she describes them as small and very unsteady. She was not really sure she wanted to follow the path of recovery. But once she repented of her sins and allowed Jesus into her life, the Lord began to reveal and confirm that this was the direction she needed to go.

Paula smiles to remember her "awakening" and the joy she experienced from knowing she was doing well under God's watchful eye. That feeling was growing from following God's direction, and it filled a void that Paula had tried to fill herself by abusing substances for many years. Paula discovered the need to do what was favorable by God every moment in her life.

At a later point in her recovery, Paula began to long for an assurance of her salvation, and she started to search for answers in that area. As she did, the Holy Spirit made her aware that now she was growing by leaps and bounds instead of small steps. Her desire to change for the better in the sight of the Lord took Paula to new levels of Christian maturity. Every minute of the day, Paula praises God for this growth in Christ because it keeps her from falling back into her old way of life.

Thank you, Father, for our convictions to do good. Thank you that we devlop a new desire in our life when we trust you. Help me to be wise and forgive me when I am foolish.

J.L.M.

> *You are my hiding place;*
> *You shall preserve me from trouble;*
> *You shall surround me with songs of deliverance.*
> —PS. 32:7

David, throughout the Psalms, put great faith in God who was his safe hiding place and his deliverer. God didn't let David down. He delivered him from his enemies. He will also daily deliver us from our sins and old behaviors.

Step Seven of the Twelve Steps speaks of humbly asking God to remove our shortcomings.* When we confess our sins to God and to others, we are admitting our weakness and showing a desire to change.

For women in recovery, this step can be tricky. Sometimes in our need to confess we may be too critical of ourselves and make mountains out of molehills. This type of confession can be too much for everyone concerned. Confessing sins doesn't mean we have to admit to every negative thought we've ever had and every wrong act we've ever committed. Instead, we need to focus on acts and thoughts that have come from premeditated, hurtful motives.

God's goal for us is spiritual growth. He wants us to have His peace. He knows that as we humbly confess our sins, the weights will be lifted. We will be surrounded with songs of deliverance.

I will confess to God today any premeditated, willful sins I have committed that I have not yet asked Him to forgive me for, also asking Him to keep me from those same sins in the future.

J.E.M.

*See page v.

In this is love, not that we loved God, but that He loved us and sent His Son to be the propitiation for our sins.
                                    —1 JOHN 4:10

It's always been interesting to me that God created us as "human beings," not "human doings." He loves and accepts us far more than we seem to be able to accept ourselves. Especially if we come from dysfunctional homes, the tendency is to figure that we won't be loved unless we're able to do. What a setup this is for becoming overachievers. The trouble is that all the doing doesn't satisfy. The affirmation we receive doesn't feel like enough, and the standards have to be constantly raised in order for us to feel valuable. We end up saying yes when we mean no. We're terrified of conflict. We feel used, exhausted, and taken advantage of. We experience little joy in living, and we develop a severe case of ingrown eyeballs—all we can see is ourselves. What's the way out? With God's help, we need to pull out of our rat race and acknowledge the emptiness inside of us. Then we need to crawl into God's lap, so to speak, and get to know how deep His love is for us. We need to find one or two friends who will accept and love us at our lowest point. Most important, we need to come to terms with the truth that we were created not primarily to do, but to be who we are—a beloved child of God.

Lord, thank you for your love. Because I have been loved, I can relax in the security of your love.

                                    J.M.C.

> *Confess your trespasses to one another, and pray*
> *for one another, that you may be healed.*
>
> —JAMES 5:16

It's not my fault." "I did my part." "Don't blame me!"
Have you ever caught yourself making any of these
statements? We cannot be in a relationship without
some of the blame belonging to us some of the time,
yet it is so difficult to admit that just maybe we could
be at fault. Many times, in fact, our claim to innocence
is the true indicator of our guilt. Whenever we find ourselves vehemently protesting that we're not to blame,
it may be time to evaluate our own denial.

Admitting our mistakes is especially crucial when
we are newly married, and it continues to be necessary for a growing relationship. It's frustrating when
we seem to be the only ones saying we are sorry, but
for our own sake we must admit our wrongs even
when our spouse is so slow to follow. God desires that
we accept responsibility for our actions so we can be in
strong fellowship with Him.

Spiritual growth comes when we confess our sins to
other people (James 5:16) and to God (1 John 1:9). Accepting responsibility for our actions can be painful,
but it paves the way for learning and developing spiritual maturity. Ownership of our mistakes allows for bitterness and resentment to be removed and gentleness
of spirit to emerge.

Father, please convict me of my sins and give me courage to admit
my wrongs to those I have hurt.

J.L.M.

*Through the Lord's mercies we are
    not consumed,
Because His compassions fail not.
They are new every morning;
Great is your faithfulness.*
                    —LAM. 3:22–23

One of the most comforting tenets of Christianity is that God provided a way for us to get to Heaven without having to be perfect. God, in His mercy, gives us a new day every day in which we can begin again to serve Him. He wants us to be righteous, but He knows we will never totally arrive.

The healthy Christian life doesn't come naturally to women in recovery. Our habit is to live in codependent, destructive relationships. We have to strive daily to develop healthy, new behaviors.

Sainthood doesn't come until Heaven. Our goal on earth is to grow toward Christ-likeness by making healthy choices—and healthy choices lead to healthy habits. As we change our behaviors in small ways, we see evidence of God's mercy.

It's easy to take backward steps. Let's determine not to fall backward today, but instead to accept His mercy this morning and go forward. God is there to lead us faithfully each step of the way.

Thank you, Lord, for being merciful, compassionate, and faithful toward me in spite of my shortcomings.

                                                J.E.M.

> *For God did not send His Son into the world to condemn the world, but that the world through Him might be saved.* —JOHN 3:17

Katy would "hide" in her room every night under the pretext of studying. In the kitchen, Katy's alcoholic dad would be screaming curses at her mother. Pots and pans would crash, dishes shatter, doors slam. Then he'd start to make his way down the hall to beat whichever kid had incurred his wrath with some minor infraction. And Katy's mother would tell the kids that everything would be all right if they just did whatever daddy wanted. That was a lie. Over time, things just got worse.

Katy's parents were toxic. Their words were poison, their vision blurred. Katy's perceptions were denied. Mistakes were not allowed. Criticism, inconsistency, violence, and denial were Katy's reality.

Even as an adult, Katy carries those condemning, critical parents with her in her head. They remind her repeatedly that she's worthless, that she'll never amount to anything. Imagine Katy's surprise when she reads our verse for today. God didn't come to earth in the form of Jesus Christ in order to condemn us, but rather to love us. Condemnation Katy is well acquainted with—but love? Truly to Katy the gospel is good news. It is radically different from the reality she has had to face. This gospel can heal the love hunger that exists in Katy's very being.

Lord, heal my humiliation with your love. Thank you, Jesus, that you don't condemn me.

J.M.C.

*I, even I, am He who blots out your
transgressions for My own sake;
And I will not remember your sins.*
—ISA. 43:25

Watching my middle daughter reminds me of myself as I grew up. But the scary part is that I treat her just like my mother did me," Bea told her friend. She couldn't seem to stop herself from criticizing her daughter. She would feel so guilty for attacking her daughter's character that she could hardly stand to be in the same room with her.

Bea began to realize how desperately she wanted things to be right between her and her own mother. She realized that she hadn't forgiven her mother and that she constantly held her mother at arm's length. She knew her mother might never change, but she still needed to forgive her. So Bea went to her mother and discussed their past relationship. Gradually, as they talked and prayed, God began to heal the relationship. Bea could not believe how much her attitude changed toward her mother. But even more amazingly, she began to see her daughter in a whole new light. Over the next few months, as she went out of her way to comfort her daughter, she could see that forgiving her mother had freed her from bondage.

Thank you, Lord, for forgiving me and for helping me to forgive others so that I may truly be free.

J.L.M.

> *Call upon Me in the day of trouble;*
> *I will deliver you, and you shall*
> *glorify Me.* —PS. 50:15

Some days are harder than others. We need God's strength every day, but some days we feel as if we have no strength left at all. It is a comforting thought that when we are weak, He can be our strength.

What do we do when trouble comes? Prayer is a positive, practical response. God is always there, waiting to hear our petitions. Each time we claim His strength and He delivers us, we bring glory to Him.

We can call on God during days of trouble. He will help us throw away those codependent behaviors that have marred our lives. He will give us strength to face the pain of our past and replace it with constructive behaviors instead of destructive ones.

Every human has a God vacuum. Don't be ashamed of yours. You can't overcome your troubles without God's help. Call on Him today. He loves you and wants to deliver you from trouble.

I will ask God today to deliver me from my troubled times, realizing He may deliver me by giving me strength to take strong steps myself.

J.E.M.

*All things were made through Him, and without
Him nothing was made that was made.*
—JOHN 1:3

Kimberly loves to weave. As she works she delights in the textures and hues of the wool. Annette plays the piano beautifully. She feels the music. Karen is an expert at decorating with wallpaper. June derives deep satisfaction from resolving tricky dilemmas in her job. Jan delights in working with clay. And all find joy in their creativity.

Creativity is part of the image of God within you, demonstrated in ways that are unique and wonderful. I don't believe it is the same as originality. Rather, I see creativity as a way of breathing new life into tasks you've had to do hundreds of times before. Greeting your husband and kids in an unexpected way—a way that brings joy and delight. Reading a story to a child in a voice you've never used before. Living life with flair—tasting it, touching it, smelling it, really seeing it.

Creativity comes to us through our Creator God. As we lose ourselves in His love, our limited interpretations and narrow focus are replaced by love, energy, and light. When that happens, everything around us— our families, homes, jobs, ministries—takes on a new hue.

Thank you, Lord, for creativity. Give me the eyes to see myself, others, my responsibilities, and my world through your love and creativity.

J.M.C.

From the end of the earth will I cry to You,
When my heart is overwhelmed;
Lead me to the rock that is higher than I.
—PS. 61:2

It was a sunny day as fair haired Alison played outside in the landscaped yard. She stayed on the grass with her Barbie doll, being very careful not to touch any of the yellow roses she had been instructed to stay away from. She was wearing her favorite red cowboy shirt, which always made her feel happy.

All of a sudden, Alison looked up and saw her father storming toward her. What had she done now? She never knew when he was going to start yelling at her. This time he shouted at her for getting fingerprints on the window of his new Mercedes.

Many years have passed, and now Alison realizes that her anorexia can be linked to her controlling father. He hasn't changed, but Alison has. She knows his anger wasn't her fault, and she has regained her health. She sees her heavenly Father as a new source of strength, and she relies on Him instead of wishing her own father were different. Alison was able to let go of her bitterness by talking through the pain and finally putting it to rest. She also talked to her father about the ways he had hurt her, but her recovery was not contingent on his apology. Alison has finally come to accept her father as he is and to pray for him.

Lord, give me your strength to overcome my painful memories.

J.L.M.

*. . . God deals with you as with sons; for what son
is there whom a father does not chasten?*
—HEB. 12:7

In history, God has acted in the role of both parent and
lover. Both of those roles are involved in the relationships God seeks to develop with us.

Babies depend totally on their parents for every
need. They would die if the parents didn't feed and
care for them. And God wants us to depend on Him for
what we need. But what is the goal of the parent? It is
to teach independence so the children will develop the
self-confidence to go out into the world. And God
wants us to grow and mature as well. Lovers have the
freedom to be independent of each other. Because of
their love for each other, however, they choose to
serve their partners. Their relationship is one of frequent giving. A healthy love relationship is one in
which giving is done not out of obligation, but out of
respect and love for the other person. God wants our
love for Him to be given that freely—not out of obligation but out of a sincere desire to love and serve Him.

*If I feel "chastened" or lovingly prodded by God today, I will respond
by realizing that it is for my own maturity rather than by getting
angry at God for not letting me stay a spiritual infant.*

J.E.M.

> *He has sent me to heal the brokenhearted.*
> —LUKE 4:18

Did you learn to trust love in your family of origin? Stacey didn't; she grew up in an alcoholic home. But life changed for Stacey at age eleven, when she spent a week at summer camp. It was a marvelous experience for Stacey. She could have a friend and be a friend there without being terrified of how her parents would act. She could walk anywhere without depending on an intoxicated parent for a ride. No one broke into her cabin at night to pull her out of bed and scream at her or hit her for something she supposedly had done.

Best of all, Stacey made a new friend named Jesus Christ. She saw that people who had experienced God's love could say "I'm sorry." She was amazed at the respectful way they talked to each other, even when they disagreed. She had always felt alone, but these people really seemed to care. In fact, her counselor wanted to meet with Stacey on a weekly basis to talk and have fun. It was almost too much for Stacey to comprehend. The best part, as far as Stacey was concerned, was that on those long fearful nights when her parents were screaming at each other, she had a friend to talk to—Jesus Christ—and she really could trust His love.

———

Lord, thank you for your presence even in the midst of my pain.
J.M.C.

Though the fig tree may not blossom,
Nor fruit be on the vines;
Though the labor of the olive may fail,
And fields yield no food;
Though the flock be cut off from the fold,
And there be no herd in the stalls—
Yet I will rejoice in the Lord,
I will joy in the God of my salvation.
          —HAB. 3:17–18

This is a portion of the prophet Habakkuk's prayer and hymn of faith. Most of us would be angry at God and blame Him if we experienced the kind of loss Habakkuk spoke of. And many have found ourselves cursing God when terrible events occur. Yet Habakkuk found joy in the God of his salvation. He seems to have focused on God's saving grace instead of life's misery.

Life can be painful, and sometimes the only thing we have going for us is the faith that God is there to comfort us. But that does not mean we should deny the pain and simply stuff our feelings inside or pretend they are not there. Just as Habakkuk did, we need to talk or write about painful events and admit them to God and significant people. Nevertheless, if we believe the truth that Jesus died for our sins, rose from the grave, and offers us the opportunity to be with Him in heaven, we always have something good to hold on to. Even as we grieve our losses, we can also find joy in the God of our salvation.

Father, help me to find joy in you, especially when life is not particularly joyful.

                              J.L.M.

> *For in much wisdom is much grief,*
> *And he who increases knowledge*
> *increases sorrow.*
> —ECCL. 1:18

Gloria had been on our psychiatry unit for a whole week. I had had four individual sessions with her, and she had been in group therapy for two and a half hours per day for all seven days.

When Gloria came into the hospital, she was suicidally depressed. Now, a week later, she felt worse. The other therapists and myself had dug up many repressed emotions in her unconscious, and she was experiencing grief as a result. She was discovering a painful, if liberating, reality: The truth will set you free—but first it will make you miserable!

I assured Gloria that the truth really does hurt, but that the only way to resolve her innermost root problems was to expose the truth and deal with it maturely and realistically. By the end of the second week, she began to feel better. By the end of the third week, she was sleeping through the night without any sleeping medication and was able to laugh, share, and feel good about herself. She had definite plans for continuing to deal with her conflicts on an outpatient basis. After four weeks she went home and has done very well for over a year now.

When I look at the truth inside myself, I will expect it to hurt, but I will not let that discourage me from progressing past and through the pain.

J.E.M.

Thus also faith by itself, if it does not have works, is dead. —JAMES 2:17

Janet had gone through a devastating series of losses. Her only son had died of a drug overdose, her father had suffered a heart attack, and she had lost her job. Janet struggled with incredible grief and a dark depression. One day, a woman from Janet's church asked how she was. When Janet replied honestly, the other woman told her sharply, "You've just got to snap out of it, Janet. If you'd just read your Bible and pray more, you'd be fine." Now Janet was left with two problems—the original depression, and the hurt, anger, and guilt brought on by this woman's insensitivity.

Janet eventually worked through her pain, and she decided to provide an antidote for such insensitive "counsel." So she organized a group of people at the church to act as a support team for people undergoing tragic circumstances. Two people were assigned to the hurting people for a month at a time. They were to phone, visit, take them for outings. At the end of the month, another two people took over. After a year, the hurting people had discovered twenty-four new friends who cared for them in tangible ways. Then, when the time was right, the hurting person became part of a twosome who would comfort someone else.

How healing faith and works can be when they work in tandem!

J.M.C.

For you, brethren, have been called to liberty; only do not use liberty as an opportunity for the flesh, but through love serve one another.

—GAL 5:13

Serving one another through love can be fulfilling. But we women sometimes tell ourselves we're serving in love when we're really playing the martyr. Our suffering in behalf of our friends, co-workers, husbands, or children can sometimes be just a selfish way to get our needs met. We may give up our time, money, and energy, in the hope that maybe someone will notice how much we have sacrificed. Unfortunately, when we bend over backward trying to make everyone else happy at our own expense, we put ourselves in the role of the victim. And no relationship is healthy when one person is acting as a victim.

Whether we are serving each other in love or merely acting as a martyr depends on our inner motive. With selfish martyrdom there's a sense of "Poor me; I work so hard." But loving service is a joyful, energizing act motivated by Christlike love. As we begin to examine our actions and rid ourselves of the victim role, we experience a freedom genuinely to serve others. This type of service both benefits others and blesses us.

Lord, I want to serve you through serving others. Help me to serve people out of an earnest, loving desire, and show me when I am acting as a martyr instead of a servant.

J.L.M.

You shall know the truth, and the truth shall make you free.   —JOHN 8:32

Fran came to see me because she had an anxiety attack and had felt very anxious for the past week. Anxiety nearly always comes from a fear of finding out the truth about one's own unconscious thoughts, feelings, and motives. As Fran's therapist, I asked about the significant people in her life. She had normal responses until I mentioned her mother whom Fran was going to visit the next week. Then Fran's neck developed red blotches, her pupils dilated, her hands got sweaty, her arms crossed, and her eyes looked away from me toward the floor. She denied any problems with her mom, but her body told me she was lying to herself. It turned out that her mother had always been very narcissistic, demanding, and conditionally accepting.

I finally convinced Fran that her coming vacation and her week of anxiety were no coincidence. She was bitter toward her mother and feared being aware of her rage. As Fran looked at the truth and wept, she knew she would have to learn to forgive her mother and to protect herself from her mother's abuse. Fran's anxiety disorder would take more than one session to resolve—probably many—but Fran was definitely on the road to recovery.

Whenever I feel anxious, I will pray for insight into the truth inside myself, then seek the truth from friends or counselors God sends my way.

                                                                    J.E.M.

> *"Be angry, and do not sin": do not let the sun go
> down on your wrath.*
> —EPH. 4:26

Samantha was in the sixth grade when she watched her father beat up her sister. It must have been an upsetting experience, but Samantha recounted it to me without emotion. She couldn't remember feeling anything. In therapy, Samantha grew to realize that, in her family, only the male adult was "allowed" to be angry. A child who expressed anger risked physical abuse. So Samantha had learned to push all emotions deep into her being—so deep that she could no longer feel them.

Our verse today is a familiar one often used in the context of relationships. Is it possible that, at yet another level, the verse means "Don't push your anger into the darkness so that it goes out of your awareness"? Fortunately our God is not a dysfunctional parent who can tolerate only our positive feelings. He invites us to express all of our feelings to Him—even our anger and fear. After all, He created us; He knows what we are feeling. And He desires that we get in touch with our own feelings. He desires honesty in our innermost being.

Thank you, Lord, that you made me to be a woman who can experience a wide range of emotions. Thank you that you are accepting of all of them.

J.M.C.

He who is slow to anger is better than the mighty,
And he who rules his spirit than he who takes
a city. —PROV. 16:32

Self-control can be a daily struggle when your child is strong-willed and active. It's easy to become irritated and lose control—to yell at your kids louder than intended or even hit them. After that, the parent usually feels guilty, and the child feels resentful. But self-control is possible. Here are a couple of suggestions to help you control your temper with your child.

First, commit yourself to relying on God daily to help you with your anger; asking a friend or family member to hold you accountable is also beneficial. Make sure you continually remind yourself that changing the way you interact with your children will take a great deal of time.

Second, decide which behaviors—such as hitting—are destructive to your child. When you feel yourself resorting to one of these behaviors, take a time-out. Go to a different room or even outside. Breathe deeply, pray, and either write down your feelings, call someone, or just talk out loud to God. As soon as you have a chance, write out what happened and, with the help of a friend or family member, make a plan for what to do next time.

———————

Father, I want to discipline my children appropriately. Please guide me and help me discipline out of love instead of anger.

J.L.M.

> *Have you found honey?*
> *Eat only as much as you need,*
> *Lest you be filled with it and vomit.*
> —PROV. 25:16

Patricia's mother and father were both physicians. They both loved her very much, but they worked long hours, received many emergency calls at inopportune times, and had to cancel many scheduled activities. Patricia had two parents who were so busy "serving mankind" that they had little time or energy left to be her parents. As a result, she craved attention and did everything she could think of to get it. She got straight As in school, became a cheerleader, and became easy prey for any good-looking athlete who said "I love you." She got pregnant, had an abortion, and developed bulimia soon afterwards.

For Patricia, food became a love substitute—her unconditionally accepting friend, mother, and father. But food also became Patricia's enemy, her addiction. She eventually ate twenty thousand calories per day and vomited them back up. Fortunately, Patricia sought help after being strongly confronted by her parents. She completed a hospital program, then two years of outpatient therapy. But family therapy was also a major help. As Patricia's parents identified their own unhealthy patterns, Patricia felt less of a need to fill the holes in her soul with food.

I will reexamine my priorities today and make drastic changes if necessary to make my own family a higher priority than rescuing others.

J.E.M.

> *But the father said to his servants, "Bring out the*
> *best robe and put it on him, and put a ring on his*
> *hand and sandals on his feet. And bring the fatted*
> *calf here and kill it, and let us eat and be merry;*
> *for this my son was dead and is alive again; he was*
> *lost and is found." And they began to be merry.*
> —LUKE 15:22–24

When Susan began her recovery process, she began to drift away from active involvement in her church. The more we talked, the more obvious it became to me that up to this point her religion had been shame-based, so she was afraid of getting closer to God.

One day we were reading the story of the prodigal son together. Susan had always related to the story— up to the point that he comes home stressing that he is unworthy. At that point she would be so overcome by her own shame that she would go no further with the story. This time, because we were reading together, we moved past the shame of the prodigal to the compassion, acceptance, and joy of the father. As we talked about the story together, Susan came to see that when she sees herself worthless, damaged, and beyond hope, she sees God as shaming, abusive, and abandoning. By contrast, when she sees God as valuing, accepting, forgiving, and loving she sees herself as valued, accepted, forgiven, and loved. Susan came to replace her shame-based identity with her God-given identity.

Thank you, Lord, that I don't have to prove myself to you. Help me to relax in your obvious joy in me and love for me.

J.M.C.

The silver-haired head is a crown of glory,
If it is found in the way of righteousness.
—PROV. 16:31

Some people's most precious memories involve having an elderly relative in the home as they grew up. An acquaintance of mine had the privilege of having her great-grandmother live with them until she died. The old woman was quite feeble and could barely walk, but she could still stand up long enough to bake chocolate-chip cookies for the kids every other Thursday. She complained that her eyes were going, but the large-print children's books she read to them were as entertaining to the great-grandmother as they were to the children.

Those of us who have the opportunity to touch the life of an elderly person are providing ourselves the opportunity to receive a special blessing. Our attention can enliven an older person's day, while we receive the gift of growth. We can learn from the wisdom of this person's experiences while giving him or her the priceless gift of our time. Our time is especially well spent with a committed elderly Christian; the faith of a righteous individual who has relied on God through years of joy, pain, birth, and death can truly be a crown of glory in the sight of God and humanity.

Lord, help me to recognize both the needs and the unique gifts of elderly individuals with whom I have the opportunity to share my time.

J.L.M.

They have struck me, but I was not hurt;
They have beaten me, but I did not feel it.
When shall I awake, that I may seek another drink?
—PROV. 23:35

Louise was an alcoholic who called herself a social drinker. She had grown up in a dysfunctional family and had a lot of unresolved pain, which she tried to kill with alcohol. Unfortunately excessive use of alcohol depletes serotonin in the brain, making emotional pain worse.

Louise's friend Judith tried to persuade Louise to join an Alcoholics Anonymous group and also get professional counseling, but Louise refused help. A week later, with a couple of Bloody Marys under her belt, Louise drove her six-year-old daughter to school. There was an accident, and little Jennifer was critically injured. She survived, but was permanently brain damaged.

Grief-stricken, Louise finally checked into our psychiatry unit to receive help for her alcoholism. Over time, she resolved the pain of her early childhood abuse. She asked God to forgive her for damaging her own daughter in the accident. She also worked through the grief process, forgiving herself. Louise must spend the rest of her life living with the consequences of her actions, but she now has resources for facing her life as a growing, emotionally healthy adult.

An ounce of prevention is worth a pound of cure, but better a pound of cure than no cure at all.

J.E.M.

> *Choose for yourselves this day whom you will
> serve, whether the gods which your fathers served
> that were on the other side of the River, or the gods
> of the Amorites, in whose land you dwell. But as
> for me and my house, we will serve the Lord.*
> —JOSH. 24:15

Two young men had heard stories for years about the wise old hermit who lived up in the mountains. Rumor had it that he was very eccentric, but there wasn't a question that the old man couldn't answer. The young men decided to test the old man's brilliance. They decided to catch a little bird and hold it with their hands. Then they would ask the hermit if the bird was dead or alive, they were going to crush it to death.

Pleased with themselves, the youths stomped up the mountain until they arrived at the hermit's cabin. When the elderly man answered their knock, the bravest one said, "Sir, we have a little bird in our hand. Is it dead or alive?" The man looked right into the eyes of both and said, "Whether that bird is dead or alive is in your hands. The choice is yours."

In your recovery process, you can choose whether you're going to go it alone or whether you're going to ask God, in the person of Jesus Christ, to help you. In that sense, the choice between life and death is yours to make.

Lord, thank you for the freedom to choose whom I will serve.

J.M.C.

*Behold, I will bring it health and healing; I will
heal them and reveal to them the abundance of
peace and truth.*   **—JER. 33:6**

If you were abused as a child, it is important to grieve
and resolve your childhood pain both for your sake
and also for your children's sake. This can be done in
several steps that are easy to explain but that take time
to carry out.

Start by praying that God will bring to your mind
any past hurt or unresolved situation. Write it down as
it comes to mind. (Don't be concerned if some hurts are
blocked and come at different times.) Second, process
the issue by writing about and talking about how you
felt and feel concerning each issue. This step can be
quite time-consuming, so don't expect a quick fix. It is
helpful to talk to a friend or a counselor, but you can
just write and talk to God if no one is available. Ask
Him to heal each hurt as you talk about it. Finally, remind yourself that God wants you to accept His forgiveness and to forgive the people who have hurt you.
Forgiveness is important for your healing because it
releases the burden you have been carrying.

*Father, I don't want my childhood pain to affect my children. Help
me to work through it so I will be healthy and my children will have
an appropriate role model.*

                            J.L.M.

> *Oh, the depth of the riches both of the wisdom and*
> *knowledge of God! How unsearchable are His*
> *judgments and His ways past finding out!*
> —ROM. 11:33

I love my own mother and father. I know I can call them on the phone to share any burden with them and they will empathize and pray for me. I also appreciate the support of my husband, children, and friends. But there is something about my relationship with God that reaches beyond all these other relationships.

God is all-knowing, all-powerful, everywhere present, and compassionate. He sees through me like an X-ray machine, and He knows a thousand times more about me than I even know about myself. He knows my hurts, my joys, my pain, my insecurities, my unconscious motives, my vacuums and emotional voids, my temptations, and—yes—even my sins and failures. And yet He calls me His daughter, loves me unconditionally, and uses a host of circumstances and people to bring comfort to my soul.

How God does all this I will never know until I die and enroll at the University of Heaven for my Ph.D. in Advanced Truth! Until then, I will enjoy the riches of knowing God while accepting the fact that His decisions (judgments) and His ways of doing things are beyond my limited human comprehension.

I will thank my awesome God today for who He is and what He means in my life.

J.E.M.

If you have faith as a mustard seed, you will say to
this mountain, "Move from here to there," and it
will move; and nothing will be impossible for you.
—MATT. 17:20

A tightrope walker had decided that for his next pub-
licity stunt he would walk across Niagara Falls. The
event was publicized nationwide, and people gathered
from miles around to watch. The tightrope walker
waved at the people and stepped onto the wire. Not a
sound was heard from the crowd as he inched his way
across that great divide and back again. Then, when
his feet were once again on terra firma, the crowds
started cheering.

The tightrope walker made his way to the microphone and asked, "How many of you believe I can
walk across Niagara Falls?" All hands were raised.
Then the tightrope walker made eye contact with one
gentleman. "You sir, do you believe I can walk across
Niagara Falls?" he asked. "Yes, yes" was the reply.
"Then you get into this wheelbarrow, sir, and I'll wheel
you across," grinned the tightrope walker. Never has a
man disappeared into a crowd so fast.

It isn't enough to say we believe. We have to be willing to risk getting into the wheelbarrow—to act on our
belief. This applies to our relationships and even with
our own recovery. It's not enough to know that there is
the possibility of help out there; we have to be able to
commit ourselves to the recovery process before we
can be healed.

Lord, I want to risk. Make me willing to be willing.

J.M.C.

> *For whatever things were written before were*
> *written for our learning, that we through the*
> *patience and comfort of the Scriptures might*
> *have hope.*
> —ROM. 15:4

Many of us find it difficult to hope in God as our heavenly Father because of our own father's failures and inconsistencies. Instead of looking to God to help us from day to day, we may have come to rely on ourselves.

God, however, never leaves us or forsakes us, and He wants us to place our hope in Him. The key to being able to do this is to confront what caused us to lose hope in the first place. That means thinking back to the original person who let us down and working through that loss. We need to discuss our pain and disappointment with someone we trust, then examine each loss and find out when we started also to mistrust God. Finally, we must begin to realize that although there are those in this sinful world who are not safe to put our hope in, God is always a dependable source of hope.

Father, please help me to separate you from the people who have failed me. I want to be able to hope again, and I pray you would reveal yourself to me.

J.L.M.

Create in me a clean heart, O God,
And renew a steadfast spirit within me.
—PS. 51:10

It is so easy for women in recovery to beat themselves for the sins of yesterday. Something down deep inside wants to convince us that because we weren't victors yesterday, we can't be victors today. Like the psalmist David, we have the duty of accepting God's cleansing. He is willing to give us a fresh start today. Will we accept it?

David should be a comfort to all of us. He committed adultery, murder and cover-up. Most of us can't top that. Yet, God called David "A man after my own heart" (see Acts 13:22). Why did God love David so much? David acknowledged his sin and knew that God would be faithful to create him anew.

We may feel unworthy of God's love today. Victory over sin may not have been evident in the last few days—or even weeks! We may have slipped back into behaviors we thought we had victory over. Guess what! God is still there. He loves us, and He's reaching out His hand. Let's take God's hand today! Let's pray and ask Him to create in us a clean heart. Let's start today anew with Christ.

I will visualize Christ as lovingly holding out His hand to renew me—then grab hold!

J.E.M.

*Then the angel said to her, "Do not be afraid, Mary,
for you have found favor with God."*

—LUKE 1:30

Nowhere in Scripture do we find God promising us security or absence of suffering. Rather, He promises His presence in whatever we face. He calls us to leave the comfortable, the familiar, and to get to the place in our daily walk where Jesus is our security. But that's risky!

Mary was promised by the angel Gabriel that she would be the mother of the Messiah. In our more romantic moments, we ponder how wonderful that would be. What an affirmation! But what a risk! When Mary said yes to God's plan, she risked ridicule. She had to bear the shame of being an unwed mother and then to spend her life watching people reject and ultimately crucify her son. Would she have taken the risk if she hadn't trusted in God's goodness?

Trust must precede risk. That is why it is necessary for us to comprehend the security found in God's accepting and forgiving love—to grasp that God loves us just as much whether we succeed or fail—before we will be free to risk.

Thank you, God, that because of Jesus' sacrifice on Calvary, I have found favor with you. Help me make that the basis of my security so that I am free to risk.

J.M.C.

The blessing of a perishing man came upon me,
And I caused the widow's heart to sing for joy.
—JOB 29:13

When a husband dies after a long illness, friends and family might discuss among themselves that "at least she was prepared" for the loss. Yet even an expected death can leave a widow feeling shocked and helpless. She may have already been handling the finances and going places alone, but she was still continually doing things for "two of us." She may have grieved and adjusted to having a terminally ill mate, but not to living totally alone.

Mary Ann would whisper, "I'm a widow; I'm by myself," and pray that she would somehow accept it. She had not realized how much she had come to rely on the visitors, cards, flowers, and prayers that kept her going during her husband's long bout with cancer. Now, several months after his death, she found people didn't call or write as much. She realized that if she were going to have fellowship, she would have to arrange it herself. Mary Ann started setting up lunch dates and shopping trips, and the people she asked began returning invitations. The more initiative Mary Ann took, the more fellowship she enjoyed. Mary Ann now enjoys the support of her new relationships, and the time spent with friends is taking away the loneliness.

Father, I pray that you will fill my lonely hours and give me the strength to reach out to others while remaining content in your presence.

J.L.M.

He who dwells in the secret place of the Most High
Shall abide under the shadow of the Almighty.
I will say of the Lord, "He is my refuge and
* my fortress;*
My God, in Him I will trust."

—PS. 91:1–2

Trusting in Christ fills the God vacuum that we all have. The Holy Spirit comes to dwell within us, and we are privileged to begin to know and understand the mind of God. This secret place should be our dwelling place, not merely a place to "stop over" when life gets rough. Let's not think of a short meeting with Christ when we're in desperate situations. Instead, let's resolve to stay in His Word and in His dwelling all the time. As we pray and talk with God daily, we will grow comfortable in His presence. We will learn to look at life through His truth instead of our own. As we dwell in His place, we will eventually be delivered from the sinful behaviors that have plagued us for so long.

When the strong winds blow in our life, we can rest assured that God is our refuge and our fortress. Let us join the psalmist in putting our trust in God. He won't let us down.

I resolve today to find God's secret place to dwell in—an intimate, moment-by-moment relationship with Him.

J.E.M.

*For all have sinned and fall short of the glory
of God.*   —ROM. 3:23

The failure rate for human beings is 100 percent. We all sin. We all make mistakes. We all fall flat on our faces. And we all have the potential for every imaginable evil.

This truth was illustrated graphically to me when my son was five years old. It was the day before Halloween, and he and his friend were sitting on the porch swing, their masks pulled up on top of their heads. They called to me, asking for some cookies, and I said no. They helped themselves anyway. I could hear the metal lid being put back on the cookie jar. So I followed them back out on the porch. As if on signal, the two little boys pulled their masks down over their eyes. Then, when they realized that I knew, they vehemently blamed each other. Young as they were, they were no strangers to guilt and deception—sin.

I, too, tend to hide behind masks and blame my guilt on others. I need to look long and hard at Calvary to see that I have the same potential for evil and deceit as the people who caused Christ to be crucified and the people who have abused me.

Remind me, Lord, that heaven is for those who know they sin and hell is for those who think they are pretty good.

                                          J.M.C.

> *Being filled with the fruits of righteousness which*
> *are by Jesus Christ, to the glory and praise of God.*
> —PHIL. 1:11

The torn piece of bread floated only for a moment before the largest duck grabbed it. It was wonderful to be able to enjoy taking the children to the park. Just a year ago, Marie knew she would have resented "wasting" time there.

Marie had two children, aged nine and five, whom it seemed she barely knew. She had always stayed home with them, but motherhood had always felt like a burden instead of a blessing to her. She had been too task oriented to relax with them, and she resented having to clean up after them.

A friend helped Marie realize that her children were more important than her schedule or her house. This wise friend convinced Marie to take some steps toward changing her attitude and getting to know her kids. Marie began by first taking the kids to a place where she wouldn't worry if they messed up or caused a commotion—the park. They then progressed to the zoo, a fast-food restaurant, the mall, and even the grocery store. Once Marie got to know and enjoy her children's personalities, she began to understand that when they made noise or a mess they were just being normal kids, not trying to make her life miserable. She now praises God for the blessings her children have brought into her life.

Father, teach me how to enjoy my children by giving me the wisdom to discern what is important in life.

J.L.M.

*Put off, concerning your former conduct, the old
man which grows corrupt according to the deceitful
lusts, and be renewed in the spirit of your mind.*
—EPH. 4:22–23

My little brother had a favorite blanket that he carried with him when he was feeling the need for security. The older he got, however, the more tattered the blanket became and the more he became ashamed to need it. Many times he would throw the blanket in his closet, determined not to carry it again. Yet, when those waves of insecurity came, it was back to the closet to look for the blanket.

Paul, in this message, encourages us to throw away our blanket of sin and be renewed in our spirit. Those old habits we hid in the closet are so easy to find. They feel so comfortable. They give us security, even though we know they aren't good for us. In our moments of insecurity we want to run to the closet and cover ourselves with the security of our old behaviors and habits. But we don't have to do that today. We have another choice. We can let God work in our lives, and we can become new women in Christ. Our security can be in God instead of our old, tattered, familiar sins.

Lord, help me today to develop my bonding with you. Help me replace the sins I run to when I am feeling insecure with the security of being your child.

J.E.M.

> *Behold what manner of love the Father has
> bestowed on us, that we should be called
> children of God!*
> —1 JOHN 3:1

Jesus delights in giving us names that we can grow into. Never does Jesus label us "sinners." We are commanded to "go and sin no more," but we are not given a derogatory label. Instead, we are called "children of God." Imagine that! Jesus affirms us, and we grow into His affirmation.

Jesus delighted in doing the same things with His disciples. Jesus changed the name Simon, meaning "reed," to Peter, meaning "rock." Instead of focusing on Peter's indecisiveness and impetuousness, Jesus focused on what Peter would become—rock solid.

Have you noticed that when you label someone, all you can see from then on is the label? You persist in seeing "Jack the drunk" or "Donna the airhead" instead of Jack and Donna, God's cherished children. Following Christ's example we need, with the eyes of faith, to see the potential for wholeness and transformation in each person, including ourselves. We need to be God's affirming voice to those around us.

Lord, thank you for the affirming people you have brought into my life; their affirmations move my eyes away from my mistakes toward my potential. Help me learn to affirm others, too.

J.M.C.

An excellent wife is the crown of her husband,
But she who causes shame is like rottenness
in his bones.
—PROV. 12:4

Acceptance of our mate begins with acceptance of God and ourselves. One of the biggest disruptors in marriage is feeling inadequate, depressed, or angry at ourselves. Imagine a wife's bringing into her new marriage an assortment of trunks and boxes full of personal problems. Then picture her spouse's bringing all of his boxes and trunks too. All this makes for a crowded existence! To further complicate things, marriage partners often try to start unpacking and fixing their mate's boxes of fears and troubles while tripping over their own.

Marital growth begins when we begin settling and unpacking our own fears and dilemmas and supportively allowing our mate to do the same. As we allow each other the space to maintain a strong relationship with Jesus Christ, our own problems have a chance to be resolved.

Father, please remind me to keep my focus on you. I want to strengthen my marriage by strengthening my relationship with you.
J.L.M.

*And He said to me, "My grace is sufficient for you,
for My strength is made perfect in weakness."
Therefore most gladly I will rather boast in my
infirmities, that the power of Christ may rest
upon me.*   —2 COR. 12:9

The apostle Paul was an excellent model for women in recovery of how to react to personal weaknesses. Not only did he not try to hide his weaknesses as we often try to do, he actually wrote about them in the Bible. And he wasn't the only one. The Bible, from Genesis to Revelation, is a story of man's weakness and God's grace.

When can God step in and take control? Is it when we, in our pride, are trying to hide our sin and our vulnerability? No! God comes in with His sufficient grace when we say we can't cope anymore. He steps in and fills the gaps. He builds the bridges so we can cross the troubled waters of our life.

Sometimes the problems in our lives won't disappear. Paul, for example, lived his whole life with his "weakness of the flesh." But he still came to a point that each of us are striving for. He gave himself humbly to God and was willing to accept whatever God chose for his life. Let's determine to accept God's grace today. He is there waiting for us to come to Him.

Lord, I lay down before you my many sins and shortcomings. Alone, I just can't get better. With your grace, I can continue on the road to recovery.

J.E.M.

For I will forgive their iniquity, and their sin I will remember no more.   —JER. 31:34

Many of us in recovery carry around a backpack of regrets. We wish we hadn't said this, done this, fallen for that line. We wish we hadn't been so irresponsible. Some of us flog ourselves on a daily basis with "if onlys" and "what ifs." It's easy to turn these regrets into excuses for not accepting responsibility. They can be an excellent justification for failure and self-pity, and they can cause us to stay dependent on others rather than facing life on our own.

God invites us tenderly to release our regrets through confession—words backed up by a change in our behavior. Then God promises to forgive us and wipe our slate clean—to remove our transgressions completely.

A priest was told that a woman in his congregation had visions. To test her he told her to ask God what the last sin the priest had confessed was. A few days later, the woman sought the priest out and told him she had followed his request. "Well, what was the last sin I confessed?" he asked. The lady smiled, "God said he couldn't remember."

If God can't remember the regrets we've confessed to Him, who are we to carry them around?

Lord, help me to use my energy on growth rather than regrets.

                                                                J.M.C.

> *I say then: Walk in the Spirit, and you shall not
> fulfill the lust of the flesh.* —GAL. 5:16

If Janet had known at age thirteen what she knows now, she probably would not have smoked that first marijuana joint with the friend she met on the Texas Gulf coast during a family vacation. Janet has had to work hard to recover from that decision and the other bad decisions that followed.

Now, thirteen years later, Janet is asking, "Why is it so hard to change?" You see, Janet started looking for joy in substances such as marijuana, alcohol, cocaine, amphetamines, and cigarettes and eventually became dependent on them. After battling her addictions for two years, she is also asking, "Why did I make so many bad decisions?"

Reading Galatians 5:16, Janet learned that we make unwise decisions partly because of our sinful nature. Fortunately for us, God loves us and offers forgiveness for our sins. Janet regrets waiting so long and going through so much difficulty to learn about God's love for her. However, because of her acceptance of God's forgiveness and her love for the Lord, her life has been changed.

Lord, thank you for your guidance and for giving me the desires of your own heart. Forgive me when I sin against you and help me to change for the better.

J.L.M.

Out of heaven He let you hear His voice, that He might instruct you. —DEUT. 4:36

An excellent swimmer, she was out in a local lake just before sunset. She could easily see the shore and was enjoying her swim. Suddenly a fog rolled in from seemingly nowhere. The swim went from leisurely to frightening. She lost all sense of direction because all landmarks had disappeared in the fog. She swam first one way and then another, unable to find her bearings. Finally, after about twenty minutes, she heard voices. She swam toward the shore with only the sound of voices to guide her.

Sometimes in life we feel all alone in the fog. We head in one direction, then another, and still can't find the safety of the shore. How will we ever find the way?

The Swiss psychiatrist Paul Tournier once said, "Where there is no longer any opportunity for doubt, there is no longer any opportunity for faith, either." The "foggy times" of our life bring us doubt, but they can also give us a chance to exercise our faith. God loves us, and the Bible gives us many examples of His concern for us. God uses natural resources, such as voices on the shore, to show us the way. I believe He also sometimes uses supernatural resources such as dreams. We will be uncertain and confused at times in our lives, but we can always be sure that God is there and He does care. One way or another, He'll provide the "voices" we need to teach us and show us the way.

What subtle "voices" from God are instructing me in my life today?

J.E.M.

> *Blessed are the peacemakers,*
> *For they shall be called sons of God.*
> —MATT. 5:9

How do you react when someone disagrees with you? Conflict in relationships causes incredible discomfort to some, whereas others can't feel at home without some controversy. Regardless of the reaction, conflict is still a part of any relationship. If it isn't, one of you is not being honest.

Whenever there was even a hint of conflict, Robin would crumble. She would do anything to avoid conflict—even sacrifice her own needs. In her mind, conflict was the ultimate enemy. Robin was a peacekeeper.

By contrast, Julie was a peacemaker. She saw conflict as an opportunity to gain greater understanding by taking an honest look at differences. She realized that her perception was limited, and she was open to discovering a more complete sense of the truth.

If you were choosing a person to be in relationship with, which woman would you choose—the one who kept you from growing or the one who challenged you to grow?

Help me today, Lord, to be a peacemaker rather than a peacekeeper in my relationships.

J.M.C.

Now faith is the substance of things hoped for, the evidence of things not seen. —HEB. 11:1

Jennifer finally decided to stop fighting God and go where He was leading her—back to school and into social work. She knew she had a great deal of life experience which God had used to prepare her for this task. However, Jennifer was plagued with the fear of failure. What if she couldn't keep up in class? What if no one hired her? It seemed much safer to remain a housewife and mother!

Jennifer knew that she would just have to take a step of faith, which to her meant acting upon the truth instead of giving in to her feelings. It was like stepping off a cliff into the unknown. But God's strength was more than enough to sustain her. Jennifer completed her degree, received her licenses, and has been working for about six years. She has been able to help many women, couples, and young people through difficult times and to win quite a few people to the Lord. She now looks forward to God's next challenge with excitement. She still has doubts and fears, but now she looks at each step as a challenge to serve God.

Father, give me the ability to act upon the truth instead of my feelings. Thank you for challenges that give me new opportunities to serve you.

J.L.M.

> *Put my tears into Your bottle;*
> *Are they not in Your book?*
> —PS. 56:8–9

Women cry more than men. Scientists say it is good for us. Our ability to let out our emotions is probably one of the factors that account for women living so much longer than men.

God knows and understands our deep pain. Think of God's pain when He allowed His only Son to die on the cross for our sins. He feels pain when we feel pain. He also offers us comfort for the pains of life. He wants to carry us through the darkness into light. When we lose loved ones, when we stumble and fall, when we disappoint ourselves, we will cry. That's a natural thing to do. But God wants to forgive us, dry our tears and carry us on. And God has promised to wipe away all our tears someday when we go to Heaven to live with Him.

In the world, we will have tribulation—that's a promise. But we have a Savior, Christ, who has overcome the world. And there is a new day coming where we will never cry again.

Thank you, Lord, for loving me so intimately and considering me so important that you even keep track of my tears.

J.E.M.

*For we are His workmanship, created in Christ
Jesus for good works, which God prepared
beforehand that we should walk in them.*
—EPH. 2:10

Great occasions for serving God come seldom, but we are surrounded by little ones on a daily basis. In our marriages, our families, our work, our friendships, we are meant to be God's hands, arms, feet, eyes, and smile as we reach out to those around us.

Those of us in recovery realize that our helping others must come out of our fullness rather than our emptiness. But that doesn't mean we should hold back from giving. In the last few years, our culture seems to have shifted from a "What can I give?" to "What can I get?" philosophy. What a disservice we end up doing to ourselves and others when we adopt that policy. Bob Hope was quoted as saying, "If you don't have generosity in your heart, you have the worst kind of heart problem."

How is your giving muscle? Is it underdeveloped, overdeveloped, or healthy? What we choose to do really isn't the issue. What's important is how much love we put into what we do.

Lord, help me to develop a healthy, giving heart.

J.M.C.

> *Give her of the fruit of her hands,*
> *And let her own words praise her*
> *in the gates.* —PROV. 31:31

Jessica was an attorney and the mother of two young daughters. Although she worked outside the home, Jessica was quite disciplined and actually spent a lot of quality time with her children. It helped that she had someone great to care for the girls and help with the cooking and cleaning. But Jessica still felt pulled. Finally she decided to be a full-time mother and practice just enough law to keep her in the field.

Jessica's husband, Dan, was delighted at her decision, even though he had supported her in her work. However, her female attorney friends felt she was letting them down. To them, her success had made a statement by proving that women could be both good moms and good attorneys.

Jessica explained to her colleagues that she wanted to stay at home not primarily because of her girls, but because of Dan. She had enough time to be an attorney and a mother, but she didn't have much left over for her husband. Now, because she has already given so much of herself to the children during the day, she is able to give Dan attention in the evening. In addition, Dan is able to spend more quality time with the kids since Jessica is not so concerned about getting hers in.

Lord, show me what priorities are important and how to divide my time appropriately.

J.L.M.

> *Who among you fears the Lord?*
> *Who obeys the voice of His Servant?*
> *Who walks in darkness*
> *And has no light?*
> *Let him trust in the name of the Lord*
> *And rely on his God.* —ISA. 50:10

The highways of life are filled with potholes. Bumps in the road often throw us into discouragement and depression, and we grow weary in the journey. But God has given us a road map for the hard roads of life—the Bible.

We've made a commitment to travel on the road to recovery. The God of the Bible is the only true Higher Power. He has promised never to leave us or forsake us. We know that God sent Christ, His only Son, to die on the cross that we might have eternal life. Now we have two choices. We can feel sorry for ourselves that we have so many bumps in our road, or we can put our trust in God and determine to follow His guidance as we journey through life, bumps and all! We can sometimes rest beside the road; God wants us to do that. But He doesn't want us to stop and dwell on our discouragement and depression. Let's keep traveling today with our map in hand and our eyes on Him.

May God grant me the strength and courage today to keep going on my lifelong journey toward wholeness.

J.E.M.

> *Who comforts us in all our tribulation, that we may*
> *be able to comfort those who are in any trouble,*
> *with the comfort with which we ourselves are*
> *comforted by God.*
> —2 COR. 1:4

Joyce and Jim left their precious two-year-old son with Jim's parents. The parents, who had guests, were preoccupied with entertaining until they suddenly realized their grandson wasn't in the room. They searched everywhere. Finally they found the little boy at the bottom of their spa—dead.

Can you imagine the anger, the guilt, the helplessness, the sadness Jim and Joyce had to face? Joyce referred to it as a hole in her heart. Sometimes they felt the feelings would smother them.

Another couple who had experienced a similar tragedy ten years earlier took Jim and Joyce under their wing. They listened to them, comforted them, sometimes fed them. Mostly, however, they were just there for them. One day Joyce cried out, "Where was God when my son died, when your daughter died?" Her friend took her in her arms and said, out of her own deeply felt experience, "He was the same place He was when His son died." And for the first time Joyce felt the comfort of knowing at a deep level that God really does understand our hurt and our pain.

Lord, use even my pain as a vehicle to help someone else. Let me be a source of comfort to them because you have been a source of comfort to me.

J.M.C.

Be strong and of good courage, do not fear nor be afraid of them; for the Lord your God, He is the One who goes with you. He will not leave you nor forsake you. —DEUT. 31:6

Debbie's husband had just died of AIDS, which he had contracted from a homosexual lover. Debbie was devastated and full of fear. In addition to feeling betrayed, she knew she was probably infected too. How could he have been so selfish? She had always tried to please him, but she must not have been woman enough for him!

Two years later, Debbie began to realize that in a sense she was *still* trying to please her dead husband; she couldn't shake the sense of rejection. Somehow God had given her a miracle; she wasn't infected with HIV, but she felt that her husband's rejection had infected her life.

Debbie began to read and meditate daily upon the Word of God. As she did, she began to understand how much God loved her. She began to feel anger and a great sadness toward her husband and all the other men in her life who had rejected her. And she began to reach out to God for help in forgiving each of the rejections in her life. She even made an effort to talk to her father. She had never felt she lived up to his expectations. Now, as they both cried, laughed, and began a mending of their relationship, Debbie could feel her sense of rejection fading away.

Lord, please help me to face my feelings of rejection so I can begin to see and feel your love for me.

J.L.M.

> *"Can anyone hide himself in secret places,*
> *So I shall not see him?" says the Lord.*
> —JER. 23:24

Stick your head in the sand and you don't have to know what's going on around you. People who play this game think that if they deny their problems or put off facing them, the problems will go away. But the problem with the head-in-the-sand trick is you eventually have to come up for air.

Sometimes we therapists feel like lifeguards going around the beach and saving people from suffocating by pulling their heads out of the sand and then some of them want to stick their heads back in! I once had a patient I had rescued say to me, "If I had known sane people were this crazy, I would have stayed crazy."

Very few problems disappear when we avoid them; we must eventually face what we're hoping will go away. Denial is like believing in magic. We somehow think that pretending a problem isn't there will cause it to be solved by someone else or simply fade away. That rarely happens.

Avoiding pain by procrastination and denial is usually the route to prolonging problems and making them worse. Let's pull our heads out of the sand and face the challenges of life today.

Denying my conflicts causes significantly more personal pain than facing them and devising plans to overcome them. I will ask God's help in facing my problems today.

J.E.M.

A merry heart does good, like medicine,
But a broken spirit dries the bones.
—PROV. 17:22

Kim and Dan were so excited! For a whole year they had been planning the vacation of a lifetime. Now they were actually on their way to Hawaii. But they had their first major argument on the plane, and the situation just went downhill from there. Their dream vacation became a nightmare—and each blamed the other. Two years later, as they sat in my office, Kim and Dan were still angry about Hawaii. Resentment over this and other issues was drying up their love for each other.

Resentment is normal when we have been hurt, but it isn't constructive. Resentment can't change the past or correct the present. It certainly doesn't make us feel better, and it puts us in the powerless position of letting others make us miserable. How much better if we would admit our hurt—to ourselves, to God, and to the person who hurt us—then consciously and continually release the hurt. Every time it rises to choke us, we need to choose to forgive. We will know that we are not carrying resentment when we can understand the other person's hurt and when we can pray honestly for his or her success. At that point, our broken, resentful spirit will once again become a merry heart.

Lord, help me to release my resentments today. Teach me to be honest about my hurts but then to choose forgiveness.

J.M.C.

> *Behold, children are a heritage from the Lord,*
> *The fruit of the womb is His reward.*
>   —PS. 127:3

Katie beamed with excitement as she watched her new baby daughter, Summer. She was filled with both excitement and trepidation because she could remember all the painful feelings she had experienced growing up and she cringed at the thought of her daughter's feeling that way. Katie could remember feelings of isolation; someone had always seemed to be displeased with her or saying how much trouble she was. She knew now that she had been very demanding and had seemed to push the other family members away with her strong will. Yet she had always longed for someone to put arms around her and tell her she was OK and lovable.

As Summer grew older, she proved to be just as demanding as Katie had been. The harder Katie tried to be loving, the harder Summer pushed her. To get strength, Katie began to pray and meditate upon God's Word. The first thing she did was to give up control and give Summer over to God. Then she made an effort to take a genuine interest in Summer's feelings and to accept Summer for who she was. Now, as Katie sits and talks with Summer on weekend visits from college, she realizes that the traits that made Summer a challenge to raise have made her a strong leader and an effective witness for the Lord.

Lord, let me see how you could use the qualities of my child to further the kingdom of God.

                                         J.L.M.

He who loves his wife loves himself.
—EPH. 5:28

Phil and Vera should have been the ideal couple. Phil thought he was perfect, and Vera knew she wasn't. Both of them thought they deserved sainthood—she for her humility, and he for his righteousness. They had been married twenty-five years when they came for marriage counseling. Their insecurities had kept them from deeply loving themselves or each other.

Phil finally figured out that his righteous cover was hiding an insecure little boy who never felt quite good enough. That's why he spent much of his life trying to convince himself and the world that he was great. He had to learn that his true righteousness could come only from Christ, who would accept him as the sinner he was.

Vera also had much to learn. Her humility, she found out, came not from a servant's heart but from a masochistic need to suffer so that people would admire her for her martyrdom. She had looked down on Phil for his egotism, but now she had to confess the pride she took in her humility. She asked God to forgive her and help her to take healthy pride in being the person He wanted her to become.

Vera and Phil know now their sainthood will only be achieved through Christ, who truly was and is perfect. Secure in Him, they can now know the beginnings of genuine love.

Lord, help me accept the real me and love others better.

J.E.M.

> *In You, O Lord, I put my trust,*
> *Let me never be ashamed;*
> *Deliver me in Your righteousness.*
> —PS. 31:1

Sonja's family never wanted her born. Her mother had made three trips to a doctor who performed abortions before she decided she couldn't carry through with it. Her father told people that Sonja wasn't his daughter. Then, when Sonja was one, he ran away, never to be heard from again.

As a baby, Sonja just lay in her crib. No one played with her. In fact, her grandmother delighted in telling her as she grew up that she would have starved if Grandma hadn't fed her. Sonja wet her pants until she was five. Her nickname was "Sad Sack." She had serious problems with her legs, but no one ever took her to see a doctor.

I met Sonja as an adult. Not surprisingly, she was having problems. She couldn't sleep. Her marriage had collapsed. She felt guilty for existing. Sonja's sense of shame was so deep that her recovery had to be slow and deep. One of the important concepts Sonja had to grasp is that even though humans shame other humans, God doesn't. He never humiliates us. He never devalues us or agrees with our self-contempt. Once Sonja grasped the depth of God's love for her, she never again felt guilty for being born.

Dear Lord, only your love can release me from my feelings of shame.

J.M.C.

Therefore whoever humbles himself as this little child is the greatest in the kingdom of heaven.
—MATT. 18:4

Have you ever sat and watched small children play? I watched a group of five-year-olds one day. They seemed to be so free with their emotions. They got angry, sad, or happy fast and were able to switch from one emotion to another quickly. One little black-eyed girl was amazingly trusting. She accepted what the teacher said as if God has just told her Himself.

Why do we as adults hide our emotions and play games with each other? Hiding our real thoughts and feelings from others seems to keep us protected, but it really stops us from receiving love. Our walls keep us from having the trusting spirit I saw in that one little girl at the playground.

It will always be necessary to protect ourselves from some things in the world. If we are going to grow closer to God, however, we must approach Him with the spirit of a little child. We must begin to share all our feelings with God. And we need to trust all of what God tells us in order to receive the full extent of His love. When we keep that in mind, we can begin to see God's love for us in all the little children.

Heavenly Father, help me to become more like a little child, sharing all my emotions openly and trusting you as my guiding light to love.

J.L.M.

> *But seek first the kingdom of God and His*
> *righteousness, and all these things shall be*
> *added to you.*
> —MATT. 6:33

Lillian was sure her plan would bring her happiness. She wasn't happy with her husband, so she had chosen to find someone else to fulfill her needs. She agreed to counseling, but her mind was made up. She would leave her husband and three children, marry her lover, and move to another state to start life afresh.

Lillian was headed for disaster for two reasons. First, she had made up her own definition of happiness. Second, she had chosen to go against her Christian faith and seek happiness above holiness, forgettng that holiness is the only way to long-term happiness.

In counseling, Lillian was confronted lovingly but firmly with the truth about relationships. She faced her childhood fantasy of "Someday my prince will come." Slowly she realized that in reality there are no princes in most people's lives, but that her husband was a reasonably good guy.

All stories don't have happy endings. This one does. Lillian is now reunited with her husband and children. She is acutely aware of what she almost lost. Her daily prayer is "Lord, this is a new day, help me to seek holiness first today. Help me to realize that I will only be truly happy as I seek to do your will each day."

Happiness is a choice, so I will choose to live for Christ's kingdom today.

J.E.M.

*Anxiety in the heart of man causes
depression,
But a good word makes it glad.*
—PROV. 12:25

We are all born with two natural fears—fear of falling and fear of loud noises. Every other fear and anxiety is learned—and it can be unlearned.

Obviously, some fear can be good; it can lead us to steer clear of danger, set goals, and make necessary changes. But fear can also be destructive. Because it causes us to cover up, deny, and wear masks, it blocks our ability to give or receive love. Fear drains us of energy and sets us up to experience the very thing we fear. It also limits our effectiveness. Some of us seem to go through life with the brakes on because we are consumed by anxiety.

How do we get rid of our fear? When a child fears a shadow or a dark shape in her room at night, the solution is to turn the light on. The fear is eliminated, because the child has seen the truth. And that's the key to conquering adult fears, too. Jesus Christ refers to Himself as Light and Truth. His love lets us see our fears for what they really are. We can own them, examine them, and decide what to do about them. An acrostic I have seen for fear is: *F*alse *E*vidence *A*ppearing *R*eal. Instead of focusing on fear, therefore, let's focus on faith instead.

Name a four-letter word for a response to difficulty. One woman said fear, *another said* love. *Which would you choose?*

J.M.C.

All your children shall be taught by the Lord,
And great shall be the peace of your children.
—ISA. 54:13

The most important thing you can do for a child in trouble is to pray for him or her. But this does not mean pray and then try to rescue the child or take care of the problem yourself. Many parents naturally want to "fix" their problem children, but one person cannot "fix" another. Instead, work on making changes in your attitude and the way you respond or react to your child.

First, resolve to let go of guilt and blame. Sure, you probably have not done everything just right in raising this child—but no parent is perfect. (And remember, you are not the only influence in your child's life.) Dwelling on the past will only keep you helpless. Concentrate instead on where you are right now and what steps you can take to make some changes and gain peace of mind.

A parent support group can be a special blessing if you have a child in trouble. After all, our children have plenty of support from their peers in acting out! A support group can give you suggestions and ideas forged in experience, and they will be an invaluable source of strength when you must take a stand with your children.

Father, provide me with friends who understand my dilemma and can support me in helping my child the best way I know how.

J.L.M.

Beloved, let us love one another, for love is of God;
and everyone who loves is born of God and knows
God.
—1 JOHN 4:7

The need to belong and be accepted is universal. We all crave the love of God and the love of humans, and rejection is one of our greatest fears.

Love for a newborn baby can mean the difference between life and death. This has been well documented in studies of orphanages where babies receive normal physical care but, because of the understaffing, are not played with or shown affection. In such situations, the babies cry at first, then seemingly give up. They become listless and lose their appetites. Many become ill, and some die. Of those who survive, many are mentally retarded or mentally ill.

But age makes little difference in the need for love. Social scientists at the University of California at Berkeley found that adults who aren't in some kind of nurturing group are just as much at risk for health problems as people who smoke, have high blood pressure, high cholesterol, or are obese. Being a loner can be deadly.

You have probably seen the bumper sticker that asks, "Have you hugged your kid today?" Answer yes! Determine to show your love to your friends and family. Think of specific ways to let them know you care. Do it today. And let them show love to you too!

Love is contagious, so I will think of several ways to pass it on today.
J.E.M.

*If someone says, "I love God," and hates his
brother, he is a liar; for he who does not love his
brother whom he has seen, how can he love God
whom he has not seen?* —1 JOHN 4:20

The following is an excerpt from a letter written by a
pastor who learned eleven years ago that his son is a
homosexual:*

Our son came home from Bible study when he was seventeen and shared with us that he was struggling with ho-
mosexuality. We have tried to preach it out of him, argue it
out of him, pray it out of him, shout it out of him, program
it out of him, and even cast it out of him. But up to this
point his orientation is the same. We have finally made an
attempt to commit ourselves to him, and him to the Lord.
When we finally learn to commit everything in life to the
Lord, we can withdraw our hurt and anger and just love
people for who they are. We have never hated or rejected
our son. Consequently we are just attempting to use this
discipline to grow more like the Lord Jesus. We often fail,
but the blessing is in the attempt. Biblical love is not to
condone behavior; it is to make complete and keep a relationship from being destroyed.

*Lord, help me remember that you called me to be a witness, not a
judge.*

J.M.C.

*A portion of this letter was printed in a newsletter put out by Spatula Minis-
tries, a ministry to families with homosexual loved ones. They can be reached
at Box 444, La Habra, CA 90631, (213) 691-7369.

The Spirit of God has made me,
And the breath of the Almighty
gives me life. —JOB 33:4

I am so tired today. I feel an incredible amount of tension and pressure at home, at work, and inside myself. I just can't seem to find any peace or rest. It's on days like this that I wonder if what I'm doing is worthwhile or if it's all in vain.

All day I watched the clock, knowing I wasn't accomplishing anything, just trying to hold on until time to go home. I struggled through dinner, groping for the right attitude. I bit my tongue more than once to keep from snapping at people I love.

Now I just sit on my back porch, watching the sunset. The sky is painted in a beautiful mural of oranges and reds. The evening birds are singing a sweet melody. The flowers give off a sweet fragrance, and the wind gently massages my face. As I ponder over the day, I begin to see how much I need to take regular time out and meditate upon God. It is incredible how being aware of His presence around me helps me to get things in perspective.

Lord, I realize that I made it through the day because you were carrying me. Thank you for your breath of life and help me to take time to meditate upon you daily.

J.L.M.

> *Remove falsehood and lies far from me.*
> —PROV. 30:8

Do the following lines sound familiar?

"I'm not perfect, so I'm no good."

"I've been rejected; something must be wrong with me."

"I'm not happy because things are always going wrong in my life."

"I am a failure because my parents didn't do a good job of raising me."

One of the first things we try to do in counseling is counteract lies like these which clients have told themselves about themselves. To function healthily, we must learn to see the true picture of ourselves and not a distorted one. We often ask patients to wear a rubber band around their wrists and tell them to snap the rubber band every time a lie about themselves goes through their heads. But sometimes it takes a lot of counseling just to get them to the point where they can identify the lies. Clients who have had a childhood of continual put-downs will carry those false messages in their heads for a lifetime if they're not interrupted and the lies replaced with the truth.

One of our main goals as women in recovery should be to change our view of ourselves. If we don't, no one else on earth will.

Lord, help me to see myself as you see me, "positionally perfect" through the blood of Christ in spite of my imperfections, and help me see my self-deceptive lies.

J.E.M.

For God has not given us a spirit of fear, but of
power and of love and of a sound mind.
—2 TIM 1:7

Heather was the first girl born in her family for five generations. As a result, her parents were overly protective of her. All her life, she received a consistent double message: "Try new things . . . but you know you won't be able to do it well. Let me help you." Small wonder that Heather's adult life became dominated by the fear that she won't be good enough.

Children raised in homes full of criticism often become critical adults with inadequate self-esteem. Fear of rejection eventually leads to fear of trying. And this was true for Heather. She would set unrealistically high standards for herself and then rationalize not meeting them. She would prepare inadequately to achieve her goals and feel justified in her low self-esteem when she failed.

Then Heather came face to face with Jesus' unconditional acceptance, and she started a journey of self-discovery. She didn't have to focus on the distorted self-image she had picked up as a child. Jesus saw just as much value in her before she reached her goal as after she had succeeded. Even when she "failed," He labeled the result as experience, not failure. Slowly her fear was replaced by an awareness of being loved. That awareness freed Heather to call on Christ's power and to work toward her goals.

Lord, thank you that your love can overcome my fear of rejection and help me learn to accept myself.

J.M.C.

Apply your heart to instruction,
And your ears to words of knowledge.
—PROV. 23:12

While attending what she thought would be a boring seminar on "How to Be an Effective Middle School Principal," Martha received some valuable insight that had nothing to do with school. She felt all right about her job as a school principal, but she felt inadequate to be the mother of her four-year-old. She couldn't believe she could manage seventy-seven teachers and not this one small child. As Martha listened, it seemed that the presenter of the seminar was talking about the way she treated her son, Mark, instead of the way she exhibited leadership at school. The presenter listed four points that Martha knew she usually lost by the time she got home: (1) Have a clear mind, (2) Have a cheerful disposition, (3) Have a discreet mouth, and (4) Have a humble spirit. Martha decided to make these points her goals as a mother. First, Martha set out to work on her grouchiness toward Mark. She made an active decision to be as polite to him as she was to her co-workers. She also decided she probably needed to get rid of the "I'm the mom, and I'm right" attitude and try and "I'm the mom and I love you" attitude. After a few months of trying to think clearly, watch her mouth, and getting rid of her bossy attitude, Martha saw distinct improvements in her relationship with Mark.

———

Father, teach me to value my position at home as much as my position at work.

J.L.M.

And forgive us our debts,
As we forgive our debtors.
—MATT. 6:12

Marla had been coming to counseling for well over a year, but she was still a very angry young woman. She had vented her feelings over and over again. One afternoon, I finally said, "Marla, you're never going to get well until you forgive." Her answer was quick and to the point, "I don't do windows, and I don't do forgiveness." I said, "Well, I guess you won't get well then." Marla left in a huff. I wondered if she would come back.

Next week, however, Marla showed up. She seemed calm and relaxed, so I asked her how the week had gone. Rather sheepishly she replied that she had had a great week. She had really thought about what I had said. And she had decided to make an effort to forgive not only others, but also herself. Marla had started on the road to forgiveness by taking the first step— making a conscious decision to begin the process of forgiveness. It is a long process that often requires peeling off layers of bitterness like tearfully peeling layers of an onion. Unlike an onion, however, our lives come out of the "peeling" process whole and intact— better than ever.

I will decide to forgive today, so the long process of forgiveness can begin to bring healing in my life.

J.E.M.

> *Yea, though I walk through the valley*
> *of the shadow of death,*
> *I will fear no evil;*
> *For You are with me;*
> *Your rod and Your staff, they*
> *comfort me.*
> —PS. 23:4

Their beautiful, vibrant, clever, precious daughter was dying. They had had so many hopes for her, had prayed for her all her twenty-three years. Now she lay helpless against the cancer in her body.

Vicki was devastated when she heard her brother had been killed in a car accident. Jerry had been her soul mate, and her best friend—the one she could talk to when the injustice of caring for their alcoholic mother became too much. Now he was gone!

How do we face the agony of death, the shock of it, the finality of it? God alone is sufficient to see us through. His presence is real. His acceptance of our tears and desolation brings healing. God is the comfort giver and strength provider in life's deepest valleys. His care is often felt through the loving support of faithful friends who accept our grief, who see that our needs are taken care of, and who don't expect us to be further along in the grieving process than we are. In the process, we often discover as we work through our grief that God has equipped us with a capacity to handle adversity and tragedy that we didn't know we had.

Thank you, God, that when I face death I do not see a hopeless end, but an endless hope. Let me demonstrate that hope in my attitudes today.

J.M.C.

*For godly sorrow produces repentance leading to
salvation, not to be regretted; but the sorrow of the
world produces death.* —2 COR. 7:10

One sign of an altered lifestyle is a feeling of sorrow
about our past. Whenever we discover that our styles
of communication or our habits are destructive and
learn new patterns, we usually feel guilty. We see our
poor judgment clearly and wish we had never made
those mistakes.

It is good to talk about those guilty feelings, but not
to agonize over or dwell on them. We cannot change
our past, but we can change our present lifestyles by
learning from our past. Dwelling on the guilt, however,
can cause us to return to the old behaviors. It is like
getting stuck on a fence with one foot on either side.
Continuing to labor over the past keeps us from climbing over the "fence" and moving onward. Instead, we
must turn our bodies and minds toward the future.
Rather than just standing there and looking back, we
need to start walking away from our old behaviors, regrets, and guilty feelings. God is ready to forgive us,
and He wants us to move on by forgiving ourselves,
using good judgment, and practicing new ways to live.

*Lord, may I admit my mistakes and release my regrets to you so I can
move on to a healthier lifestyle.*

J.L.M.

Since you have purified your souls in obeying the truth through the Spirit in sincere love of the brethren, love one another fervently with a pure heart.
—1 PETER 1:22

Laura, one of my clients, shared a dream with me: "I dreamed I was acting in a series of plays. One woman always showed up early for the shows, bringing a tape recorder. She listened to every word of every play. When there was a comedy, she laughed. When there was a sad drama, she cried. And she came to every one of the plays, not a select few. Then one day some people came and took all the costumes away. They took the curtains down. They even removed the scripts. The only thing left was a bare stage and a lone actress—me."

Laura looked at me with tears in her eyes and said, "Well, tape machine lady, no one has ever sat through every act of every play before. What are you going to do now that I have no costumes, no script, and no curtain to hide behind? I'm just me, and I'm not sure who I am." With tears of my own, I told her, "We are now ready for the real show to begin."

I felt deeply privileged to be involved in helping Laura learn to accept herself as she is. But the privilege of helping others accept themselves is not reserved for therapists. Laura is doing it, too, as she learns to become more accepting of the people in her life—loving them with a sincere, unconditional love.

Do I love my family and friends for who they really are—without the curtains, costumes, or script?

J.E.M.

My heart is severely pained within me.
—PS. 55:4

A Chinese woman had lost her only son in an accident. She thought the grief would suffocate her. So she went to the holy man in her village and asked him what she could do to ease the pain. He suggested that she go out and find a mustard seed from a home that had no pain.

The first place she came to was a mansion. Thinking, "They couldn't possibly have any problems here," she knocked on their door. "Pardon me," she said, "I need to get a mustard seed from a home that has no problems in order to ease my pain." "Oh," the man at door replied, "you came to the wrong house." And with that he started to tell her all his problems. "Well," she thought, "I've had some experience with problems. It will help this man if I listen." So she listened awhile before continuing her quest.

You probably know what happened. No matter where she went, to the rich or to the poor, she couldn't find her mustard seed. But she did find the truth that, when we help others, somehow our pain lessens. A dear friend of mine, who lost her husband a year ago, learned that truth as well. She told me that when she is tempted to debilitating grief, she just "pushes her walls out." That is, she reaches out to someone else who is also in pain, and they comfort each other.

Lord, help me "push my walls out" when my "heart is severely pained."

J.M.C.

> *Remove from me the way of lying,*
> *And grant me Your law graciously.*
> —PS. 119:29

I must be kind to all people" said Jerri. But as Jerri kept talking, it became clear that she took this to mean she had to do what others wanted in order to get their approval. I started thinking about how we all tend to take a simple truth and then add our own set of rules and regulations to it. We develop a clouded perspective.

As Jerri began exploring her attitudes and feelings, she began to realize that she felt a lot of anger and resentment toward a couple of the people in her life, especially Sara. But surely she couldn't be mad at Sara! She was a godly woman, a strong leader at church. Jerri told herself, "I must have made these feelings up." But her husband helped her see that the anger came from following her twisted definition of being kind. She would do anything Sara asked—and swallow her resentment. Jerri's husband pointed out that she needed to set appropriate boundaries with Sara.

Two months later, Jerri felt much better because she had been able to tell Sara no a few times. She and Sara had actually become better friends, and she found that Sara respected her more. Jerri now reads her Bible and asks God to help her see things through His eyes instead of her own clouded vision.

Father, help me to be able to see the truth, so that the lies I have clung to won't destroy me.

J.L.M.

For I say, through the grace given to me, to everyone who is among you, not to think of himself more highly than he ought to think, but to think soberly, as God has dealt to each one a measure of faith.
—ROM. 12:3

Self-esteem has been defined as how you feel about yourself. If I came to your home for a visit today and asked you to write down all of your good qualities, how long would it take you to come up with your list? What if I asked you to list all of your negative or bad qualities. Which question would give you the most trouble?

Women in recovery usually have self-esteem work to do. Low self-esteem breeds victimization, distorted and ruined relationships, and failure in the workplace.

A group of boys got together to form a club. They talked about what the rules for their club would be and, after much thought, came up with this list:

1. Nobody act too big.

2. Nobody act too small.

3. Everybody act medium.

I like those rules. Healthy self-esteem frees us to be "medium"—without superiority or inferiority feelings, honest about weaknesses and proud of strengths, and secure in the worth that comes from being a child of God.

My goal today will be to see myself as God sees me and to love myself anyway—like God loves me.

J.E.M.

Bear one another's burdens and so fulfill the law of Christ.
—GAL. 6:2

Susan was in a state of shock. She had arrived home from work to find a note from her husband, saying that he was in love with someone else and wanted out of the marriage. Susan was devastated by this turn of events. She had been totally in the dark about her husband's involvement with another woman. But she was also determined not to face this crisis alone. She phoned five of her closest friends and asked them to meet her for lunch. She looked her friends in the eye and told them of the devastation she was feeling. She confessed her feelings of abandonment, anger, shock, and mistrust. She also told her friends that she couldn't make it through this crisis without their support. She asked them to agree to meet her for one breakfast a week for a year.

The Greek word translated "burden" in this passage refers to a giant boulder. Some of life's realities really do feel like crushing boulders—and we cannot carry them alone. Only when we allow our friends to help us carry our boulders can we make it. We really do need each other.

If I have a "boulder" in my life, Lord, help me risk vulnerability so that someone else can help me carry it. Keep my eyes and ears alert to opportunities to help others carry their crushing loads.

J.M.C.

Leave your fatherless children,
I will preserve them alive;
And let your widows trust in Me.
—JER. 49:11

Just when we think we're at a point where we can carry on after being widowed, small occurrences may trigger a sudden wave of grief. It may happen the first time we take the car in to be fixed and need a ride to work or back home. Or it may come when we are in the middle of fixing dinner, run out of milk, and need someone to run to the store. These unexpected reminders of loss can bring an outpouring of tears and a sense of utmost sadness.

When Jan looks back to that time in her life, she realized God was the only one who got through to her. At first, she had blamed Him for "taking" Robert. She had tried to avoid Him and deprive herself of the comfort she so desperately desired. Finally, however, she turned back to God, and He comforted her. She felt a security in Him through reading scripture and meditating on it. Jan now shares with other widows how important it is to stay in fellowship with the Lord. She tells women to go ahead and talk to God about their anger—He knows their heart anyway—instead of running from Him. She tells them that her loneliest hours were the ones she sat rocking by herself, but her deepest comfort came when she leaned on the Lord.

Lord, I hurt and need you to comfort me because I've separated myself from you. Please forgive me for my bitterness and be a part of my grieving process.

J.L.M.

> *Now to Him who is able to do exceedingly*
> *abundantly above all that we ask or think,*
> *according to the power that works in us.*
> —EPH. 3:20

One of the biggest problems with a woman's image of God is confusing Him with her earthly father. We find in counseling that the more godly the client's father was, the easier it is for the client to trust and rely on God. But the reverse is also true. Women with inadequate fathers have a hard time relating to a heavenly Father.

Many women have grown up with no father, or their father was uncaring and detached. But God knows when each of us gets up and goes to bed. He knows every word we speak and even understands our every thought.

Earthly fathers who are inconsistent produce insecure children; their children can't depend on them. But God is consistent. He is never moody, always faithful, never changing. We can be secure in Him.

Many women felt, while growing up, that their fathers were too busy to meet their needs. But God is a close father. He is never too busy to listen to our prayers and sympathize with our pain.

Many earthly fathers are incapable of carrying out their parental responsibilities. But God is completely capable to fulfill every obligation. He is a kind of parent every child longs for—and every one of us can trust.

God is everything I need in a father. I will learn to trust in Him.

J.E.M.

This is the day which the Lord has made;
We will rejoice and be glad in it.
—PS. 118:24

Today is God's good gift to us. What are we going to do with it? Are we going to fill it with regrets about the past or hope for the future? Are we going to fill it with bitterness or kindness? Are we going to face it with griping or gratitude?

Life is a sacred gift. If you don't believe that, take the time to talk to someone who is dying! Those who are facing death so often tell us not to fear that our life will end so much that it will never begin. True, life isn't always what we want, but it's what we've got.

Let's make the most of it today. Take the time to smell the flowers, to touch a child, to reach out in love. Take time to laugh, to feel, to create, to be quiet, to be grateful, to learn. Exercise your soul emotionally and spiritually. Surprise someone. Work hard, play hard— be young at heart.

Take the time to live!

Lord, help me to live today as if I were going to die tomorrow.
                                                          J.M.C.

Thus says the Lord:
"Cursed is the man who trusts in man
And makes flesh his strength,
Whose heart departs from the Lord."
—JER. 17:5

Margaret was very depressed because she had been rejected in so many relationships. She had been rejected by her father because she wasn't the son he wanted. Then, after twelve years of marriage and two children, Margaret's husband left her for a younger woman. She felt as if something must be wrong with her—maybe God didn't want her either. She had been depending on her husband to meet her needs and he was no longer around, so she was totally lost.

At church, Margaret heard today's scripture, and the words stuck in her mind. She realized she had been trusting and looking to "man" for support and validation instead of allowing herself to receive the free gift of God's love. Determined to change, she began exploring God's love and trying to apply it to her life. Then one night several months later, she awoke in the middle of the night and realized that for the first time she was able to look at herself as God would. She felt so much understanding, compassion, and love for herself. After all, God knew all the facts about her, and He still loved her. Margaret realized that deep inside she had a quiet strength that God had placed in her and that God had been with her through all her suffering.

Lord, help me to stop the curse I have placed on myself by "trusting in man" instead of your free gift of love.

J.L.M.

God longs to be gracious to you;
he rises to show you compassion.
—ISA. 30:18 NIV

Grace means getting what we need instead of what we deserve—and God offers such grace to us freely. His grace is unconditional, unlimited, and also unending. And as today's verse shows, God longs to be gracious to us.

What has grace done in our lives? God's saving grace has taken away all our guilt (Eph. 1:7–8). Salvation is based not on our works, but on God's grace and mercy. And grace reshapes our lives daily, freeing us from our pasts to live in the future. God's grace takes away the hurt in our lives and helps us in time of need (Heb. 4:16).

Although God's grace is freely offered, accepting it is our choice. God never forces grace on us; we can choose instead to live with our guilt. If we do, we may develop a bitter spirit (see Heb. 10:15). A real key to receiving grace is to be humble enough to admit we need it (James 4:7).

What can we do with grace, now that we have it? We can learn to be gracious to others, as God has been to us. We can also daily determine to share the story of God's grace.

I will walk *grace today.*
I will talk *grace today.*
I will accept *God's grace today.*

J.E.M.

*Take heed to yourselves. If your brother sins against
you, rebuke him; and if he repents, forgive him.
And if he sins against you seven times in a day,
and seven times in a day returns to you, saying,
"I repent," you shall forgive him.*

—LUKE 17:3–4

Richard didn't know how much more he could take
from Karyl. Last night he had endured a torrent of bitter words, a long list of grievances, and a catalog of all
his faults. Now Karyl was glaring at him, and the tirade
was about to begin again. Richard put up his hand.
"Honey," he said, "if you're going to scream at me, we
can't discuss this. I'll be in the other room until you
calm down, and then we can talk." With that he went
into their bedroom and shut the door, leaving Karyl
alone with her fury.

Forgiveness and reconciliation are two different
things. If people abuse us, we are to limit the abuse by
speaking the truth in love. Richard did a great job of
this with Karyl. Even though we are open to reconciliation, we don't willingly put ourselves in the path of
abuse again until we see that the other person has
truly repented. This doesn't mean a cheap "I'm sorry"
that invites the abuse to happen again in ten minutes.
Instead, the abuser must choose to turn away from the
abusive behavior. Our part is to put away all judgment
and condemnation, to forgive in our hearts and be
ready to reconcile when the time comes.

*Lord, help me have a heart for forgiveness even while protecting my-
self from abuse.*

J.M.C.

The Lord is my strength and song,
And He has become my salvation;
He is my God, and I will praise Him;
My father's God, and I will exalt Him.
—EX. 15:2

Marilee was exhausted. She worked all day as a bank teller. Then she headed home to help with her two boys' homework, cook, clean, and then start all over again the next day. Her husband, Doug, helped, but his load was heavy too. There just didn't seem to be enough hours in the day.

Marilee began to pray about her long days and to talk with her husband about the situation. Then she realized she could prioritize her day to be better prepared mentally and emotionally. She decided that, no matter how busy her day was, her relationship with Christ had to come first. Her relationship with her family would come second and her job next. She had been trying to keep everything perfectly balanced, which was impossible. Marilee began to start each day with prayer and Bible study. This practice gave her a peace of mind that enabled her to move more calmly throughout the day. In addition, as Marilee directed her thoughts toward the Lord, her daily tasks became less of a priority and the people in her days became more of a priority.

Lord, help me remember my priorities. Putting you first in my life will give me strength through the hectic times.

J.L.M.

> *And after my skin is destroyed, this I know,*
> *That in my flesh I shall see God.*
> —JOB 19:26

Life should be easy" is a prevalent belief even among Christians. Many people search constantly for an easy way to get through life. They are disappointed time after time as they are reminded daily that life is usually difficult and often excruciating.

Today a promise in the Bible that we can cling to is from Romans 8:28: "And we know that all things work together for good to those who love God, to those who are the called according to His purpose." God has never promised that we won't have trials in this life. God has promised that He'll turn the bad things into good if we press on through the pain to find the good. And He has made it clear that the greatest good will come *after* our earthly life is over.

Joni Erickson Tada is a good example for all of us. When she was paralyzed as a teenager, she believed God's promise that things could still work together for the good. She worked through and moved beyond the "life should be easy" lie. Joni came from a low point of bitterness to a place of complete surrender to God's way. As a result, her life has touched millions. And she looks forward to an eternity in which she will leave her wheelchair and rejoice in God's infinite goodness.

My life as a believer consists of an infinite number of years of perfect joy and love—but starting off with seventy or eighty years of intermittent pain. I can live with that!

J.E.M.

He heals the brokenhearted
And binds up their wounds.
—PS. 147:3

Ben Hooper, a two-term governor of Tennessee, used to tell this story about his humble beginnings and the preacher who changed his life:

> I was born an illegitimate child. I never knew who my parents were. I had no friends. I always felt as if people were talking behind my back, wondering who my parents were.
>
> One day a new preacher came to town, so I went to check him out. He was good, so I went back again and again. But I always arrived late and left early so I wouldn't have to talk with anyone.
>
> Then one Sunday I was so caught up in the message I forgot to leave. Before I knew it, people were in the aisles and I was trapped. Suddenly I felt a big hand on my shoulder. It was the preacher man. He looked right at me and asked, "Who are you, son? Whose family do you belong to?" I shivered when I heard those questions. But before I could answer, the preacher said, "I know whose family you're in. There's a distinct family resemblance. You're a child of God."

Lord, make me aware of who I am in you. Thank you for healing my wounds by putting me in a healthy family—your family.

J.M.C.

*Greatly desiring to see you, being mindful of your
tears, that I may be filled with joy.*
—2 TIM. 1:4

Cathy's days were models of organization. She was
active in her work and in all her children's school activities. She and her husband spent time together.
Their life was full and rich, if not especially joyful.
Then her small daughter had to be hospitalized. Cathy
started spending hours, days, then weeks at the hospital. Her busy schedule fell by the wayside. And for the
first time in years, she began to spend quality time
with God. She began to see how, although she had
been really efficient at daily living, she had been missing something. She had not been sharing God's love
and His eternal gift with others.

At the hospital, Cathy began to go around visiting
other children, playing with them, telling them stories,
and sharing God's love. As her daughter got better,
they both began sharing and giving their time. For the
first time, Cathy felt the special joy of staying close to
her heavenly Father. Instead of just spending time
making sure everything is in order, she was spreading
God's Word and taking time to show His love.

*God, please forgive me for turning away from your love for so long. I
want to spend "quality time" with you and know the joy of sharing
your love.*

J.L.M.

*Now to Him who is able to keep
  you from stumbling
And to present you faultless
Before the presence of His glory
  with exceeding joy. . . .*
—JUDE 1:24

People are not naturally moral. History proves it, our own nature shows it, and the Bible tells us from cover to cover that stumbling is part of our natural condition. History, for example, is filled with wars, greed, deceit, and hatred. Our present generation has witnessed the Holocaust, the threat of nuclear war, public corruption, private betrayal. And if we really look within ourselves, we have to admit to self-destructive habits and tendencies. Physically, we often don't take care of ourselves as well as we could. Mentally, we view ourselves with such distortion that we often need professional help to sort truth from error. Morally, we take shortcuts, hold grudges, tell lies—on a small scale if not a large one.

Christ would not have had to die if people were basically good. But when we depend on Christ's substitution for us, we do become good in His sight. We read in today's verse that some day Christ will introduce us to the Father as faultless—and He'll do it with great joy.

Today I will visualize Christ as proudly introducing me to the Father—and rejoice that His sacrifice makes it possible for me to be good.

J.E.M.

> *A wholesome tongue is a tree of life,*
> *But perverseness in it breaks the spirit.*
> —PROV. 15:4

Christi was mortified. When she got up to give a speech in English class, her mind went absolutely blank. Terrified, she looked out at a sea of faces. She wanted to sink through the floor. Unfortunately, she had to stay around to hear her teacher say, "Well, I just hope you're not planning on being a public speaker!"

Public humiliation hurts. And this was not the first time Christi had experienced it. At age three, she had wet her underpants at a family gathering. With everyone watching, her mother had shaken her head and said, "Christi, I can't believe you wet your pants again. How could you? You're such a baby." Christi had felt deeply shamed. From that point on, in fact, she had come to see herself as fundamentally and irreparably deficient.

When we as adults have to reprimand or correct children, we need to separate the children's performance from their personhood. Then it is crucial that, even if we criticize the performance, we praise the children themselves. When our children made a mistake or a foolish decision, we taught them to give themselves an imaginary kiss or pat on the back before facing their consequences. We wanted them to be able to fail without ever thinking they were failures.

Lord, teach me to speak with a wholesome tongue as I separate the person from the performance. And help me to see myself as a person of value, even when I've made a mistake.

J.M.C.

My soul melts from heaviness;
Strengthen me according to Your word.
—PS. 119:28

As the compulsive overeater gives up control of her compulsion, she begins to experience feelings that have been numbed by her food binges. Living with those feelings is frightening.

The overeater must come to understand that she has been feeding something other than hunger pains; she has also been attempting to feed emotional pains and fill unmet longings. Stuffing oneself with food is an effective way of hiding from hurt, anger, rejection, or some other painful emotions. As the cycle stops, the person is faced with addressing her feelings head on. And unless she finds a healthy way of coping with those emotions, she is likely to fall back on her old habits or to develop another addiction.

This is a crucial point in recovery. The compulsive overeater must learn how to express emotions through talking, writing, or praying instead of eating. If she can find a way to face her feelings, she will be on her way down the track to recovery.

Father, I pray you would guide me as I learn how to express my feelings and deal with all my emotions without bingeing and purging.

J.L.M.

*Therefore a man shall . . . be joined to his wife,
and they shall become one flesh.* —GEN. 2:24

What you see is what you get."

"If you don't like me the way I am, leave."

"You knew what I was like when you married me."

All these statements are part of the "I shouldn't have to change" lie. Today's verse says that when we marry, we become one flesh. To do that, we obviously have to change. And change must happen if we want to grow in our relationships to each other. Change doesn't mean that one partner puts his or her brain into neutral and lets the other partner do all the thinking. But a beautiful change occurs in a marriage when each partner humbly sees characteristics in his or her partner that are worth emulating. For instance, if one member of the couple is a listener and one is a talker, wonderful things can happen when they observe these strengths in each other. The talker learns to talk a little less and the listener learns to listen less and talk more. They grow together as one complements the other.

Growing in any relationship means changing. How beautiful a newborn baby is—but how sad it would be if the new baby never changed its appearance. And how sad it would be if a new relationship just aged, but never grew and changed.

Growth means change. What would be a reasonable goal for change in my own life today?

J.E.M.

Commit your way to the Lord,
Trust also in Him,
And He shall bring it to pass.
—PS. 37:5

I think that I've lost my faith in God," Sue stammered. "I accepted Him as my Savior when I was a little child, but now I don't know what to believe. He isn't here anymore. Why?" With that she yanked the drapes closed and slumped into a chair.

Sue's cancer was spreading rapidly. She was in her mid-thirties—a loving wife, the involved mother of two little girls, a wonderful friend. And now we were trying to face her death together. Questions and thoughts kept tumbling out. "Who will take care of my daughters? Who will they go to when they have a heartache? Can Dave make it on his own? I won't be there for birthdays, graduations, weddings, grandchildren. I feel cheated. And on top of all this"—she wheeled and spoke sharply—"God isn't here."

I just held my trembling friend in silence. I had no answers. Suddenly through the drawn drapes came one tiny shaft of sunlight, and I had an idea. "Sue," I said softly, "the fact that you've pulled the drapes shut doesn't mean the sun isn't shining." I could feel Sue relax in my arms. "I see," she said, "I see."

Lord, thank you that your constant presence lights up my life. I commit myself to you today.

J.M.C.

> *A man's pride will bring him low,*
> *But the humble in spirit will retain honor.*
> —PROV. 29:23

When I begin to look around at how much of myself interferes with my walk with God, I wonder how I am going to begin to receive all God wants to give me. This thought came into my mind after a minor incident this morning. A colleague made a joke about my being late for work. This hurt my feelings. But instead of letting the other person know how I felt, I got nervous. I started thinking of ways to justify myself.

I know better! I know I am worthy because I am a child of God. And I know the best way to settle a misunderstanding with a friend. But my pride and my need to prove my self-worth got in the way of my good judgment.

It amazes me how pride rears its ugly head over the most petty events. To remain humble in spirit, I must renew my mind daily. I must seek God with all my heart, seeking to know Him. And I can't begin to know God in this way until I have been completely broken of self. When I come to the end of all my own resources, all my strength—when all I have is God's love and strength—then I catch a glimpse of His love.

Oh Lord, protect me from pride and self-justification. Help me to be broken of self, so that you can reveal your love to me.

J.L.M.

The Spirit Himself bears witness with our spirit that
we are children of God. —ROM. 8:16

Self-worth is best built on how God sees us. God knows everything about us, and He loves us more than anyone on earth ever could. When we begin to understand God's view of who we are, we will then feel free to accomplish the things God wants us to accomplish with our lives. We live in a world that yells, "Dress for success. Dress to impress. If you have it, flaunt it; if you don't, fake it. Look out for number one." But God tells us that building our self-worth on people and accomplishments is like the foolish man who built his house upon the sand (see Matt. 7:24–27). The wise man built his house upon the rock, and that's where our self-worth will be built when we accept God's view of us.

Southern California, where I live, is full of people trying to impress others and to prove that they are somebody. We don't have to do that. God is already impressed with us. We already are somebody—His children. And He has equipped each of us to accomplish His plan for our lives today.

I will rethink my schedule for today, eliminating those activities designed to impress men but keeping those that will truly impress God.

J.E.M.

> *A word fitly spoken is like*
> *apples of gold*
> *In settings of silver.*
> —PROV. 25:11

Once a year we have a triathlon in the area where I live. In this grueling competition, men and women bike for forty kilometers, swim one and a half kilometers, then run ten kilometers. Spectators usually line the route. As competitors pass them, they yell out encouraging words: "Keep going!" "You can do it!" "Just a little further!" I've been told by competitors that those words give them a fresh burst of energy. Encouragement is such an upper.

By contrast, discouraging words become a self-fulfilling prophecy. Eve grew up in a home where she was constantly criticized. *Clumsy, awkward, dumb, lazy, fat,* and *timid* were words used to describe Eve on a regular basis. The verbal bombardment never let up, and Eve's spirit was eventually broken. She really believed the distorted image that her parents reflected to her—and she lived up to that image.

Words are so powerful. They can be used to encourage, affirm, and build up or they can tear down, discourage, and destroy. Build up or tear down—the choice is ours.

Lord, help my words today to reflect hope, love, and encouragement to the people in my life. Help me remember that it doesn't take a lot of muscle to give a heart a lift.

J.M.C.

For He satisfies the longing soul,
And fills the hungry soul with goodness.
—PS. 107:9

Elaine sat in the waiting room at the hospital, picking at her nail polish and feeling both happy and resentful. At the moment, Elaine's younger sister was delivering her third child. Forty-one-year-old Elaine had never been married and was unable to bear children.

Elaine used to blame God for her condition. She also used to sabotage any relationship that started to get serious. But after her last breakup, Elaine realized something was wrong. She had always told people that her relationships didn't work out because she couldn't have any children. But maybe they failed because she wouldn't accept herself or allow people to accept her!

Elaine began to pray that she could accept herself for who she was. She then began acting upon her prayer by taking an initiative to develop friendships. As Elaine began to accept herself, she no longer pushed others away, and she wasn't so worried about not having children. Through God's love and guidance, Elaine enjoys her new self and feels excited about living without the continual fear of rejection. She even believes she is worthy of another's love for her. And she has begun making inquiries about taking in a foster child.

Lord, help me accept myself and my limitations, then reach out to others.

J.L.M.

> *Let each one give . . . not grudgingly or of*
> *necessity; for God loves a cheerful giver.*
> —2 COR. 9:7

Giving is a perplexing problem for women in recovery. It seems like we've been giving too much our whole lives, and that doesn't feel good at all. So, what are we supposed to do, quit giving? No! We must re-learn *how* to give! So many times in the past, we gave with an outlook of wanting others to see how much we were giving so they would applaud and ask admiringly, "How could you ever give so much?" Or we would give because we thought we had to in order to be loved—but resented the giving.

God loves a cheerful giver. Let's search our hearts and consult with wise friends and decide daily how much we can give of ourselves to others. Our goal in giving should be to do it willingly, not reluctantly or under pressure. Hopefully, we can retrain our heart feelings so that we can decide from our hearts what to give cheerfully and joyfully.

We're also told in 1 Chronicles 29:18–20 to give expectantly. This is a confusing thought for some of us. Perhaps it will help to think of the differences between "expect" and "demand." To *expect* God to give back to us as we have given is to do as He has told us. To *demand* that God give certain things to us because we have given to Him will certainly end in disappointment.

When we give to God today, we can expect to receive His gifts in our tomorrows.

J.E.M.

*Let no corrupt communication proceed out of your
mouth, but what is good for necessary edification,
that it may impart grace to the hearers.*
—EPH. 4:29

A question we need to ask ourselves before we communicate is, "Who is going to benefit from what I'm going to say?" If the answer is "no one," then perhaps the words would be better left unsaid.

Men often joke about how much women talk, and yet I haven't run into a man who believed a woman talked too much if she was in the process of telling him how wonderful he was. Not all communication can be direct affirmation, however. There are times when we have to speak what is true rather than what sounds good to the person we are in relationship with. But because so many of us in recovery have been injured by thoughtless words, we are often afraid of confrontation. We don't know how to confront in a loving way.

I believe great communication is a combination of truth, tact, and timing. Contemplate before you communicate; don't just blurt out your frustrations. Someone has said that tact is the ability to close your mouth before someone else wants to. Another way to look at it is making a point without making an enemy. An important question to ask in order to judge timing is "Can this person hear this truth at this time?" Truth and tact and timing make for great communication.

Lord, help me to offer truth, tact, and timing so that other people can hear the message I am attempting to communicate.

J.M.C.

> *This is the message which we have heard from*
> *Him and declare to you, that God is light and in*
> *Him is no darkness at all. If we say that we have*
> *fellowship with Him, and walk in darkness, we lie*
> *and do not practice the truth.*
>
> —1 JOHN 1:5–6

During those times when I see God all around, it's hard to comprehend how at other times I can feel totally alone. Scripture says that when I accepted Christ, I began walking in light. So when darkness hits, I feel totally abandoned and afraid. If God's purpose is to use me to further His kingdom, why would He allow me to feel such darkness?

Then the answer comes to me. If I'm in the dark, it's because I have strayed off on a path of my own choosing, seeking my own gain. I know this because 1 John 1:5 says that God is light and in Him is no darkness at all.

I know that my darkness isn't of God. But I also know God is by me in this time of darkness. I thank Him for giving me an eternal perspective by allowing me a glimpse of what hell is like. I pray that no one would ever have to experience that kind of eternity. And I realize that experiencing this kind of pain gives me compassion and understanding for others in pain. It also teaches me to be vulnerable with others in His kingdom, who comfort me and help me return to the light.

Thank you, Lord, for being the Light that helps me not to believe the lies of the world, but hold on to the truth.

J.L.M.

Let patience have its perfect work, that you may be perfect and complete, lacking nothing.
—JAMES 1:4

One of the hardest things we have to do in life is learning to live with and love ourselves in a healthy way. How can we do this? One of the keys is patience.

Patience is a virtue few of us have enough of, especially with ourselves. "Be patient; God isn't finished with me yet" is a saying we should repeat to ourselves daily.

It helps to keep an eternal perspective. We won't be "finished" in this lifetime. But with God's help, we can keep headed in that direction, especially as we persevere in recovery. And we can take comfort in His promise that "the God of all grace, who called us to His eternal glory . . . [will] perfect, establish, strengthen, and settle" us. With that kind of promise, we can afford to be patient.

God wants us to acknowledge His part in our lives and be grateful for the good we see. But our tendency is to judge ourselves by how far we have to go rather than how far we've come. Let's thank God daily for the progress we're making—and resolve to keep moving, with His love and guidance.

Today I will try to be patient with myself and others, knowing that God is patient with me. I will thank Him for the good work He is doing in my life.

J.E.M.

> *Therefore we do not lose heart. Even though our outward man is perishing, yet the inward man is being renewed day by day.* —2 COR. 4:16

It takes me longer to get ready every morning than it used to. Have you noticed that, too? When I travel, my heaviest suitcase has my beauty supplies in it. A friend of mine says that "as the years zoom by, I begin to think that I'm in a war to keep my mind together, my body functioning, my teeth in, my hair on, and my weight off."

The truth is there comes a time when each of us has to face the physical realities that growing older brings. Yet even as we face these changes and limitations, we can be growing stronger in our hearts and souls.

As I pull away daily to be quiet and to focus on Christ instead of my circumstances, I find myself refreshed. As I fill my mind with God's Word, pray, and meditate, I am renewed. God grows in me an inner quietness and strength.

When I try to be beautiful independently of God's resources, I put all my emphasis on externals. But the problem is that my exterior is showing the wear and tear of life. How much better if the effort I put into making myself look good is supported by an equally developed internal depth. If that happens, I will be a beautiful woman regardless of my age.

Today, Lord, help me put as much effort into developing my inner beauty as I do my outer beauty.

J.M.C.

Counsel is mine, and sound wisdom;
I am understanding, I have strength.
—PROV. 8:14

I'm just watching my weight." "You're supposed to exercise to be healthy." "I don't have any problems." Denial is a key component of anorexia nervosa. Even those who have developed severe malnutrition tend to deny that the weight loss is a danger. It usually takes months for an anorexic to even admit she has a problem. Then comes the long period of denying that the problem is directly related to family or personal struggles.

Healing cannot progress until denial is broken through and the "uncovering" stage begins. The anorexic must discover the emotional needs that lie behind her excessive dieting and exercise. She may have restricted her food intake because she felt that was the only thing she could control. Many anorexics have been sexually abused; others have grown up in perfectionistic or controlling homes.

Once the anorexic uncovers the pain behind her behavior and gives up her efforts to control, healing can begin. Emotional nourishment and physical nourishment combine to help the anorexic feel stronger, think more clearly, and understand herself better. Recovery is on its way.

Father, please break through my denial and help me see the root causes of my problem so I may try to resolve the issues and be the healthy individual you desire me to be.

J.L.M.

> *Do all things without murmuring and disputing.*
> —PHIL. 2:14

Have you ever been invited to a pity party? As children, we teased complainers by accusing them of doing that. Feeling excessively sorry for ourselves and sharing it with others is a common ailment of our society. We cry "unfair" when life throws us curves. We readily take on the martyr's role and complain that no one really appreciates us. We become cynical and try to convince others and ourselves that nothing will ever get better. We become perfectionistic with ourselves and others and conjure up unrealistic expectations, then complain when those expectations aren't met.

One of the most important tasks of recovery is learning to state our feelings honestly—but that's not the same as "complaining and disputing." So how can we hush the whiner, the martyr, the cynic and the perfectionist that live deep inside us? First, let's admit that our complaining spirit is a problem. Excess complaints are a way of ducking responsibility for our problems. Instead of complaining, we must own our problems—and then we can begin to solve them. In addition, we need to work toward an attitude of thankfulness instead of self-pity. God made us, loves us, and sent His Son to die for us. When we look at our lives from that perspective, it's hard to stay at a pity party.

I will ask God today to help me sort out my legitimate, assertive complaints from my excessive, demanding gripes.

J.E.M.

Casting all your care upon Him, for He cares for you.
                                    —1 PETER 5:7

Jesus Christ is such a healthy example of a care giver. When He deals with us, He comes alongside us. In fact, He became a human being and related to us as human beings. We didn't have to become more spiritual to reach Him. He became human to touch us.

When He was on earth, Jesus accepted His human limitations. He chose twelve disciples to assist Him in His work. He took time to rest, to eat, to relate with friends, and to renew Himself. He often would pull away to pray even when the people were pressuring Him to give more. When He did give to others, it was out of fullness rather than emptiness—out of love, not duty.

Jesus respects our boundaries. He never forces Himself on us, and He never pressures us to see things His way. He supports us and loves us even while He allows us to face the consequences of our choices. Because Jesus is this kind of a care giver, we feel enriched after being with Him, and our self-respect is increased.

Not only is this Jesus an incredible model for each of us as we give care to others, He is a trustworthy Lord on whom we can cast our burdens.

Jesus, today as I reach out to others in my life, help me to model my care giving after yours.

                                    J.M.C.

> *To the Lord our God belong mercy and forgiveness,*
> *though we have rebelled against Him.*
> —DAN. 9:9

In recovery, alcoholic moms usually carry excruciating guilt about the humiliating ways our children have seen us. We feel awkward about taking charge of the household and the discipline when our children have been the ones caring for us, our homes, and themselves. However, it is important to ask forgiveness from God and our families and to forgive ourselves. And it is never too late to offer the love and support our children crave.

Preparing our children by explaining the new changes helps them adjust. We can sit down and explain to the children that Mom has been ill, but is now recovering and ready to be their mother. This will help them understand why our behavior will be different. We can also assure them that we will be watching over them now instead of their watching over us. Most important, we want to let them know that we feel good about the changes, that God is pleased with us and that, with His help, we will continue to grow together.

Father, give me the courage to take care of my children after they have been used to caring for me.

J.L.M.

And forgive us our sins,
For we also forgive everyone
who is indebted to us.
—LUKE 11:4

One of the seemingly magic steps in counseling is the area of forgiveness. Depressions lift when the bricks of unforgiveness are thrown out of the "grudge back-pack" we all seem to carry around.

Two of the questions we frequently ask our clients are "Whom are you blaming?" and "Toward whom are you feeling bitter?" Blaming others or ourselves for our unhappiness puts us in a paralyzing position. We must see blame as a form of unforgiveness. Let's determine to throw away the "blame bricks" from our grudge backpack.

Bitterness is another load of bricks many of us carry. Do we keep score and hold onto our hurts? If we do, we're holding onto bitterness. The weight of "bitter-ness bricks" certainly keeps many women slowed down on the journey to good mental health. We can choose today to throw away the bricks of blaming and bitterness through forgiveness for ourselves and others.

I can only release bitterness and blame through continual, daily re-forgiveness.

J.E.M.

> *But when you do a charitable deed, do not let your*
> *left hand know what your right hand is doing, that*
> *your charitable deed may be in secret; and your*
> *Father who sees in secret will Himself reward you*
> *openly.*
> —MATT. 6:3–4

Years ago, when my husband was working on his doctorate, the Immigration Department told me I could not continue my teaching career because of my nationality. What a shock that was to our financial plans! Dave didn't qualify for Canadian student loans because he was studying out of the country, and he didn't qualify for American ones because he was a Canadian.

My husband was allowed to work twenty hours a week on campus; we took out a second mortgage on our house; and we lived off credit cards. But by the time we were entering the last year of Dave's program, we were heavily in debt and questioning whether we could hold on much longer.

One day we found a stamped letter with no return address on it in our mailbox. I opened it to find a typed Scripture passage and a check for one hundred dollars. Every month of that last year, the same gift arrived in the mail. The letter was never signed. To this day I have no idea who sent those hundred-dollar bills. God's love was made tangible in our lives through someone's generosity. But our desire to give to others increased because of those gifts.

William Wordsworth is quoted as saying that the "best portion of a good life" is the "little, nameless, unremembered, acts of kindness and of love."

J.M.C.

> *I have not spoken in secret,*
> *In a dark place of the earth;*
> *I did not say to the seed of Jacob,*
> *"Seek Me in vain";*
> *I, the Lord, speak righteousness,*
> *I declare things that are right.*
> —ISA. 45:19

The secret that separated us from friends and family made our relationships essentially dishonest. Bulimia is often totally hidden. No one may suspect the binge-ing and purging; frequently parents or even husbands don't have a clue. But God knew we had a problem and, even though we denied it, we knew.

Now that we are in recovery, the real test is trying to be honest with ourselves. This means admitting mistakes to ourselves, forgiving ourselves and asking for help. It means giving up on expecting others to read our minds and know what we need. No one should have to drag things out of us anymore; it is our responsibility to tell others what is bothering us or what we think, feel, or want.

Like any addiction, bulimia creates a false identity. Revealing the true us is scary but, if taken very slowly, results in the blessing of true intimacy. This is exciting since we don't have any big secret to hide anymore and we really want to be close to people. Just being able to be ourselves, with nothing to hide, is a new freedom.

Father, help me to develop intimacy by being honest about what I really think and feel with those you show me I can trust.

J.L.M.

> *The ear that hears the reproof*
> *of life*
> *Will abide among the wise.*
> —PROV. 15:31

We are wise when we learn from the experiences which we have in life, but we're even wiser when we can learn from someone else's experiences. Accepting criticism is one way of doing this.

Why do we resist criticism? Usually, pride is the core of the resistance. Pride makes us defensive and unteachable. And what is underneath pride? Usually severe insecurity lies beneath the veneer of pride. Before we can accept criticism, we need to examine who we are and acknowledge our underlying insecurity.

At the same time, we must also bear in mind that criticism is seldom totally true. Critics are only people, and there are no perfect people. We must keep in mind that all critics speak only from their own limited perspectives. But we can still learn and grow from imperfect criticisms if we will acknowledge that God teaches us through imperfect vessels. We must learn to sift out the truth from the criticism we receive and then let the rest go.

Learning from criticism is a wise thing, so I will keep my ears open for it today.

J.E.M.

And you, fathers, do not provoke your children to wrath, but bring them up in the training and admonition of the Lord. —EPH. 6:4

Anna sought counseling because she had just opened her home to a sister, who was relocating from a distant state, and her family. Watching her sister's interactions with the sister's children, Anna came face to face with her own childhood. Anna's mother and father had used cruel and unnecessary means of punishment. They had beat her with a broom, locked her out of the house, and forced her to crouch with her feet and hands touching the floor for hours at a time. But she had repressed these terrifying memories until she watched her sister punishing rather than disciplining her children.

Meeting with Anna, I realized afresh that when parents provoke their children to anger, the cycle can continue for generations. Because the children have no safe place to take the anger, it is swallowed, repressed. Perhaps it lies dormant for years. When those children become parents, however, they are all too likely to follow the only parenting model they have and to take out their anger on *their* children. The good news is that the vicious cycle can be broken. The better news is that if we choose not to provoke our children to anger, the cycle never has to begin.

Lord, help me face my own anger so that I will not provoke my own children to anger.

J.M.C.

> *If you abide in Me, and My Words abide in you,*
> *you will ask what you desire, and it shall be done*
> *for you.*
> —JOHN 15:7

As Dawn drove her little red Honda to her mother-in-law's house, she wondered what the day would bring. Dawn had been married to this woman's son for ten years, yet she still felt like an outsider. And when Dawn and her husband, Rick, announced their decision not to have children, her in-law relationships had become more tense.

Dawn felt anxious over confronting her mother-in-law, but she knew that she could no longer ignore the comments such as, "God meant for you to have children." Dawn was visiting her mother-in-law specifically to ask her to accept their decision and to accept Dawn herself. She prayed that the Lord would help the two of them begin a new relationship.

As Dawn and Rick's mother ate lunch together, Dawn groped for the right words to say. As she told her mother-in-law how hurt she was by her comments, Dawn realized that for the first time she was sharing her feelings with this woman. Amazingly, Rick's mother switched her tone when Dawn expressed her honest thoughts. She apologized for her words and admitted she had been rude to Dawn; she also admitted she felt rejected by Dawn. As the two shared their feelings, they made a decision to start being honest with each other and to treat each other with respect.

God, help me face the daily fears I try to avoid.

J.L.M.

*Whoever listens to me will dwell safely,
And will be secure, without fear of evil.*
—PROV. 1:33

Have you ever been in a storm at sea? My husband and I were on a ship once in the waters of the Mediterranean. The sea was supposed to have been calm, but something happened and the waters were tossing our ship (which held about four hundred people) back and forth as though it were a toy.

Some of the people on that boat felt fine. Not me—I was seasick. My husband went to the ship's doctor and got me some medicine. I took the medicine, rested a few hours, and felt much better.

Life's storms are like the storm that came up that night—unpredictable. We don't know how they will change our lives. The same storm might barely affect one person, yet throw another person completely off balance.

The storms of life are inevitable and impartial. Every person alive will encounter several. It's how we weather the storms that shows what kind of people we are.

Weathering the storms of life takes fortitude. But let's remember not to panic or be afraid. God is our captain. He's close, He cares, and He's in control.

I will think now about the current storms raging in my life, then listen for what my heavenly Captain would advise me to do for those situations.

J.E.M.

> *Teach me good judgment and knowledge,*
> *For I believe Your commandments.*
> —PS. 119:66

A baby enters this world with an emotional hand out-stretched; she needs love, comfort, food, and protection. When these needs are not met, the infant learns that the world is a terrifying and lonely place. She learns to distrust relationships and perhaps even to deny her need for them. Dana was such a baby. When she was born, her mother handed her to an older brother and never touched her again. The father was an absent workaholic. Any nurturing was done by the brother, who eventually abused Dana sexually.

Understandably, Dana had problems with relationships. As together we remembered the atrocities done to Dana, grieved them, and then slowly let go of them, Dana came to recognize her need for a healthy model of relationship. She attached herself to a Christian family who reached out to her, loved her, and acknowledged that her needs were legitimate. She began the process of learning to trust herself, others, and God. And the more she came to understand that God's ways are so different from our dysfunctional ways, the more she grew in knowledge and good judgment.

Lord, today I ask you to help me to exercise good judgment. Help me to react not out of my dysfunction, but out of love. Bring healthy models of your love into my life. Thank you, Jesus.

J.M.C.

The Lord God is my strength;
He will make my feet like deer's feet,
And He will make me walk on my high hills.
—HAB. 3:19

As I walk into my bedroom," said Dana, "I am struck by how delightful my room is in the early morning, with the leafy shadows dancing outside my window. I used to love morning as a child, and I was always excited to start a new day. . . ." Then, suddenly, Dana's mood switched. "It's so unfair!" she cried angrily. "I feel like I've been robbed of all the joy and love that filled me before. I want that back!"

Dana's cancer had only recently been diagnosed. Always strong in her faith and filled with exuberance, she now felt little but anger and resentment. But emotional healing was ahead for Dana. After allowing herself to grieve for her lost health, she began slowly to regain her enthusiasm for life. She made it a point to spend time with nature, and she also found many new ways to serve the Lord. Gradually she stopped being preoccupied with her illness and started sharing with other cancer patients about the joy and the life-sustaining gift of Jesus Christ. Now, years later, Dana has recovered from her cancer and continues to share with others about what life and God have to offer.

Lord, remind me through the beauty of your world and the love of your people that you are my strength for now and eternity.

J.L.M.

> *But God demonstrates His own love toward us, in*
> *that while we were still sinners, Christ died for us.*
> —ROM. 5:8

The "voice" speaks to me at the most inopportune times and in the most out-of-the-way places. Sometimes it screams, and sometimes it whispers. It's not always there, but I feel its presence much of the time. It's the voice that whispers, "You're not quite good enough."

As a woman in recovery, this voice is one I'm trying to silence. Daily I remind myself that God accepts me where I am and as I am. God doesn't expect perfection, and neither should I. Christ died because I wasn't perfect. Because of His sacrifice, God has forgiven every past, present, and future sin. I can rest in His love and calmly, not frantically, strive to accomplish what He wants me to accomplish today. If I'm good enough for God, through Christ, then I must be truly good enough.

That voice that is whispering "You're not quite good enough" is whispering a lie.

Perfection is only found in heaven. But because Christ died for me, I am good enough for God.

J.E.M.

*A man [woman] of great wrath will suffer
punishment;
For if you rescue him, you will have to
do it again.* —PROV. 19:19

A man told me about a scene he witnessed many times as he grew up. His father had an incredible temper. His favorite place to use it was at the kitchen table. Something would be missing from the meal, or someone would act in a way that wouldn't please him, and the man would pick up the ketchup bottle and throw it at the wall. It would break, and ketchup would splatter everywhere. For twenty-five years his wife would quietly get up from the table, pick up the broken glass, and wash up the ketchup.

One day at lunch, the father had another outburst. The ketchup bottle went flying. Everyone waited for mother to clean it up. Instead, she said, "We're having guests over for dinner tonight. I wonder what they will think of the new design on our kitchen wall." With that she got up quietly and left the room. For the first time in twenty-five years of marriage, the man got up and cleaned up the ketchup. His wife had stopped accepting his temper as her responsibility. She had decided that her husband must face his own consequences. If she continued to rescue him, she would have to do it again and again and again for the next twenty-five years.

Lord, help me to own what is my responsibility. Teach me to not get in the way of others' accepting their own responsibility.

J.M.C.

> *And our hope for you is steadfast, because we*
> *know that as you are partakers of the sufferings,*
> *so also you will partake of the consolation.*
> —2 COR. 1:7

One day, Angela was beaming because her husband had finally decided they could try to have another child. The next day, she was distraught because she had learned she couldn't have any more children. Years before, Angela had an abortion, and now she couldn't get it out of her mind. That must have been the child God would have wanted her to have—and she killed it for the sake of convenience.

Angela knew God had forgiven her long ago, but she couldn't forgive herself. In her pain, she started shutting all her emotions down; she couldn't accept love and comfort. But when Angela finally began to pray and to express her feelings to God, she realized that God had put very special people in her life and that she needed to reach out and receive comfort from them. She talked to her friend down the street, and she asked her husband to hold her as she cried. Angela discovered that God's comfort is all around us; she just needed to reach out and accept it. It took awhile, but Angela finally managed to forgive herself and to be content with the children she now has.

Lord, thank you for my friends and family who comfort me in my time of need. And help me to remember that you are always here for me too.

J.L.M.

Bear one another's burdens, and so fulfill the law of Christ.
—GAL. 6:2

The Greek word translated "burdens" in this verse actually has the meaning of "overburdens." And that more specific meaning can be a real help for women in recovery who are trying to achieve a balance between giving to others and saying no.

Imagine carrying a hundred-pound pack on your back. Someone your size comes along carrying a twenty-five pound pack and asks if you will take half the contents of her pack to carry on top of yours. Clearly, that's not appropriate.

We aren't asked to carry *all* of other people's burdens; we're asked to help them out when their load is just too much for them. We are also urged to seek help when our own burden becomes too much. A woman who is developing interdependence is a woman who is able to give help when it is truly needed and seek help when her own load becomes too much for her to carry.

God wants each of us to grow, and the burdens of our lives are His teaching tools. Let's daily ask ourselves if we are hindering others by bearing burdens God wants them to bear or hindering ourselves by putting the burden God wants us to carry on someone else's back.

Lord, give me the strength to carry the load you have given me, the compassion to help others with their overloads, and the humility to seek help when I really need it.

J.E.M.

> He who rebukes a man will find more
>   favor afterward
> Than he who flatters with the tongue.
>   —PROV. 28:23

Trust is always built through truth telling. Carmelle hadn't learned this lesson because she feared conflict. She would go along with anything her husband, John, said, even if she disagreed. For example, John might suggest that they go out to eat at a Mexican restaurant, and Carmelle would go along, even though she hated Mexican food. Carmelle would be miserable. And John would be in the dark; he didn't even know that Carmelle had yielded. Unfortunately, the same thing would happen with more important issues too.

Carmelle's philosophy was peace at any price, but she was unable to see that peace at any price is a counterfeit peace. Carmelle was not really avoiding conflict; she was just postponing a major eruption. When we "stuff" our feelings, our bitterness grows over time and finally spews all over the people in our life—even those who don't deserve to be confronted. How much healthier it is to speak the truth consistently in our relationships. Doing this may bring some initial discomfort. But intimacy can't happen without honesty, and honesty just can't be voiced without some conflict.

Lord, help me to express the truth in all my relationships today. Help me to speak honestly, deal honestly, and live honestly.

                                          J.M.C.

O my God, I trust in You;
Let me not be ashamed;
Let not my enemies triumph over me.
—PS. 25:2

So many people have told me about the difficulties they have standing up for the Lord. They often give the excuse that they don't want to offend anyone. But they feel ashamed because of their silence.

Consider this scenario. You go out to eat with a few people from work. Everyone orders wine, so you do, too, even though you usually don't drink. Right away you start asking yourself "Why?" Then, after dinner, they want to go to a movie, and they pick one with explicit sex and violence. You think it's exploitive, but you can't seem to open your mouth to object. The next day, you are ashamed and angry at yourself for not standing up for what you believe.

As we approach God and read the Scriptures about such situations, we realize that often we have trouble speaking up because we don't trust God to give us the boldness we need. When we get into such a situation again, we can overcome by reminding ourselves that we can trust in God to help us and that taking stands is a part of being an individual. Our opinion is just as important as someone else's. Often, expressing our views gives someone else the courage to express theirs. We also feel triumphant, unashamed, and self-assured.

Lord, please strengthen my trust in you. Help me to meditate on your Word at all times so I will not be ashamed about the principles you have instilled in me.

J.L.M.

*How much more shall the blood of Christ, who
through the eternal Spirit offered Himself without
spot to God, purge your conscience from dead
works to serve the living God.* —HEB. 9:14

One of the most damaging lies we can believe is,
"God's love must be earned." Many times this belief
has come from a background in which either the
church, the family, or both has taught in subtle and not-
so-subtle ways that our actions affect whether or not
God loves us. And we have fallen into the reverse trap
of thinking that the more we sin, the more God hates
us. The "tapes" in our head continually blast, "You
blew it again, so God hates you." Well, God does hate
sin, but He loves us sinners!

When we live with such a distorted ideal of God, we
either give up or back so far away from "religion" so
that we no longer try to live the Christian life. It is only
when we truly understand that God's love is unchang-
ing that we can begin to have the freedom God wants
us to have. God wants us to live a godly life, as free
from sin as possible. And His forgiveness makes it possible for us to try. When we sin, as God knows we will,
we can come to Him and ask for forgiveness. We will
still suffer the consequences of our sin, but God has
graciously provided a way for us to start over, again
and again.

*God's love can't be earned. He gives it freely when we accept the
provision Christ made on the cross.*

J.E.M.

*There is one who speaks like the piercings
  of a sword,
But the tongue of the wise promotes health.*
—PROV. 12:18

Our words can draw someone near or drive someone away. They can undergird or undercut, bolster or belittle, welcome or wound. Words demonstrate whether we are more concerned with kindness or correctness, reconciliation or record keeping, lecturing or listening. They also indicate whether we view our children, husbands, or friends as our enemies or our friends.

Our words betray, as little else does, the value we put on relationship. When an acquaintance arrives unexpectedly, when your husband appears without notice, when your children come home from school, what attitude do your words convey? When you are in the middle of an errand or a project, what do your words indicate to other people? These attitudes of ours are highly contagious. Like the measles, they reproduce themselves a hundredfold in our lives, and they spread into the world around us.

God, when you created me, you gave me a mouth that closes and ears that don't. Help me to remember that truth. Grant me wisdom as to when and how I open my mouth.

J.M.C.

> *And the apostles said to the Lord, "Increase*
> *our faith."*
> —LUKE 17:5

If the Lord has been faithful to reveal His promises to me and to prove His faithfulness, then why do I sometimes waiver in believing and trusting in Him? I often find that I hope in Christ's coming for eternal life but doubt that God came to bring me an abundant life *right now*. In other words, I tend to refuse God's grace for the present, accepting it only as part of a distant obscure future.

It's not uncommon to claim the promises of God but lack the faith to apply them to the here and now. We may truly believe that the Lord will provide for us . . . then hold back our tithe checks because we "need" it for something else. Or we may share with others about how God forgives everyone who asks, then refuse to accept His forgiveness when we sin against Him. But faith means believing God is here for us today! It means trusting in Him right now to help us through a meeting! It means praying in the car on the way to work instead of limiting prayer to church and bedside.

More than anything, faith is a continual process. That means I can rest assured that, even when my faith is lacking, God is with me—and I will get another chance tomorrow.

Father, thank you for being with me even when my faith waivers.

J.L.M.

All we like sheep have gone astray;
We have turned, every one, to his own way;
And the Lord has laid on Him the iniquity
  of us all.   —ISA. 53:6

We are so often guilty of pulling God down to a human level. When we sin, for instance, we think, "If I can't forgive myself, God can't forgive me either." Somehow, in our distorted way of thinking, we think that asking for forgiveness is not enough; we think we should continue to suffer. We commit a sin and then ask God to forgive us. God has done His part; He has "laid on [Jesus] the iniquity of us all." He forgives us. But we act like we don't really believe that is all there is to it. Consciously or unconsciously, we decide that we deserve to suffer more for the sin we've already confessed and asked forgiveness for. We go into periods of self-hatred and depression. We deplete our energy in unforgiveness toward ourselves. Then we have no energy left to begin again to live a healthy, balanced life, much less to reach out in love to others.

God is love, and He wants us to live a life filled with His love. God has provided a way for us to live that kind of life on this earth; He offers forgiveness to all who ask. If God forgives us, isn't it time to forgive ourselves?

God the Father already laid all our sins on Jesus, so I will just say "Thanks." I will not play God by continuing to punish myself once I have been forgiven.

                                        J.E.M.

> *I waited patiently for the Lord;*
> *And He inclined to me,*
> *And heard my cry.*
> *He also brought me out of a*
>   *horrible pit,*
> *Out of the miry clay,*
> *And set my feet upon a rock,*
> *And established my steps.*
> —PS. 40:1–2

A woman fell into a pit and couldn't get herself out.

A *subjective person* came along and said, "I feel for you, down there."

An *objective* person came along and said, "It's logical that someone would fall down there."

A *Pharisee* said, "Only bad people fall into a pit."

An *alcoholic* said, "What pit?"

A *news reporter* wanted the exclusive story on her pit.

A *fundamentalist* said, "You deserve your pit."

An *IRS* man asked if she was paying taxes on the pit.

A *self-pitying* person said, "You haven't seen anything until you've seen *my pit!*"

An *optimist* said, "Things could be worse."

A *pessimist* said, "Things will get worse!"

Jesus, seeing the woman, took her by the hand and *lifted her out* of the pit.

SOURCE UNKNOWN

Thank you, Lord, for being a God of action who lifts people up rather than dragging them down. You are my Rock. I am established on you.

J.M.C.

For I am persuaded that neither death nor life, nor angels nor principalities nor powers, nor things present nor things to come, nor height nor depth, nor any other created thing, shall be able to separate us from the love of God which is in Christ Jesus our Lord.   —ROM. 8:38–39

When I was a child, my dog Rudy and I were inseparable. He was just a black mutt I found as a stray, but I didn't care; I just loved him. Rudy and I walked together on my paper route for five years. Together we went to the store, to my friends' houses, on vacation. I even used to go scrunch up with him in his doghouse (he had an extra big one). I talked to him, trained him, and spoiled him.

When I turned sixteen, I gave up my paper route to take a "real job" at Burger King. I no longer took my friend walking every day, and I often was too busy to play with him. But that dog never forgot or was too busy for me. I knew he would sacrifice his life for me if he thought I was in danger.

Rudy was just a dog, but in a way his love gives me a picture of Christ's love for me. Rudy showed me an unfailing loyalty and unconditional love. He loved me even when I didn't deserve it and when I turned away from him. Rudy has since passed away. But I am thankful for all the ways he continues to remind me of God's special blessings and faithful love.

Lord, thank you for the ways you revealed yourself through your creation. More than that, thank you for loving me unconditionally and never giving up on me.

J.L.M.

> *But [Job] said to her, "Shall we indeed accept good*
> *from God, and shall we not accept adversity?" In*
> *all this Job did not sin with his lips.*
>
> —JOB 2:10

Some people come to God with the mistaken notion that He will protect them from pain and suffering while they're on earth. If we look around, however, we'll see some of the most godly people suffering through pain that is beyond our comprehension. Since the Fall, life has been and will continue to be difficult. Faith makes life on earth bearable, but faith does *not* take away the inevitable pain we experience as we journey through life.

Elisabeth Elliot deals with the problem of pain and suffering by asking us if we would like to be spiritual dwarfs. She then explains that growth comes through pain. We can choose to grow and learn from difficult situations, or we can decide that bitter is better and live as a spiritual dwarf.

Pain and suffering are an inevitable part of life. Let's learn from our pain, grow from it, and then go on in our walk with God as spiritually "bigger" people.

I will take God's hand when my life's journey takes me through some pain and suffering.

J.E.M.

*Man looks at the outward appearance, but the Lord
looks at the heart.*   —1 SAM. 16:7

Amy is a classic beauty. Her shiny black hair cas-
cades down her back. Her clothing is fashionable, her
makeup impeccable. I have watched heads turn as she
walks into our office complex. Amy has told me she
sometimes spends up to two hours getting ready to
leave her house. She will try on many outfits until she
settles on the "perfect" one. She is constantly sending
away for one beauty product after another. The result
of all her emphasis on her external beauty is quite
breathtaking.

One more thing about Amy: she is physically abusive in relationships. When she gets angry, she throws
frying pans, knives—and anything available at her husband. She pounds him with her fists and pulls his hair.
All is not quite so beautiful under Amy's surface.

In recovery, we learn that true beauty always begins
on the inside and moves outward. Our soul needs to
become beautiful through the love and forgiveness of
Jesus Christ washing over it. It needs to be nourished
through times of prayer, meditation, and quietness.
Then our external self begins to reflect the beauty of
what's inside.

---

*Lord, help me to live today from the inside out. Let my external ap-
pearance be just a reflection of my internal beauty.*

J.M.C.

> *Be kindly affectionate to one another with brotherly*
> *love, in honor giving preference to one another.*
> —ROM. 12:10

Both of my grandfathers passed away before I knew them. But a man who lived up the street from me has been a friend and a grandfather figure to me over the years. I remember going to his house as a child, along with my dog and other neighborhood children, to visit him and his dachshund. He would tell exciting stories about his days as foreman of the Warren Livestock Ranch in Wyoming. And he always had treats for the children and for my dog.

As I got older and passed by his house each day near the end of my paper route, he would invite me in to warm up from the cold—and, of course, for a snack. Sometimes he let me read the stories that would go into a book he was writing, or he would show me part of an arrowhead collection, or we would just visit.

I was honored to be this man's friend—and I still am. Now in his nineties, he continues to touch the lives of others. All the time he took with me showed me how much it means to children for us to give of ourselves. I will never forget his kindness, and I hope I can touch someone's life the way he touched mine.

Father, thank you for friends who have shown love to me. I ask that you will help me be the same kind of friend to others.

J.L.M.

How can you say to your brother, "Let me remove the speck from your eye"; and look, a plank is in your own eye?

—MATT. 7:4

I often ask my clients, "Describe the type of person you hate to be around." Connie's answer came quickly: "That's easy. I hate hypocrites!" The promptness of her answer didn't surprise me. Connie herself was struggling with an intense form of hypocrisy—a multiple personality disorder.

One of Connie's personalities smoked marijuana at a downtown park on Saturdays. On Sundays, another one of her personalities passed out tracts to the drug users at the same park. Needless to say, life was very confusing for Connie. She would leave my office and ask me if she would see me next week. I would have to answer that I didn't know, because I wouldn't know from week to week which personality would come for therapy. I'm sure the secretaries thought it was strange when Connie and I took two or three extra chairs into my office each week. I had her change chairs as she changed personalities.

Your answer to the question of what type of person you dislike being around probably won't be as dramatic as Connie's was, but it can certainly help you get some insight into yourself. As you answer the question, look into your heart for bits and pieces of that person within you.

The truth about myself will set me free to be more accepting of other imperfect people—especially those with similar faults.

J.E.M.

> *I ackowledged my sin to You,*
> *And my iniquity I have not hidden.*
> *I said, "I will confess my transgressions*
> *to the Lord,"*
> *And You forgave the iniquity of my sin.*
> —PS. 32:5

Gwenne came to see me in a panic. She had just been hired by a graphic design firm. Now she was facing a major deadline, and she was not going to make it because she had spent too much time with her boyfriend.

Gwenne had been raised by an alcoholic father who was very argumentative and manipulative. Most of her life, Gwenne had watched her dad relinquish all personal responsibility for his behavior. Now she was tempted to do the same thing.

"It's not fair; the deadline was too short," Gwenne ranted. "I'll quit my job and show him." Then she tried another tactic. "I'll fall on the ground. I'll beg. I'll kiss his ring." Finally, however, Gwenne looked at me and said, "I'm going to have to make an appointment with my boss and see if he will extend my deadline. If he won't, I will just have to face the consequences."

Gwenne had moved from manipulation to honesty. In our relationship with God, we must be willing to do the same thing. We must face ourselves, confess our sins, and ask for forgiveness and cleansing. God grants that to us out of His character of love, not as a result of our manipulation.

Lord, thank you for your forgiveness and cleansing. Thank you for the self-respect I gain when I face you and confess my sins.

J.M.C.

This Book of the Law shall not depart from your mouth, but you shall meditate in it day and night, that you may observe to do according to all that is written in it. For then you will make your way prosperous, and then you will have good success.
—JOSH. 1:8

I have always been so proud of my older brothers. As a child, I adored them; I would do anything to get them to include me in their activities. I can remember feeling so proud when they would actually let me ride bikes with them. Even when they teased me unmercifully, I continued to go back for more.

Fortunately, I grew out of that craving "little sister" stage and developed an equal relationship with each of my brothers. I could do this because, as I grew older, I began to respect myself and become an individual. I no longer believed their thoughts, friends, and activities were more interesting or important than mine.

Sadly, many women relate to men like "little sisters" rather than equals. A woman may disregard herself completely and sacrifice her identity to get love and affection from a man. And she may continue to return to him even after being repeatedly rejected. Such an unhealthy craving can be healed as a woman begins to take her focus off the man and place her attention on Christ. That way, she begins to develop self-respect, to feel secure and to trust that she is a significant individual. And she begins to relate to man as an equal.

Lord, thank you for making me who I am. Help me respect myself and turn to you for support.

J.L.M.

> *But he who looks into the perfect law of liberty and*
> *continues in it, and is not a forgetful hearer but a*
> *doer of the work, this one will be blessed in what*
> *he does.*
> —JAMES 1:25

I ask a question early in therapy that always helps me assess my client's mental health. I ask her (or him) to imagine three pictures of herself hanging on the wall— one of how she sees herself, one of how she thinks others see her, and the third of how she believes God sees her. The closer the three pictures come to looking alike, the more whole or integrated the patient is likely to be and the less work we will have to do in therapy.

A simple way to describe what goes on behind the counselor's doors is to say that we are working toward the insightful *integration* of body, soul, and spirit. This "integration work" (as masterfully described by Henry Cloud in his book, *When Your World Makes No Sense*) typically centers around four *Bs*. Clients must learn to establish *boundaries*—to avoid being enmeshed with others. They must learn to *bond* with others and love them in a healthy way. They must learn to accept their *badness* along with their goodness and to rethink who the *boss* of their life is. (Is their life being run by illogical and sick voices from childhood?)

What do your three pictures look like? What is the state of your four *Bs*? Determine in your heart to work on those areas that help you develop into a healthy, integrated woman.

Good mental health is a choice, but it takes a lot of emotional and spiritual work.

J.E.M.

> *And when He had sent them away, He departed to*
> *the mountain to pray.* —MARK 6:46

Often we are helped in our journey towards health when we encounter people who have discovered the secret of renewing themselves in order to give to others. Irene played such a role in my life.

Irene ran a pottery business from her home. She had four children in the space of seven years. Needless to say, her days were full to overflowing. One day I asked her the secret of her energy. Her answer astounded me. "Oh," she said, "from noon until twelve-thirty every day, I retreat to my bedroom. First, I make certain the children are well taken care of. Then I take a cup of steaming hot tea into the bedroom and I lock the door. I put my feet up, drink my tea, and talk to God. It helps restore my perspective and remind me that love is the reason I am doing all I am doing. At first the children didn't understand; they would knock on my door and ask me what I was doing in there. My answer to them was always the same, "I'm making you a better mother."

As I left Irene's house that day I wondered, what am I doing to renew myself and to make myself a better person?

Help me today, Lord, to take the time to get charged up before I charge out. Help me see that when I take time for myself I am not taking it away from anyone else.

J.M.C.

Beware, brethren, lest there be in any of you an evil heart of unbelief in departing from the living God; but exhort one another daily, while it is called "Today," lest any of you be hardened through the deceitfulness of sin.

—HEB. 3:12–13

After Jane left the small town where she grew up, she realized how much her Aunt Alicia had helped with her spiritual and emotional growth. Aunt Alicia was patient with Jane, but she also knew when to push her. Jane remembers a particular day when she had given up on herself and her aunt confronted her about her attitude. Jane stormed out of her aunt's house and didn't return for two months. But Aunt Alicia waited patiently for her to come back and then welcomed her with open arms.

Just as Jane's aunt confronted her, God confronts us about our behavior. He may gently nudge us, or He may have to get our attention in a stronger way—and it is important to listen to Him. He may use our jobs, other people, our thoughts, or many other circumstances to speak to us. Sometimes I think God speaks to me by using significant people like Jane's Aunt Alicia. At other times I get ideas that I know are from the Lord, and often God speaks to me through my gut-level feelings. However the Lord communicates with me, I am thankful that He continues to teach me.

Lord, thank you for those special people you place in our lives, and thank you for giving me new opportunities to grow closer to you.

J.L.M.

> *. . . Visiting the iniquity of the fathers upon the children and the children's children to the third and the fourth generation.* —EX. 34:7

In therapy, we call them family traditions. They are the negative thought processes and behavior patterns that are passed on from generation to generation. Often, we end up passing on to our children the very messages we hate the most in our own lives.

Laureen was in her middle thirties when I first saw her. Anger overflowed as she told me how her mother had blamed her for everything bad that happened in her life. Laureen's mother was pregnant when she married Laureen's father. Somehow that became Laureen's fault. Her mother smoked a pack of cigarettes every day and eventually got emphysema—and she smoked, she said, because Laureen made her nervous. What a burden for a little girl to bear!

Laureen married and moved far away from her mother, but she could never move away from that voice inside of her that kept yelling, "It's all your fault!" When Laureen's children were born, she passed that message of blame along to them both verbally and nonverbally. By the time I started seeing Laureen, a third generation was already struggling with the psychological fallout of blame passed from mother to daughter to child. Intensive family therapy was needed to break the tradition.

What family traditions are you ready to end today?

J.E.M.

> *Beloved, do not avenge yourselves, but rather give*
> *place to wrath; for it is written, "Vengeance is*
> *Mine, I will repay," says the Lord. . . . Do not be*
> *overcome by evil, but overcome evil with good.*
> —ROM. 12:19, 21

Judy is furious with Art. For years her life centered around the care and feeding of his ego. In giving in to his demands, she feels, she lost her own identity. Now, instead of facing the hard reality that she *allowed* him to do that, Judy prefers to focus on Art's wrongs, which were many. She is preoccupied with getting even. Judy's comments go like this. "He made me hurt so much. I want to see him hurt. . . . I'm going to find all the people who hurt Art in the business, and I'm going to form friendships with them. That should hurt him."

Judy needs to learn that revenge always boomerangs. She needs to take ownership for both the way the marriage was and the way it is today. She must face herself and realize that she is responsible only for her own actions and reactions. And then—for her own sake as well as Art's—she needs to give up her right to revenge and leave the judgment to God. Only then will she be able to overcome the evil in her life with good.

Lord, it's so natural to want to get even with people who hurt me. Help me remember that, in seeking revenge, I am only hurting myself. Help me learn, instead, to take responsibility, turn my pain over to you, and move on.

J.M.C.

If any of you lacks wisdom, let him ask of God,
who gives to all liberally and without reproach,
and it will be given to him. —JAMES 1:5

Sandra had always been a devoted wife. She prayed for her husband every day. She raised three fine boys. And she did quite well as a realtor. She always tried to be obedient to God. And yet she continued to feel controlled and smothered by her husband. It seemed that the more she gave, the more he took. And he refused to go see a marriage counselor or the pastor. Where could Sandra turn?

Finally, after much thought and prayer, Sandra decided to move out. She still loved her husband, but putting space between them seemed her only positive option. Her husband was angry at first and tried some of his controlling tricks, such as not allowing her to have any of their money. Two weeks after Sandra moved out, however, her husband finally decided to talk things over. He agreed to counseling. They started communicating differently and going out on dates. Sandra came to understand that much of his controlling behavior stemmed from his fear of losing her. And her husband began to acknowledge his controlling behavior and took steps to back off. Finally, three months after moving out, Sandra moved home again. She and her husband, with God's help, are working to rebuild their marriage.

Lord, help me to seek your wisdom and follow after you. Please give me a peace about which way I should turn and what direction I should take.

J.L.M.

So teach us to number our days,
That we may gain a heart of wisdom.
—PS. 90:12

Jim Elliot was one of six missionaries killed many years ago by the Auca Indians in South America. He was not even thirty when he died. Many would say that his was a wasted life, but there is certainly another way to look at his life story. Elisabeth Elliot, his wife, included this excerpt from his journal in a book she wrote about Jim's life: "He is no fool who gives what he cannot keep to gain what he cannot lose." Jim Elliot was a man who numbered his days and used the time he had to help mankind. Jim Elliot was no fool.

I tend to rush through my own life at such a fast pace. And I sometimes forget to ask whether my priorities for my life match my priorities for the day. When it comes to the things that matter most, I tend to say, like Scarlet O'Hara in *Gone With the Wind*, "I'll worry about it tomorrow." I'll spend time with my mate and family, start exercising, start eating healthily, become more active at church later. Right now, I'm too busy just getting through the day.

I need to determine to number my days—to remember my time is limited and make it count for something. Yes, I will get sidetracked and blown off course sometimes. But if I wake up each day and dedicate that day to the Lord, He will help me. I'm not ready to live until I'm ready to die. Are you?

Lord, please help me to experience a balanced, meaningful life today.

J.E.M.

As iron sharpens iron,
So a man sharpens the countenance
of his friend.   —PROV. 27:17

Samantha was thrilled when Larry gave her a beautiful diamond engagement ring. As the weeks went by, however, she started to grow skittish. Did she really want to give up her independence to get married? How could she be sure that Larry was the one? What if she got pregnant and then something happened to Larry? Eventually Samantha gave the ring back, saying that she needed more time.

But time wasn't really the issue here. Samantha, like many others, feels pulled between her urge to merge and her desire to stay independent. She tends to focus on the potential problems in a relationship to avoid having to share, compromise, and maybe even yield at times.

Samantha needs to find a model of a healthy growing relationship in which both partners are enhanced rather than absorbed. She also has to abandon the currently popular myth that love stifles one's individuality and standing alone enhances one's growth. Autonomy often just binds people to their own smallness. We don't necessarily have to marry in order to become the best we can be, but we do need to learn how to love.

Help me to seek out relationships, Lord, in which I can be totally myself and the other people can be totally themselves.

J.M.C.

> *Cast your burden on the Lord*
> *And He shall sustain you;*
> *He shall never permit the righteous*
> *to be moved.* —PS. 55:22

Three years ago, my friend and her husband brought his eighty-three-year-old mother to live with them rather than have her go to a nursing home. Now they sometimes wonder if they made a mistake. This woman constantly complains that the food is cold, the food is too well done, the house is hot, the house is too cold . . . and the list goes on. She always seems to push all the right buttons. But my friend and her husband truly believe God is training, teaching, and refining them through this experience. When the anger comes, they turn to the Lord and admit their weakness in being able to deal with his mother. Theirs is a day-to-day struggle that is possible only through Christ's strength—not theirs.

As we care for those around us who may be sick or not so easy to relate to, we quickly come to terms with the absolute necessity of casting our burdens on God and allowing Him to sustain us. The Lord is there for us to talk to about how to confront or how to keep quiet; He is there to listen to our frustrations; and He provides His Word for us to read and learn from. As we address difficult people each day, it is good to remember how much we need the Lord's guidance—and how faithfully He provides it.

───────────

Lord, give me the strength to care for those around me with the same tenderness and compassion that you show towards me.

J.L.M.

The Lord does not see as man sees, for man looks at the outward appearance, but the Lord looks at the heart.
                                      —1 SAM. 16:7

Mark, our third-born, decided to enter the world a little early—three weeks before his due date. The first two children had been two or three weeks late, so the weekend of Mark's arrival we had felt no qualms about taking our children camping. We arrived at the campground, which was about an hour and a half from home, when I had a strange sensation, as pregnant women often do. Then my water broke. We explained to the children that we had to pack up and head back home.

During our ninety-minute ride home, my brain clicked off the list of chores to be done before I could go to the hospital. I was concerned that I wasn't yet prepared for a visit by my mother; for instance, my oven had not been cleaned yet. So I got home, packed my bags for the hospital, unpacked everything from the camping trip, and proceeded to clean the oven as labor proceeded.

I cringe a little today at that memory of cleaning my oven. I see it as a picture of my own insecurity, which motivated me to obsess on the outward appearance of my house at a time when I should have been focusing on the arrival of a new family member. I was trying to impress my mother, who loved me whether my oven was clean or not!

Today I will not focus on the external, but rather on who I am in my heart—as the Lord does.

                                                      J.E.M.

> *Moreover if your brother sins against you, go and
> tell him his fault between you and him alone. If
> he hears you, you have gained your brother. But
> if he will not hear you, take with you one or
> two more . . .*
> —MATT. 18:15–16

There are times when we must take steps to limit the
evil someone is imparting our way. Sally found this out
the hard way when her husband, Jeff, turned to alcohol. Jeff's binges terrified his family. He would throw things,
put his fist through walls, and insist on driving drunk.
He would also ignore all financial responsibilities.

At first Sally enabled Jeff's habit. She would lie for
him, pour out his alcohol, and deny to herself and the
children that he had a problem. Through the support
of friends and a therapist, however, Sally started to
face the truth and to set limits. First, she told her husband how hurtful his choices were to her and the children. Because he was in denial, he just laughed at her.
So she next confronted Jeff along with two or three
other people who were important to him. This experience was very unsettling for Jeff, but it helped him begin to face himself.

Had Sally nagged and been vindictive about Jeff's
problem, or continued to cover for him, she and her
daughters would probably still be suffering and stuck
today. Instead, she set limits that brought change, love,
and growth.

*Lord, help me face the truth about myself and those I care about. If
evil comes my way, help me to limit it and to maintain healthy
boundaries.*

J.M.C.

So God created man in His own image; in the image of God He created him; male and female He created them. —GEN. 1:27

God displayed amazing creativity in making the universe. Some of His unique creatures—fireflies, flamingos, aardvarks, kangaroos—make me wonder how He ever thought of it all! And because God created us in His image, we are creative too. But most of us don't come close to using our full creativity. We get caught in one-dimensional thinking, assuming that there are only a few ways to accomplish our goals and quickly giving up if those don't work. We become so critical of ourselves that we don't allow for spontaneity or imagination, or we attempt only what we know will be successful.

Just as our Lord designed us creatively, we can use our talents creatively. Trying new activities—dance, art, photography, or even flying—or developing imaginative thoughts and attitudes can be stimulating and promote our self-worth. And using our creativity helps us solve our problems. When we begin to see that our problems can be approached more than one way, we begin to overcome our feelings of hopelessness and inadequacy and open up to God's creative possibilities in our lives.

Lord, please forgive me when I give up and lose hope because I'm stuck in one way of thinking. Help me to remember how creative you are, and that you created me in your image, so I can try different ways of problem solving.

J.L.M.

> *Come to Me, all you who labor and are heavy laden, and I will give you rest. Take my yoke upon you and learn from Me. . . . For My yoke is easy and My burden is light.* —MATT. 11:28–30

We call her "Masochistic Mary." She feels it is her duty in life to meet all the needs of everyone she meets. Mary feels that every call is a call from God. Her life is in shambles because there is no balance. She runs from activity to activity frantically trying to do it all.

What's wrong with Mary? She hasn't learned that God has not called her to do everything, but only to do her part. Mary spins her wheels worrying about how much there is to do, how little time there is to do it, and how tired she's becoming. Mary is well on her way to the two *B*s of unbalanced living: *bitterness* and *burnout*.

Can you identify with Masochistic Mary? Do you end every day feeling guilty for all the things that are still on your "to do" list—yet still feel compelled to add to the list?

Christ doesn't want us to be worried about how much we do; He is more concerned with what we do. He wants us to listen for *His* call, not *everyone's* call, when we're deciding how to live our lives. When we look for quality in life, we find the two *P*s: *peace* and *power*.

God never called us to do it all. He calls us to do only our light and easy part.

J.E.M.

*On the next day, when he departed, he took out
two denarii, gave them to the innkeeper, and said
to him, "Take care of him; and whatever more you
spend, when I come again, I will repay you."*
—LUKE 10:35

June's nickname was "Mom." When she was around, people with needs seemed to come out of the woodwork. She would listen for hours on the phone and meet with people at all hours of the day and night—all the while ignoring the fact that she was neglecting her own family. In fact, June was giving away so much that her family had to take care of her. And many of the people who were sucking June's energy were self-centered people who had no intention of changing.

What a contrast the good Samaritan was to June. While traveling he came across a man who had a legitimate need, and he helped him. He took the injured man to an inn, paid for his care, and returned a few days later to check on him. But the good Samaritan also knew how much he could help and still take responsibility for his own life. June had completely lost sight of her personal responsibilities, and so her helping was hindering both herself and others, especially her family. The question that she never seemed to face because she was so busy living vicariously through others was what would happen if she ever started living her own life.

Lord, in my enthusiasm to reach out and help others, keep my perspective clear enough that I don't lose sight of my personal responsibilities. Help me to live my own life.

J.M.C.

But these are the ones sown on good ground, those who hear the word, accept it, and bear fruit: some thirtyfold, some sixty, and some a hundred.

—MARK 4:20

This verse in Mark is part of a parable spoken by Jesus on different types of people who receive the teachings of Christ. Another portion of the parable compares people who fall away to seeds that don't do well in stony, thorny ground. This verse, however, talks about individuals who, like seeds in good ground, accept Jesus Christ and grow in Him.

The way parents care for their children can cultivate "good ground" for the gospel in the children's lives. Because of the love my parents showed me, for example, I was able to believe and trust in God when the story of Jesus Christ was first introduced to me. My parents never took my brothers and me to church or spoke about God. Yet they loved, accepted, and supported me. I trusted them and felt secure in their love. I knew they wanted good things for me and would never harm me. Because of their love and care, when my neighbors took me to church, I was able to receive the message that God also loved me and wanted good things for me. Parents who are faithful, loving, and consistent are preparing their children to accept and grow in Christ's love.

Lord, help me to cultivate a healthy attitude toward you in my children by loving and caring for them with the same tenderness and mercy you show me.

J.L.M.

Listen to counsel and receive instruction,
That you may be wise in your latter days.
—PROV. 19:20

Yesterday morning I woke up with brown hair. Today I awakened to brownish, reddish, blondish hair. My beautician must have looked at the wrong card when she was mixing the formula for my hair. She is usually very professional about getting the right color. So, to tell the truth, I gave little attention to my new color as I paid her and left the salon. My husband and children complimented me on my hairstyle, and I was feeling pretty good about it. Then this morning, on my daily walk with my trustworthy friend, the real truth came out. "What did she put on your hair?" she asked. I mumbled something, and then my friend told me I must do something to get my hair back to its normal color.

I had been confronted with truth, and now I was faced with a decision. My first thought was "No, I'll leave it brownish, reddish, blondish, and then I'll have an excuse to go buy some new clothes to match it. Everyone knows the clothes that go with brown hair wouldn't go with my new color." My second thought was "Perhaps I should call my beautician and try to get my old color back." I went with the second option. Buying new clothes to match my new hair color would not really have been a wise decision—and I am certain my husband would agree!

When confronted with truth today, I will face it and try to make a wise decision concerning it.

J.E.M.

> *He who trusts in his riches will fall,*
> *But the righteous will flourish like foliage.*
> —PROV. 11:28

From the window the mother watched as her five-year-old daughter bounced out the doorway to play. Under the child's arm was a big bucket full of Legos. It wasn't five minutes until the mother heard cries from the front yard. Rushing out the door, she saw her child protecting her supply of Legos and the other children crying because they couldn't play with the brightly colored blocks. Quickly the mother walked over to her daughter and said, "You don't have to share if you don't want to, honey. But if you don't, you're going to end up completely alone with your toys."

What a graphic picture that mother painted of so many in our culture. They have been able to collect the best that the world can offer them materially, and yet they are all alone. Perhaps they put off relationships in order to climb the corporate ladder. Or they used people and loved things, only to realize they have been sold a false bill of goods.

When we get to the bottom line of what is precious in life, it is relationship. Things are to be used. People are to be valued.

Lord, help me to value people and nurture relationships today even as I work toward my goals.

J.M.C.

The Lord is merciful and gracious,
Slow to anger, and abounding in mercy.
He will not always strive with us,
Nor will He keep His anger forever.
—PS. 103:8–9

Anger creates a dilemma for many of us. Some women storm around in a rage, and some keep it all inside. But both of these extremes are unhealthy to us and those around us. Rage is clearly explosive, addictive, and hurtful. But holding anger in leads to dishonesty, blocked communication, and such physical problems as depression, eating disorders, and headaches. Besides, anger can't be pushed under completely. It may not come out in words, but it usually comes out through actions, jokes, or facial expressions. Or we may slyly express our anger by manipulating others; this is called passive aggression.

Expressing our anger appropriately means using "I feel" statements followed by an explanation—for instance: "I feel angry because you accepted the invitation without checking with me." "I feel" statements communicate honestly but without blame, accusation, or finger pointing. Once we have communicated our anger in this way, we can proceed to let go of it—to choose forgiveness.

Father, just as you don't keep your anger toward me forever, help me to appropriately release mine so I can move on without holding grudges or making myself sick.

J.L.M.

Even in laughter the heart may sorrow,
And the end of mirth may be grief.
—PROV. 14:13

The Martins lived in a small home in the suburbs. From the outside, nothing about the house looked strange or out of the ordinary—but inside was a different story. The Martins had an eight-ton elephant residing in their living room.

No one in the family said anything about the presence of the pachyderm. In fact, the whole family sat on the couch and watched television through the elephant's legs. Mrs. Martin cleaned massive messes and even dusted around the animal. His trunk often reached to the dining room table to get food, ruining more than a few meals. The family ignored the elephant and did their best to go on as if nothing was wrong.

Finally, however, the elephant could no longer be ignored. The carpet was ruined. The couch sagged. Fleas were all over the premises, and the neighbors were beginning to complain of the stench.

Of course, this is not a true story. It is an illustration of what happens to problems in a dysfunctional family; they are overlooked or just denied. No matter what the problem—alcoholism, depression, physical abuse, or mental abuse—problems begin to smell when they are not dealt with.

Lord, help me face problems in my family and do something about them before they reach "elephantissimal" proportions.

                                                                J.E.M.

The thief does not come except to steal, and to kill, and to destroy. I have come that they may have life, and that they may have it more abundantly.
—JOHN 10:10

No woman wants to spend the majority of her time being or feeling out of control. She doesn't want to be bullied by her emotions, whipped by her guilt, and defeated by her "if onlys." Yet the "thief"—Satan—delights when we lose hope, question God, dwell on our inadequacies, deny our need for relationship, or destroy the relationships we have. He cheers on our critical self-talk because when we talk death, destruction, and negativity we're doing his work for him.

By contrast, when we ask Jesus Christ into our life, we discover the unbeatable combination of grace and truth. God's grace, given flesh by Jesus Christ, always affirms our value—always loves and never condemns. Truly God's grace provides a place of safety in a dysfunctional world. Accepting that grace enables me to face the truth about myself. I don't have to pretend I am perfect in order to be loved, I don't have to deny my mistakes or cover my failures, and I don't have to run away from weakness in myself. I can face my strength and my weakness, my goodness and my badness in the knowledge that God accepts and loves me in my totality. What good news that is. What freedom to be myself flows from this truth.

Abundant life is the result of accepting God's grace and truth about who I am.

J.M.C.

For we walk by faith not by sight.
—2 COR. 5:7

Faith is not something we can define logically. It is trusting that things are going to work out when all seems to indicate failure. It is believing in solutions when we feel discouraged and unable to come up with any plans and relying on the fact that God is there for us even when we cannot feel His presence.

Many things in our life may seem questionable or unsure; we may not know for certain what will happen or what trial may be encountered. It is the hope that things are going to work out—that Christ is there for us and hears our prayers—that enables us to keep going. When we are recovering from a damaged past, our faith may provide our only motivation to continue the upward journey. At first, we may simply have enough faith to believe we can make it through a day. But as we exercise our faith, it will become stronger and stronger.

We may be like the mountain climber who is in the middle of her first big climb and cannot see the top, but inches on anyway. Each time she reaches a new height, she believes another climb is possible. Our recovery goals are achieved when we, like the climber, step out—even though afraid—and persevere. As we continue "climbing," our faith becomes our freedom and our guide.

Lord, thank you for never giving up on me. I want to keep reaching out and relying on you.

J.L.M.

Behold, I stand at the door and knock. If anyone hears My voice and opens the door, I will come in to him and dine with him, and he with Me.
—REV. 3:20

Judy had stars in her eyes when she came for counseling. She had her future well planned. She would leave the small town she lived in, with its petty problems and head for the big city, where she could start anew with a new apartment and new friends. But this was not the first time Judy had started over. She was thirty-five, and she had moved ten times in the past twelve years. Each time she was sure this move would be "it."

Through counseling, Judy found there was a big difference between dreaming about the future and then living in it. She began to see how she was wasting today by continually dreaming about tomorrow. She had been blaming her unhappiness on her environmental location rather then searching for happiness within herself with the help of Almighty God.

Judy made a conscious choice to begin to live in the present. She forgave those who had hurt her in the past. She also decided to face the pain of daily living in the here and now while grieving over the death of her idealized future. She is striving to have hope for the future, while still learning from the past and living in the future.

———————

Before I think seriously about changing locations, churches, jobs, or mates, I will take a little walk and talk with Jesus and look into my own heart to search for the real roots of my discontent.

J.E.M.

*Therefore a man shall leave his father and
mother . . .*
—GEN. 2:24

Dina shuffled into the office. She was in her mid-forties, significantly overweight, and deeply troubled. She felt utterly alone, even though she lived with her elderly parents, had a good job, and was active in some social circles. In the core of her being was a gnawing emptiness.

As we became better acquainted, Dina shared her failed attempts to leave home. For one seemingly legitimate reason after another, her parents had blocked her healthy moves toward independence. So Dina had stayed home and denied her own needs. But in taking responsibility for her parents' happiness, she had lost hers. She was eternally locked into the role of child.

This was never God's design for the family! God planned for the child role to be a temporary one. The family is the place where we grow up, learn how to be people, and practice relating to others. It is where we learn to be emotionally dependent on others and yet functionally independent. Eventually, however, we are to leave our father and mother. That is why healthy parents give their children both roots and wings.

Lord, help me in little ways today to release my white-knuckled grip on life. Teach me the secret of letting go. Help me to hold a child's hand but not imprison her spirit.

J.M.C.

No temptation has overtaken you except such as is common to man; but God is faithful, who will not allow you to be tempted beyond what you are able, but with the temptation will also make the way of escape, that you may be able to bear it.

—1 COR. 10:13

God promises He won't give us more than we can handle. Sometimes we think that means God will miraculously remove the obstacle in our path or remove us from the struggle. But that's not the way it usually happens.

It is wise for us, therefore, to consider all the ways God and others can help us. God never said that we must contend alone.

Each year, when some birds begin their task of migration, they group together and fly in formation to their designated goal. They don't go by themselves! They face this enormous task together. It is as if they know they have to stick together in order to make it. We humans, on the other hand, tend to isolate ourselves and set out alone to face difficult tasks. Pride— or the embarrassment of telling others about our stumbling blocks—keeps us from asking for help. When we allow people we trust to help us with our struggles, we get support as well as accountability. When we include God and others, our problems become manageable.

Lord, help me think of all the different ways you can help me with my temptations and problems. Give me the courage to allow others to help me face and overcome obstacles.

J.L.M.

"For I know the thoughts that I think toward you, says the Lord, thoughts of peace and not of evil, to give you a future and a hope." —JER. 29:11

Are you hopeful or hopeless? Little children are the picture of hopefulness. Their eyes are bright and their hearts are trusting. But hope sometimes gets lost under the pain of our ongoing lives. When hope is lost, how can we get it back?

One of the fruits of recovery is a renewal of hope. The regrowth of hope can be compared to the growth of a seed into a fruit-bearing tree. A seed must be planted before it can grow. Hope also must be planted as a seed in our hearts before it can grow. Releasing negative thoughts from my past plants seeds of hope for my future. A seed must be watered and tended, and hope must also be nourished with care. The weeds of unbelief and unforgiveness must be pruned from our hearts so that hope may grow. And just as a tree cannot grow without the help of the sun, hope can't grow without the help of the *Son*. Hope grows anew in our lives as we open ourselves to the light of His love.

Hope grows with help from the Son as He shines His light on our hearts.

J.E.M.

And at the ninth hour Jesus cried with a loud voice, saying, "Eloi, Eloi, lama sabachthani?" which is translated, "My God, My God, why have You forsaken Me?"
—MARK 15:34

Karon had been in therapy just a short time when she had a dream. She saw herself in the middle of a crowd of familiar faces—her abusive father, her siblings, and her alcoholic grandparents—and God was holding her hand. But suddenly Karon was separated from God and lost in the crowd—"abandoned and absolutely alone."

Even though Karon had a relationship with Jesus Christ, she still believed in a God who abandons people when they most need Him. That is not surprising, given that Karon was raised in an abandoning, abusive home. But now that Karon was in recovery—now that she was reading her Bible, going to church, and praying—she thought she should be over her feelings of abandonment.

Recovery is a spiritual journey, but it helps to know that times of spiritual distress often appear along the way. When Jesus was on the cross, He didn't deny His feelings of fear and abandonment; He felt them all the way up to His death. And following His example, people like Karon can walk the path that leads to grace and truth.

Thank you, Lord, for your vulnerability. Thanks that you struggled in the same ways I do. Thank you that you faced your feelings rather than running away from them.

J.M.C.

> *The work of righteousness will be peace,*
> *And the effect of righteousness, quietness*
> *and assurance forever.* —ISA. 32:17

I remember participating at my first gymnastics meet as a child. The first day, we competed on the uneven parallel bars, and an older neighbor girl won first place. The next day, we were to perform our floor routines on the large blue mats. I was ready. In fact, I can still remember the routine: step, kick, lunge, forward roll, and so on. Then I saw all the people looking at me, and I froze. I totally forgot a routine that I knew in my sleep. I floundered and tried to fake it, but nothing came to me. That event took me years to overcome. After that day I started avoiding being in front of crowds, and over time my fear worsened. As an adult, however, I have learned it is OK to fail, that taking risks is a healthy behavior—and I have worked to overcome my fear.

My boss recently told me that his son, a professional athlete, has discovered that the best way for him to work on his self-assurance is to work on his righteousness. When he focuses on developing righteousness through prayer and Bible study, his assurance naturally follows. Now, whenever I need assurance, I try to think back to Isaiah 32:17 and begin to focus on the Lord. As I do this, my fears are calmed. I begin to feel an assurance that only Christ is capable of bringing.

Lord, I want to seek after your righteousness. Remind me that true peace, quietness, and assurance are only found through you.

J.L.M.

For God so loved the world that He gave His only begotten Son, that whoever believes in Him should not perish but have everlasting life.
—JOHN 3:16

The world as we know it is a dysfunctional place. Not one of us is a perfect person, spouse, child, parent, or friend, even though many of us spend a lifetime pretending we can be.

Into this world of denial God sent the Truth—His perfect Son. Why? Because God desired relationship with us. He knew we could only find healing in the context of a healthy love relationship—a relationship in which we could face the truth about ourselves and know that we were loved at the same time. The truth sets us free, but it must be represented in the context of grace or it is too harsh for us to receive.

Love is the motive for the greatest invitation we will ever receive. God's Son, the greatest gift, was willingly sacrificed for you and me. When we accept God's Son as our Savior, we receive the greatest gift from the greatest Giver. This gift is for us today, and it also covers our tomorrows. That reality provides us with the greatest joy we will ever know.

Rejoice, you are loved!

J.M.C.

"When He, the spirit of truth, has come, He will guide you into all truth."   —JOHN 16:13

One of Priscilla's more painful memories of childhood was the day her mother locked her and her younger brother out of the house for two or three hours. Fire ants stung Priscilla, so she knocked on the door, but her mother would not let her in. Talking to Priscilla, I felt her intense anger toward a mother who could care so little for her children. How could a mother be so cruel?

A few years later, I asked Bill, Priscilla's younger brother, if he remembered that incident. Yes, he remembered being locked out of the house for a couple of hours on a Saturday morning. But he also told me about the wonderful surprise the children had found when they reentered the house. Their mother had transformed their home into a birthday surprise party for Bill. Priscilla had never mentioned a party. Bill hardly remembered the pain. Priscilla only remembered the pain of being left outside, unprotected.

As a counselor, I learned an important lesson from these two stories. Both people told the truth; they just saw it differently. We see truth through such clouded "glasses" that a great deal of our bitterness may be based on misperceptions. But we find health by seeking truth and forgiving both our real and imagined abusers.

I will seek the truth—seek to forgive—today.

                                                    J.E.M.

If My people who are called by My name will
humble themselves, and pray and seek My face. . . .
then I will hear from heaven, and will forgive their
sin and heal their land. Now My eyes will be open
and My ears attentive to prayer made in this place.
—2 CHRON. 7:14–15

The presence of humility in our lives takes away our self-centeredness and gives us a sense of awe and respect for God. Humility is like the realization we have when we watch crashing waves at the ocean or rapid currents in a fast flowing river—we cannot for a minute think we are stronger than life itself.

Giving up our demanding attitude and defiant nature allows us to become vulnerable to a reality greater than ourselves. And this vulnerability opens us up to a reverence for God and allows us to accept His guidance as we put our own willfulness aside. Becoming vulnerable may mean we can call someone on the phone and talk to them about a struggle or ask them for help. It may mean apologizing for a cutting remark we made to a loved one or admitting we were wrong. Humility opens us up to an honest relationship with God, others, and ourselves. We let down our protective guard and are able to admit our weakness, seek God, and seek the help of others.

Lord, I humble myself before you and pray that I will turn from my prideful ways. I want to respect you as my Creator and seek your guidance every day of my life.

J.L.M.

> *For a righteous man may*
> *fall seven times*
> *And rise again.*
> —PROV. 24:16

As a child, I loved to cross streams by stepping on the stones so I would not get wet. But sometimes the rocks were so slippery that I fell in the water anyway. Mistakes can be like that—either stepping stones or slipping stones.

Think with me about two people who used their mistakes as stepping stones. A chemist invented a glue that was too weak for the specific purpose he was developing it for. With the "failure," with the "wrong glue," he developed the "stick-on" notes we now use daily. A secretary who made many mistakes typing mixed white paint and water together and created correction fluid or white-out.

It takes courage to make mistakes. In a recent poll by a leading newspaper, fear of failure was listed as the number-one fear. Next time you're afraid to try something because of the fear of making a mistake, ask yourself, "Would I rather fail or never try?" If I don't try, I'll never know if I could have accomplished the feat or if I could think of a good use for my mistake.

Question: What does God call someone who falls seven times, but, rises up again to keep trying? Answer: Righteous.

J.E.M.

> *And we desire that each one of you show the same
> diligence to the full assurance of hope until the
> end, that you do not become sluggish, but imitate
> those who through faith and patience inherit the
> promises.*
> —HEB. 6:11–12

Peter Marshall, the former chaplain of the United
States Senate, used to tell the story of a quiet old man
who lived high in the Alps above an Austrian village.
For many years he had been paid by the villagers to
clear away the debris from the mountain springs that
fed the sparkling stream flowing through town. Then
one evening, when the town met to revise its budget,
someone questioned the salary figure being paid to the
obscure keeper of the spring. By unanimous vote they
dispensed with the old man's services.

For several weeks everything was as before. But in
early autumn the trees began to shed their leaves.
Small branches fell into the pools, hindering the flow of
the water. One afternoon someone noticed a slight
yellow-brown tint to the spring. A couple of days later,
the water was much darker. Within one week, a slimy
film covered sections of the water along the bank, and
a foul odor was noticeable. Disease and sickness struck
the village.

Needless to say, the embarrassed council called a
special meeting and hired the old man back. Within a
few weeks, the river began to clear, and the water
flowed freely once more.

Thank you, Lord, that your love wasn't meant to be stagnant or passive. Help me to do what I can to keep the stream flowing.

J.M.C.

> *Let us draw near with a true heart in full assurance*
> *of faith, having our hearts sprinkled from an evil*
> *conscience and our bodies washed with pure water.*
> *Let us hold fast the confession of our hope without*
> *wavering, for He who promised us is faithful.*
> —HEB. 10:22–23

We will never "arrive" in this life because we live in a world of sin. Yet, the closer we are to God, the more Christlike we'll become. Our verses for today offer some excellent advice for drawing closer to God especially suited to women in recovery.

A first piece of advice mentioned in these verses is to have a "true heart." We women in recovery often have difficulty being truthful with ourselves, and we sometimes find it difficult to be truthful with others. The second recommendation is having full assurance of faith. This means trust, and trust is also a challenge for women in recovery. Broken trusts have been a way of life for us, so we have a difficult time trusting anyone or anything. The third recommendation in these verses is letting go of guilt—a clearly difficult act to women for whom guilt is a way of life.

But the fourth piece of advice mentioned in these verses is what makes the others possible, even for women in recovery. We must be "washed with pure water"—choosing to benefit from the cleansing of the cross. When we choose to accept what He has done for us, we are enabled to be truthful, trust God, and give up our guilt, thus drawing closer to Him!

I will choose to draw near to God today.

J.E.M.

And let the peace of God rule in your hearts, to
which also you were called in one body; and
be thankful.   —COL. 3:15

Being thankful and letting the peace of God rule in our hearts require a conscious decision on our part. In order to enjoy inner peace and thanksgiving, we must commit our lives to Jesus Christ and look for ways to keep a calmness of mind and spirit. Many Christians love the Lord but experience little peace because of the busyness of their lives and their inability to let peace fill them.

To establish a quietness and harmony within, we can begin each day with prayer and reading the Scripture. To remind us throughout the day that a peaceful attitude is desirable, we can try to be aware of the beauty around us, seeing it as symbolic of God's provision. Wherever we may be, whatever time of day, we can observe beauty in our relationships and surroundings. Taking a few seconds to find something enriching in our environment prompts us to pause a moment, to slow down. This may mean lingering over a meal while visiting with a friend or sitting in the car to learn an enjoyable song on the radio even after we have reached our destination. The peace of God and a spirit of thanksgiving are gifts we receive when we set our minds on Christ and continually refocus on Him throughout each day.

Father, I will make a decision today to look for reminders of you and refocus my busyness to your tranquility.

J.L.M.

About the Authors

Janet Congo is a professional therapist associated with the Minirth-Meier Stoop Clinic in Laguna Hills, California. A former university teacher, she received her M.A. from Pepperdine University. She codirects personal-growth seminars and has appeared as a guest on radio and television talks shows. She is the author of *Free to Be God's Woman, Less Stress,* and *Free to Soar* and a contributor to *A Walk with the Serenity Prayer.*

Julie Mask is a licensed professional counselor associated with the Minirth-Meier Tunnell & Wilson Clinic in San Antonio, Texas. After receiving her M.A. in counseling from Texas Women's University, she worked with victims of family violence at The Family Place in Dallas, Texas. She is currently working on her doctorate from Oxford Graduate School.

Jan Meier is a marriage and family therapist practicing in El Toro, California. She received the M.S. in Early Childhood Education from State College of Arkansas and is currently working on a doctorate in marriage and family therapy at East Texas State University. Her husband, Paul Meier, is cofounder of the nationally distributed Minirth-Meier Clinic.